T0116296

"Sandlin deftly synthesizes and illuminates the duality of his title—both the tornado itself, which early settlers in America referred to as 'the Storm King'; and the individuals who made it their life's work to document, predict, and better understand those despots of the plains. . . . Sandlin makes talking about the weather much more than a conversational nicety—he makes it come brilliantly to life."

—*Publishers Weekly* (starred review)

"[A] well-constructed history of the politics and personalities of weather."   —*Kirkus Reviews*

LEE SANDLIN

STORM KINGS

Lee Sandlin is the author of *Wicked River: The Mississippi When It Last Ran Wild* and *The Distancers: An American Memoir*. He lives in Chicago.

www.leesandlin.com

Also by Lee Sandlin

The Distancers: An American Memoir

Wicked River:
The Mississippi When It Last Ran Wild

LEE SANDLIN

STORM KINGS

America's First Tornado Chasers

VINTAGE BOOKS

A DIVISION OF RANDOM HOUSE LLC

NEW YORK

FIRST VINTAGE BOOKS EDITION, MARCH 2014

Map reprinted from Professional Papers of the Signal Service, No. IV: Tornadoes of
May 29th and 30th, 1879, in Kansas, Nebraska, Missouri, and Iowa,
by Sergeant J. P. Finley. Courtesy of Robert J. Herman, Wamego, Kansas.

The Library of Congress has cataloged the Pantheon edition as follows:
Sandlin, Lee.
Storm Kings : America's first tornado chasers / Lee Sandlin.
p. cm.
I. Tornadoes. 2. Storm chasers. I. Title.
QC955.S26 2013   551.55'3092273—dc23 2012027314

Vintage Trade Paperback ISBN: 978-0-307-47358-5
eBook ISBN: 978-0-307-90816-2

Author photograph © Frank Blau Photography
Book design by Kristen Bearse

www.vintagebooks.com

For Joanne Fox
toujours fidèle

The wind blows as it wills, and you hear the sound of its passage, but you cannot say where it comes from or where it goes. This is how it is for the children of the wind.

—John 3:8

The wind blows over the lake and stirs the surface of the water. Thus visible effects of the invisible manifest themselves.
—*I Ching,* hexagram 61, "Inner Truth,"
Wilhelm/Baynes commentary

He cometh in terror, the vast mountains shake,
The citadel flames, and earth's huge pillars quake;
The proudest achievements of man are his spoil,
He wars with the forest, and tears up the soil . . .
The grandest, the strongest, the stateliest thing,
Must bow to the nod of the "Old Storm King."
—G. Linnaeus Banks,
Bentley's Miscellany, 1847

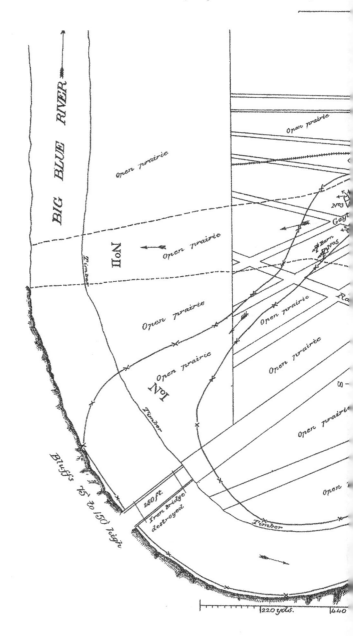

BIG BLUE RIVER

Open prairie

Open prairie

IIoN

Open prairie

Open prairie

Open prairie

No I

Timber

Open prairie

Open prairie

Open prairie

Open prairie

Open prairie

Open

Bluffs 75 to 150 high

250 ft.
from bridge
destroyed

Timber

Timber

Gayt

Ra

220 yds.   440

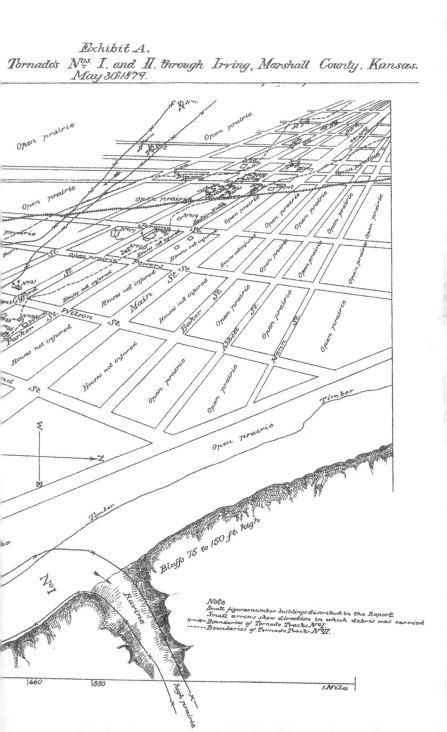

Exhibit A.

Tornado's Nos. I, and II, through Irving, Marshall County, Kansas.
May 30th 1879.

Note
Small figures number buildings described in the Report.
Small arrows show direction in which debris was carried.
—x—x— Boundaries of Tornado Tracks. No I.
------ Boundaries of Tornado Tracks. No II.

Contents

Part IV The Mystery of Severe Storms

There is an old country-and-western song my father liked called "Ghost Riders in the Sky." My father had been born and raised in rural Oklahoma during the Dust Bowl years and had spent his adolescence working at cattle ranches in Colorado and Wyoming; in his later life he was fond of saying that he had been one of the last of the old-fashioned cowboys, and he often recited scraps of cowboy poetry or retold the spooky folklore he'd heard from the other ranch hands. "Ghost Riders in the Sky" was a perfect example. It's about a cowboy who has a terrifying vision: he sees the souls of damned cowboys riding through the night in an eternal chase after a stampede of supernatural cattle. One of these spectral cowboys breaks off the pursuit long enough to warn the singer to repent his evil ways, or else, after he dies, he will join them "trying to catch the Devil's herd across these endless skies."

I don't remember my father ever connecting this stampede to tornadoes. But then, he didn't have to. I made the connection myself the first time I heard him sing the song, and it's stayed with me ever since. He was constantly telling me scary stories about tornadoes. He made them sound like a regular feature of his childhood landscape. The way he described it, anywhere on the Great Plains, if you raised your eyes to the horizon, you might somewhere in the vast flat distance see a funnel cloud beginning to form. He talked about all the different and bizarre shapes they took: grand swooping curves of impossible architecture, furious little whirlwinds like the clouds of dust above cartoon fistfights. He repeatedly told me about the closest call he'd ever had with a tornado—a blustery summer day when he and his friends had been playing baseball and a tornado had come roaring across the outfield; they'd had to hide in the dugout, clinging to the underside of the bench, to keep from being sucked into the funnel. But his favorite stories were about the nights he and his family had spent cowering in their snug lantern-lit storm cellar as the world outside had torn itself apart in the frenzy of a prairie thunderstorm: at some point his mother would raise a finger for silence, and they'd hear amid the roar of the wind and the crashes and bangs of thunder a sinister new sound, a deep throbbing and a high-pitched shriek like an airplane engine revving up. "And that," my father would conclude with satisfaction, "was the tornado."

I was spellbound by these stories, but I was also baffled by them. I never got that clear an idea of what a tornado really was. We lived then in northern Illinois, a place that was supposedly tornado heavy, but I had only seen one unmistakable tornado in my life, and that was in *The Wizard of Oz*. Few sights in any movie, or for that matter in the real world, have ever scared me as deeply as that. My father had no patience for it, though. He passed through the living room as my mother and brother and I were staring at the television screen in rapt horror, and he lingered only long enough to emit a snort of contempt. "Nah, that's no tornado," he said. "You should see a real tornado."

Each spring the science class at my elementary school would spend a day on the subject of tornadoes. The teacher would show us a filmstrip that had a lot of cartoon images of spiral-shaped clouds looming over prairie farmhouses. There were also photographs of crew-cut men with white shirts, black ties, and horn-rimmed glasses, clustered in muddy fields around weather balloons. But only a few of the images were of actual tornadoes; in those days, the 1960s, a clear photograph of a tornado was as rare as one of a flying saucer.

The filmstrip's narrator instructed us solemnly on the rules of tornado safety. There was one infallible warning sign that a tornado was coming, he said: the clouds took on a greenish glow. Tornadoes also caused an electrical disturbance that could be picked up by some TV sets, so if your TV screen grew mysteriously brighter during a storm, that was a clear signal a tornado was somewhere nearby. Then he explained why tornadoes were so destructive: there was a near vacuum at the heart of the funnel, so when it passed overhead, the air pressure trapped inside your house burst outward like an explosion. The most sensible precaution you could take, therefore, was to open your windows to equalize the air pressure. After you did so, only then should you take shelter, and the one safe place to hide was the southwest corner of the basement.

The viewing of this filmstrip turned me into a kind of amateur tornado warden. Whenever there was a storm, I kept my eyes peeled for the warning signs. But where were they? Spring after spring, tornado season after tornado season, I never saw a hint of a green glow in the sky. The closest I came to a tornado was one sultry April afternoon when I was twelve: a severe storm came through the Chicago suburbs, and a tornado touched down several miles away. The next day the newspapers ran an amateur photograph: it showed a blurry smear of buildings and streetlights, while against the horizon stood an indistinct gray cone of smoke towering up to the sky like a supervillain menacing a cartoon city. I tore it out of the paper and tacked it up on my bedroom wall, as though it were a wanted poster.

I did reports for school on tornadoes; I had all the key tornado facts memorized so that I could talk about wind speeds and air pressure with the least provocation. One afternoon in late spring when I was twelve, a storm built up in the west, and the sky around it turned a weird sickly yellow. My teacher, who knew about my obsession—pretty much everybody in the school did—asked me seriously whether that color sky meant a tornado was coming. I said authoritatively that yellow skies meant hail; green was the color of tornadoes. It was the proudest moment of my life.

I even had dreams about tornadoes. The dreams were all pretty much identical: they began with a feeling of horrible dread. I knew, with absolute certainty, that a tornado was approaching. I couldn't see it; nothing about the scene looked sinister; but it was already too late to escape. Sometimes I'd be the only one who knew, and I'd try in vain to warn everybody of the imminence of disaster. It never did any good; nobody would pay any attention to me. The dream always ended the same way: I was standing at a window, looking out at the sky, all hope lost, and just as the tornado was about to appear, I'd wake up.

I think I was at the height of my tornado passion the summer I was twelve. That was when my family went to visit my father's old home in Oklahoma, where my grandmother still lived. I spent the whole drive there staring at the clouds and expecting each one of them to transform before my eyes into a tornado. But somehow Oklahoma proved to be deficient in tornadoes. The skies were a ceaseless stampede of white cumulus, and some of them did occasionally puff up into thunderheads, but there were no funnel clouds reaching down to touch the earth. The tabletop flatness of the plains was broken by nothing out to the horizon except oil derricks.

I began to suspect that my father had been goosing his memories in order to scare me; he did always like scaring me. The night of our arrival, though, as we sat together on the front porch, a gigantic line of storms came rolling up over the southwestern sky. I had never seen anything in the world so large; it was like a tidal wave about to wash the plains clean. The sight inspired my father with something like nostalgia. This was just the kind of weather, he told me, that in his childhood had sent the whole family scurrying to the storm cellar for the night.

Did that mean there would be a tornado? I asked. It was the wrong question. I couldn't keep a quaver of fear out of my voice, and however much my father liked to scare me, I was supposed to bear up under it with stoic impassivity. He soon clumped off to bed and left me to the view. I watched for several minutes more as the storm advanced. Little flickers of yellow lightning were bursting silently all along the billows and crests like artillery fire; by the time I went to bed, I could hear the first mutterings of thunder.

Later that night I woke to find that the storm was exploding directly over my head. The thunder was making the walls quiver; the wind was in a fury, and it felt as if necessary things in the house were all bending over and were about to break. Rain rattled the windows like peltings of glass beads. The lightning bolts flared like searchlights. I went stumbling out of bed in a panic and fell forward down the hallway toward my parents' room. I had the idea that we might have only a few minutes to reach the storm cellar. But at their door I froze; as frightened as I was by the storm, my father scared me more. I huddled up against the doorway and strangely, unwillingly, fell asleep.

That's where my parents found me in the morning. Neither of them made any remarks about it. If my father had figured out what had happened, there would have been hell to pay, but I caught a break. He and my mother both just assumed I'd been sleepwalking.

That morning my grandmother took me on a little tour of the house and the yard. I expected to find a scene of total devastation, but everything was in its place: all the trees still had their branches, the flowers were charmingly mussed and gleamed with raindrops. My grandmother made no acknowledgment of the storm at all; as far as I could tell, she thought it was just a typical summer shower. She was much more interested in showing off all the improvements my father had been making for her on the property. He had even installed an automatic sprinkler system so she could see her gardens watered while she watched from her favorite chair in the living room.

By the back fence, though, there was a curious antique. The slope of a low green mound under a stand of trees was set with a weather-beaten door, like an escape hatch from a grave. My grandmother explained that this was the storm cellar. I eagerly asked to see it; she was baffled by my interest and seemed rather embarrassed to show me anything so quaint, but she swung the door up with practiced ease. A few crude wooden steps led down into the dark. My grandmother picked up a flashlight that was hanging on a post and was pleased to see that the batteries were still good. As we stooped together under the rooted, cool earth of the mound, she shone the light around for me. There were several shelves that held rows of glass storage jars; the glass was so cloudy and sooty it was impossible to tell what was in them. On one shelf was a box of corroded batteries, a stack of sooty candles, and a fossilized portable radio. In the middle of the dirt floor was a rotting table and a couple of half-collapsed chairs. The whole place looked as though nobody had bothered to take shelter there in decades.

The basics of tornadoes are not especially mysterious. The simplest way to think about them is to picture a pot of water on a stove. The essential thing is that the burners on the stove are heating the pot from the bottom up. This means that a layer of hot water is forming below a layer of cold water. As a result, the hot water is rising up but is being blocked by the cold water above it. That's an inherently unstable arrangement. At a certain point, as the heat intensifies, bubbles will begin to float from the hot zone through the cold zone to the surface. But these bubbles don't pop into existence randomly, all through the pot—at least not at first. Instead, a line of bubbles will appear in one specific place and rise up as though deliberately moving in single file.

This line of bubbles is created by a process called convection. "Convection" is a term for the concerted movement of a small group of molecules within the larger shapeless mass of a fluid or a gas. Several different things can cause convection, but one of the most common is heat transfer. In the case of the pot on the stove, the column of rising bubbles is transferring the heat through the cold layer without disturbing the rest of the water. The column is formed in this way because it requires less energy than a diffused heating of all the molecules in the liquid, and the rule in the physical world is that whatever takes the least energy is the thing that happens. (Only as the heat from the burners continues to warm the water does the process of convection at last get overwhelmed, resulting in the general indiscriminate hubbub of a boiling pot.)

The earth's atmosphere can be imagined in the same terms. Sunlight warms the earth, and the earth radiates the heat back out into the atmosphere; so it often happens that the lowest layer of air is warmer than the air directly above it. Convection columns will spontaneously arise in the atmosphere in order to transfer the hot molecules near the earth into the higher altitudes. These convection columns may take a variety of forms—the most dramatic and violent being the tornado. A tornado can be thought of as a last-ditch safety valve; it comes into existence only when the atmosphere is growing catastrophically unstable. It's a kind of emergency self-regulating mechanism that funnels huge volumes of hot air upward as fast as possible and restores the atmosphere to equilibrium.

Tornadoes can, in theory, form anywhere, and they have been observed all over the world (on every continent except Antarctica). But they are most common in the American prairie states. This is because of a fluke of geography. The extreme atmospheric instability that gives rise to the tornado generally happens only when a very large area of hot humid air is overrun by an equally large area of colder drier air. On other continents, the mountainous terrain tends to scatter flowing air masses into confused and irregular forms, but in the central plateau of North America, where the flat landscape extends for thousands of miles in all directions, vast air masses come into contact with each other with a kind of abstract purity as though in a continent-wide experimental laboratory. More than a thousand tornadoes touch down in America every year. This may seem like an appallingly large number, but in fact almost all these tornadoes are weak and brief-lived. The average tornado is less than a hundred yards wide, with winds well under a hundred miles an hour; it skims across the ground for a mile or two and dissipates without doing significant damage. Even in the area of the country where tornadoes are most common—Oklahoma, Kansas, Iowa, the region known as Tornado Alley—a really violent tornado is rare. My father's stories aside, the truth is that the majority of people in Tornado Alley go their whole lives without so much as glimpsing one.

The history of the American interior is in part a history of tornadoes. It's a curious kind of history, though, in that it consists largely of obliviousness and denial. The truth is that while midwesterners are afraid of tornadoes, and lots of them grow up as I did, obsessed with them and having recurring nightmares about them, the Midwest has been settled, developed, and generally overbuilt under the working assumption that tornadoes don't pose any serious danger. Simple shelters from tornadoes by and large do not exist. The advice about hiding in a corner of the basement, even if it were valid (which, as it happens, it isn't), can't be put into practice when the typical midwestern suburban house doesn't have a basement. And while storm cellars used to be common in the rural Midwest, many—perhaps most—have fallen into disuse, and few new ones are built. Those who are frightened of tornadoes find themselves in a situation like that of my recurring nightmare, of trying to alert people to a danger they won't recognize.

To the tornado obsessed, the very thing that makes everyone else so complacent is just what's so frightening: the tornado's elusiveness. It's not just that tornadoes are rare. It's that one can happen right in front of you and you still might not realize what you're seeing. They flash past with little or no warning. They can arrive hidden within curtains of falling rain or occluded by clouds of dust and debris. Some have moved at more than sixty miles an hour and have skimmed through entire towns before anyone outside the immediate damage zone even realized they were there. Sometimes it's only the amount of wreckage afterward, and the confused memories of the survivors that they had heard some gigantic, mysterious roar at the same instant, that confirmed that there really had been a tornado at all.

That wreckage, of course, is another reason the tornado can take such a hold on the imagination: tornadoes are so fantastically destructive. Before tornadoes were routinely captured on video, the main visual documentation of their existence was of their aftermath. Some of the earliest photographs and newsreels of the American Midwest are scenes of tornado damage. The images, even now, are grotesque and horrifying. Schools and churches become skeletal apparitions; heavy Victorian furniture is dangling from trees; a potbellied stove sits in a pig wallow; a town has become a plateau of splintered timber. They seem almost like examples of old American tall-tale art—the surreal postcards once sold as novelties, where solemn men in bowler hats inspected impossibly vast pumpkins and strawberries: comic boasts about the strangeness of life in the American heartland.

But the deepest mystery of the tornado is its actual physical presence. This is something that even now no video image can capture. A tornado funnel has an unforgettable quality of the surreal, or the hyper-real: its unimaginable size (tens of thousands of feet high), its apparent solidity, and its terrifyingly rapid movement all make it appear like a religious vision. A tornado seems to be not a cloud but some sort of inconceivable created structure—one that reaches up from the ground to the heavens as though extending from this world to the next. You can't help but see it as essentially supernatural.

The man who wrote "Ghost Riders in the Sky," Stan Jones, said it was based on an old cowboy legend. He'd heard it in his boyhood from an elderly cowhand, and he had no idea how much further it went back. The truth is that it can be taken back quite a long way: to medieval Europe and to the legend of the Wild Hunt. This was another story about strange huntsmen eternally riding after supernatural prey. In various versions of the legend, the huntsmen were demons, or ghosts, or fairies; they were led by Odin or Satan or King Arthur (or all three); they were hunting a supernatural horse, or a wild boar, or wood nymphs who took the form of windblown leaves. The sight of the Wild Hunt was often taken as a presage of disaster, of a coming war or a plague; almost always it meant doom for the eyewitness, who would be stolen away in sleep to join in the hunt himself.

The modern-day equivalent of the Wild Hunt can be seen on the highways of the American heartland every spring. They are caravans of station wagons and vans and SUVs, taking atmospheric soundings with their latest meteorological software, tracking dry lines and vortex signatures, searching for the mysterious and elusive terror of the funnel cloud. It seems like the latest and most cutting-edge kind of entertainment, but it, too, is a hunt that's been going on for a very long time. The contemporary tornado chasers are only the latest in a centuries-deep tradition of obsessive hunting. People rode after funnel clouds on horseback; they traced out damage tracks on foot, through unmapped forests and limitless swamps; they spent years sifting through paper archives, looking for the eyewitness testimony that would bring them closer to the unimaginable reality of the storm.

Most of those early hunters are forgotten now, but they used to be celebrities. James Espy, whose pursuit of the secrets of the tornado led him to be called the Storm King, was at one point the best-known scientist in America; his debates with other scientists were followed by newspapers as though they were boxing matches. John Park Finley traveled the country in the late nineteenth century to lecture on the unsuspected dangers of tornadoes and stirred up so much controversy that his career ended in a highly public shipwreck. And there were many others—professional meteorologists and obsessive amateurs, even a

Founding Father, people who risked their lives, wrecked their careers, and lost lifelong friends in poisonous feuds, all for the sake of that ever-receding quarry.

Their stories are mostly buried and have to be rooted out from all kinds of obscure sources: military field reports, privately printed pamphlets, family documents, unpublished memoirs, letters to editors, newspaper interviews, transcripts of courts-martial, congressional testimonies. But from them a strange kind of history does emerge—not a succession of blandly uplifting technological triumphs, but something more ambiguous: a story of doubts and blind guesses, grinding stupidity and unaccountable insight, horrifying violence and mysterious beauty. It's just what you'd expect from a hunt that's still thundering onward across those endless skies.

Prologue

The Pillar in the Storm

On May 8, 1680, on the outskirts of Cambridge, Massachusetts, a farmer named Samuel Stone saw a strange cloud appear in the northwestern sky. Stone later remembered the day as unusually hot, with a strong southwest wind blowing. Two things made him notice the cloud: it was moving toward him—which is to say, it was traveling against the wind—and it was singing.

In those days, people weren't necessarily shocked by strange apparitions in the sky. That was a time when scientific knowledge of the atmosphere was essentially nonexistent; there was no firm distinction drawn among clouds, comets, rainbows, the northern lights, and visions of heaven. They were all called meteors, which roughly meant "something transitory in the upper air." Meteors came in countless odd and often sinister forms. A comet was usually taken as a sign of disaster; a passing cloud shaped like a face or a hand could put a whole town in a panic. There were credible stories of ghostly armies seen fighting along the horizon at night and of demonic laughter falling from the moon. Samuel Stone doubtless thought the singing cloud was just another of these meteors.

Still, he called his son over, and the two stood in the middle of a field and watched as the cloud approached them. When it was directly overhead, its singing—a kind of buzzing ululation, like a trumpet— was suddenly answered from somewhere on the ground nearby. In a meadow beyond the fences, a little whirlwind had sprung up. The whirlwind came rushing across the fields, scattering the mown grass and weeds everywhere in wild spirals. It swept past the two men and charged up the hill toward their house. It was swelling up and growing stronger as it passed. By the time it reached the hilltop, it was uprooting and overturning trees. It crested the hilltop—missing the house but hitting the barn full on. The barn was a heavy construction of planking and trestles; the whirlwind ripped off the roof as though flicking at a stray leaf. The roof hung in midair for a moment and then fell to the earth with a thud so big it could be felt for a mile around.

Stone and his son raced up the hill. The rest of the family came cautiously out of the house. Nobody had been hurt, but they had all been terrified by the noise. They were astonished by the sight of the barn roof; the shriek of the whirlwind had been so loud that they hadn't even heard the crash.

The whole group stood together on the hilltop and watched the whirlwind skim off into the distance. It churned across a wide field of Indian corn, casting huge black plumes to either side. Then it floated up into the middle air and skipped along a line of hilltops. A half mile or so farther on, it reached down toward the earth again. They couldn't see what happened to it after that.

Stone's neighbor to the east, Matthew Bridge, took up the story. Bridge said that he, his son, and his servant John Robbins were working in the fields when they saw something moving rapidly over the ground straight toward them. It was a pitch-dark, billowing cloud about a hundred yards wide. It was sucking up everything in its path as it advanced: bushes were being ripped out of the soil by the roots, ancient fallen trees were rising into the air and tumbling up into the blackness, large rocks and boulders were soaring skyward like some kind of mysterious avalanche in reverse. So many leaves and tree branches were swirling in the heights, Bridge said, "the top and sides of the cloud looked like a greenwood."

The three men stared at the cloud in wonderment until it was almost on top of them. Then they all made a break toward the house for shelter. But it was too late; midway across the open field, they were engulfed. They threw themselves to the ground in the middle of a stand of bushes. The cloud roared around them and lashed them with a torrent of flying debris. Robbins couldn't hold on; he let go with a despairing cry and was sucked into the blast. As the shriek of the wind reached a crescendo, Bridge couldn't stop himself from looking up. The air was black as night, but within its surging fury he could make out something strange. There was a revolving glow at the heart of the cloud. Bridge described it as "a light pillar, about eight or ten foot diameter, which seemed like a screw or solid body."

Then the cloud and the glowing pillar were gone. Bridge and his son shook free from the branches and clods of dirt and rose shakily to their feet. Robbins was nowhere to be seen. They found him a little later on the far side of the field. Almost every inch of his body was bruised, almost every bone was broken, and he was dead.

The cloud had already roared on out of sight. Bridge and his son began following its trail; they were soon joined by the Stone family, who'd come riding over from their farm. The line of damage led out of the cleared land at the edge of town back into the dense woodlands. It went on for more than a mile: the trees were all downed as though swept by a gigantic broom. The track of the cloud spread out the deeper it went, until it was a couple hundred yards wide. It finally dwindled away in the depths of a swamp bristling with hundreds of spruce trees.

Nobody in the group had any notion of what the cloud was. They'd never seen anything like it in their lives. So Bridge and Stone turned to the best-educated man they knew, the pastor of the local church. He had no idea what it could be, either; he might have been inclined to disbelieve the men if he hadn't seen the track of damage himself. So he wrote out a detailed summary of their story, and he mailed it to the only man in the American colonies he thought might have a better clue: the celebrated Puritan preacher Increase Mather.

Mather was famous in those days for his hellfire sermonizing (he was the father of Cotton Mather, who inherited his style), but he was also known for his interest in odd and unusual events. He called these events "illustrious providences," by which he meant something roughly like "memorable occurrences." In one of his books he defined illustrious providences this way: "tempests, floods, earthquakes, thunders as are unusual, strange apparitions, witchcrafts, diabolical possessions, remarkable judgements upon noted sinners, and answers of prayer." He had been collecting these stories for years. He gathered them from newspapers, from anecdotes in classical literature, from contemporary journals and books of letters (he was an omnivorous reader; he owned books on everything from medicine in the ancient world to a salacious contemporary story about the lives of London prostitutes). He knew stories about magical amulets, stories about strange plants and animals growing in people's bodies, stories about people who broke into a sweat when a cat entered a room unseen, and one story about a man who, presented with a meal of pork, broke into hysterical laughter.

Mather was particularly fascinated by stories about the weather. He held to the common Christian view of those days that storms were the work of Lucifer, "prince of the powers of the air"; in one of his sermons he pictured Lucifer dwelling amid the fumes and smoke of a thunderstorm like an alchemist in his laboratory. But he also loved any weather story that was odd and inexplicable. He was intrigued by rainstones, for instance. These were mysterious rocks that fell from the sky at the height of thunderstorms. One rainstone was a hunk of iron that weighed fifty pounds; another proved to be a kind of brass that was impervious to the hottest forge; and Mather also had a report of a town in Germany that was once pelted with a shower of rainstones "of a green and partly cerulean color . . . with metallic sparks like gold intermixed."

But he was most curious about American weather. He had a notion that the weather in North America was more violent than it was anywhere else in the world. There was no way to tell this for sure; nobody was keeping weather records. And anyway, the weather in America, like almost everything else about America, was still almost wholly unknown; the colonies were still only a thin scattering of clearings between the ocean and a vast unmapped forest. Still, Mather (who had been born in the colonies) kept hearing from recent arrivals that the weather back home in Europe was nowhere near as extreme as it was in the New World, and he had duly collected several instances of American weather that seemed to be uniquely violent: hailstorms so severe that they'd caused fatalities, and winter storms that left entire towns encased in ice. He knew many instances of New England storms with deadly lightning, including one case where a lightning bolt had blasted through a church window and melted a man's hair to a pillar.

The story from Cambridge of the strange cloud with the glowing pillar within it was a natural for Mather's collection. Mather made room for it in the book he was writing—a survey of his oddest stories, which he titled *An Essay for the Recording of Illustrious Providences.* He admitted that he had no idea what the cloud was. Nor did he have any stories that were quite like it. The closest he could get was a story about a strange nighttime incident in the forests of Massachusetts—an event that was described as "a dreadful havoc." There were no eyewitnesses, but when people went into the forest the next morning, they found that thousands of trees had been downed. Was this another instance of the pillar in the cloud? Was this another uniquely American kind of storm? Mather refused to speculate. He cut the discussion off with a curt dismissal: "Thus about strange storms." Then he changed the subject to earthquakes.

But he couldn't shake the thought of the storm. There was one more authority he could consult: the recently founded Royal Society of London. It was an organization devoted to what was then known as natural philosophy and is now called the sciences—archaeology, chemistry, physics, astronomy, meteorology: anything at all that involved the physical world. He sent the society's members a long summary of the strange cloud. They were baffled by the story, too. But they published it in the next issue of their journal, *Philosophical Transactions.* (The journal's full name was *Philosophical Transactions, Giving Some Accompt of the Present Undertakings, Studies, and Labours of the Ingenious in Many Considerable Parts of the World.*)

Amid the riotous clutter of reporting in the journal's pages, the latest news and speculations about eclipses, microbes, disastrous frosts, "the Sepulchral Lamps of the Ancients," and "an anatomy of a Monstrous Pig," Mather's letter went unnoticed. It stayed buried in the back issues for more than seventy years, until it was found by another, much more famous investigator of illustrious providences—Benjamin Franklin.

PART I

THE THUNDER HOUSE

I

The Electricians

Among the popular entertainers and traveling acts in eighteenth-century America were performers known as electricians. They gave lectures on the subject of static electricity. That may sound like the height of tedium, but back then static electricity was a wholly mysterious phenomenon, and the lectures included spectacular demonstrations of its unusual properties. The electricians had arrays of metal wheels that shot off multicolored sparks when they were spun. They had long glass tubes called auroras that glowed in the dark and, when rubbed vigorously with silk cloth, could draw up metal filings as though they were magnets. They had Leyden jars—ceramic bottles with coils of copper wire that could store and release static charges. The lectures of the electricians were dazzling shows, punctuated by furious sizzlings and loud banging flashes that would make the ladies in the audience scream in delighted terror and could even force grunts of alarm from the most stoic of the men.

In 1743, a Scottish electrician named Dr. Archibald Spencer performed in Boston. Dr. Spencer's act was more serious than that of most electricians. He had an elaborate theory about the nature of electricity that he would describe at great length between the special effects. Spencer's theory was based on the idea that electricity was a "subtle fluid." This was a term borrowed from Renaissance alchemy; it meant a fluid that was weightless, invisible, and, under normal circumstances, undetectable. Spencer believed that the subtle fluid of electricity was a hidden fire emitted by the sun, which scorched the eyes and was thus responsible for every form of eye disease. (The electrical theory of disease was a particular interest of Spencer's, since he'd been trained as a physician.) He also believed electrical fluid was present everywhere in earth's atmosphere. It revealed itself in countless tiny ways. A recently fired bullet, for instance, was hot to the touch: this was because of its passage through the electrical fluid. A strong wind was fiery on the cheeks even on the coldest days: that was an electrical fluid burn. But the presence of the fluid was most apparent in a thunderstorm. The air, Spencer explained, was filled with ice crystals, which during storms were melted by the heat of the electrical fluid: the melted water fell as rain, the dissolving crystals released lightning bolts, and the thunderclap was the rush of air into the vacuum the crystals left behind.

Dr. Spencer was careful not to neglect his props. Within the blaze of stage fire, he showed how common objects, from amber to hemp twine, were alive with electrical fluid. He set up a large table and covered its surface with flakes of brass and gold; then he very slowly drew across it a gleaming aurora tube, and the glittering flakes, to the astonishment of the audience, would twitch and crawl and swirl up into the air. At the climax of his talk, Spencer had all but a few of the candles put out. In the dimness, a strange apparition could be made out: a young boy was floating in midair. (He was held up by silk ropes suspended from the ceiling.) Spencer stood beside the boy's feet, holding out one of the aurora tubes. He intoned that the fire of electrical fluid suffused the entire universe and was spontaneously produced by all bodies everywhere on earth. He would now prove its presence right before the spectators' eyes. He waved the aurora tube back and forth, and then, after a hushed interval, wild crackling bolts shot out from the boy's head and outstretched hands.

In the audience at the Boston performance was a celebrity: Ben Franklin. He was then in his late thirties. Almost everything that he is known for today—the inventions and scientific discoveries, the revolutionary politics, the long illustrious career as a diplomat—was still in his future. In 1743 he was a successful printer and newspaper publisher, and he was famous because he was the editor of *Poor Richard's Almanack,* the great best seller of colonial America. The book had earned him so much money that he was already thinking of retiring, and he was looking idly around for a hobby to pass the time.

Franklin was spellbound by Spencer's show. Immediately afterward he introduced himself and offered to serve as a theatrical agent if Spencer ever came to Philadelphia. Spencer decided to take him up on it. Franklin proved to be as good as his word. He threw himself into the job. He booked lecture halls, arranged for private performances for Philadelphia's aristocracy, talked the shows up in his newspaper, *The Pennsylvania Gazette,* and sold the tickets himself. He enjoyed himself so much that he thought of going on the road with Spencer as his full-time agent.

But that was when Spencer made a confession. He was weary of the traveling life. He wanted to give up his act and return to his old career as a physician. Franklin wasn't fazed. He at once decided to buy out Spencer's props, master his stage techniques, and become an electrician himself.

For a man who'd gotten rich extolling the virtues of temperance, prudence, and industry, Franklin was notorious among his friends for his wild and whirling enthusiasms. Each new idea may have looked from the outside like the soul of sober practicality, but it would last only as long as his excitement did and would be petulantly dropped as soon as he met with boredom or criticism or practical difficulty. Ocean navigation, the cultivation of hybrid grains, the ideal design for kitchen stoves—he seemed to take up subjects at random, burst out with a fireworks shower of innovative ideas, and then move on.

His passion for electricity was almost throttled as soon as it began. His first look at what he'd bought was dismaying. Spencer's props were shoddily made, and most of them were falling apart; Spencer himself, beneath his grand theorizing, proved to have no idea at all how any of them worked. The aurora tube, for instance: it was just a long, featureless hollow glass pipe, open at one end. Why it displayed such curious powers when rubbed by a silk cloth Spencer couldn't begin to guess. In the same way, he could tell Franklin authoritatively that static charges were seen to best advantage in closed rooms lit by masses of candles and wouldn't appear at all in the open air. But why was it true? Spencer could only shrug. Franklin wasn't deterred. He was still in his first flush of excitement over the project; he decided to commission replacements for all Spencer's gear and master the electrical trade from scratch.

Philadelphia, like most colonial towns, wasn't stratified into commercial and residential districts as cities are today; every street was a jumble of houses, stores, taverns, market stands, smithies, and workshops. Franklin could buy almost anything America had for sale within shouting distance of his front door. He hired a local potter who could fire the ceramic Leyden jars in large quantities. Glassmaking at that time was mostly done overseas, but Franklin found an ironworker who had some experience blowing glass and commissioned a sample set of aurora tubes from him, and when those proved satisfactory, he began snowing the man under with fresh orders. It was later said that Franklin created Philadelphia's glassmaking industry single-handedly.

Franklin wasn't one to keep his passions to himself. When he had a new hobby, everybody was expected to take part—family, household servants, friends, neighbors, and random passersby. They became spectators, assistants, collaborators, and sometimes unwilling subjects. Franklin's house became America's first experimental laboratory in electrical research. The parlor was the theater where he'd reveal his latest innovations. One time he showed a large, lumbering marionette of a spider that would jump and jiggle and dance with alarming energy whenever it was goosed with a charged copper wire. Another time it was a Bible with raised metal lettering on the cover: when the curtains were drawn and the candles put out, the holy word could be seen burning weirdly in the dark and shooting out sparks whenever anybody got too close. The most elaborate stunt was called "The Lady's Kiss." The lady in question would sit in a chair while several aurora tubes were passed over and around her. Then a succession of young men would attempt to kiss her. Each time, the crackling static discharge from her lips and forehead would knock the suitor flat to the floor.

Franklin's friends and collaborators started calling themselves the American Philosophical Society. Franklin used this grand title as his entrée to correspondence with the leading natural philosophers in Europe. He admitted that he felt out of his depth in such company: he was just an amateur playing around with toys; he really knew even less about the mystery of static charges than Spencer did. But he soon discovered that none of his illustrious correspondents were that much more knowledgeable about the subject than he was. They were eager to hear of his experiments, no matter how frivolous or extravagant they seemed. Some of his letters were read aloud at meetings of the Royal Society of London and found their way into its journal, *Philosophical Transactions* (which was still going strong, after seventy-five years; in fact it's still being published today).

The letters brimmed over with dazzling new ideas. Franklin was the first person to grasp the existence of conservation of charge, one of the core principles of modern physics. He discovered the phenomenon of electrical polarity: he named the two poles positive and negative, and represented them with a plus and a minus, as is still routinely done today. The loud bangs and crashes from discharging Leyden jars reminded him of an artillery battery firing, which is why, more than two centuries later, we call the successors of Leyden jars batteries.

But there was something else in his letters, especially after the first few years: a growing impatience. By the end of the 1740s, he was complaining that he couldn't come up with any practical use for electricity, except the creation of new parlor tricks. Grasping at straws, he wrote to one correspondent that he'd found it was possible to kill turkeys and other small fowl with electrical current—a breakthrough that might, he hoped, result in a juicier and more tender bird.

It was only in this mood of frustration that he at last took up the larger question of what electricity was.

He had only a few notions. He was inclined to think that Dr. Spencer had been right: electricity was a "subtle fluid" that imbued the whole universe. That led him to consider a novel idea: whether static electricity might be related to lightning.

Lightning was at that point still mysterious. It was generally believed to be some form of fire; lightning strikes did start fires, after all, and they often left behind the smell of brimstone. But lightning also deranged compasses and lodestones, as a strong static charge sometimes would, and also the two phenomena just looked so similar it was hard to believe they weren't related. So Franklin weighed the evidence. He knew by then that static electricity was created by friction—the friction of a silk cloth rubbed on an aurora tube, for instance, or of a cat's fur petted in a dry room on a winter's day. Could lightning simply be the same phenomenon of friction occurring on a much grander scale? If so, then where did the friction come from? This could be explained by the theory, first published by the Swiss mathematician Daniel Bernoulli less than twenty years earlier, that the atmosphere was made up of countless discrete molecules jostling against each other. Franklin got the idea that the atmosphere might be a kind of ocean of electrical charge, where shapeless domains of positive and negative energy, generated by friction, were continuously arising and dissipating.

The idea wasn't wholly original with him; many natural philosophers were investigating the nature of the atmosphere then, and they had begun to think along similar lines. The difference was that Franklin immediately saw a way of testing it.

He outlined his idea in a series of letters to his correspondents at the Royal Society. He proposed that a platform be erected at the top of a cathedral spire. A man should be stationed there with a metal rod; Franklin thought the rod should be thirty or forty feet long. If the theory was right and lightning was caused by the agitation of air molecules, then the static charge should be greatest when the air was at its most turbulent, and that seemed most obviously to be during a thunderstorm. Therefore the man on the platform should wait till a storm approached and then hold the rod up as high toward the clouds as he could. An electric charge should flow down the rod to its base, and a Leyden jar connected to the rod with a wire would collect it. (There was, Franklin conceded, some small danger in the experiment; he recommended that the platform be insulated and the man wear insulated gloves and boots.)

Franklin regretted that he was unable to carry the experiment out himself. He was up against a practical problem: at that time, Philadelphia simply didn't have any cathedrals or towers that were tall enough. All he could do was invite the members of the Royal Society to try it themselves, in one of England's old cathedral towns.

He sent off the letters. He knew it would be months before he would get any response. And as he waited, it occurred to him for the first time that there was another, much simpler way of sampling the electrical energy of the sky.

So this was how the most famous moment of his life came about.

On a blustery afternoon in the spring of 1752, he and his son William went riding around the open country outside Philadelphia, looking for a suitable place to fly a kite. The kite was one that Franklin had constructed himself. He'd stretched silk cloth across a wooden frame—silk was a tougher material than parchment paper, which is what kites were usually made from—and alongside its knotted tail he'd hung a metal wire. The kite string was several hundred yards of hemp twine, and at the other end of the roll he'd tied a large iron key.

Franklin and his son found a wide windswept pasturage near a stand of trees. They set up their experiment there during a golden late-afternoon lull between storms. The sky overhead was mottled white and blue; a strong fresh spring wind was blowing. Even though the kite was heavy, it went up almost at once. Big purplish clouds were building again in the southwest, and a few sprinkles were already blowing across the field. They waited. The rain was falling in fitful gusts. Franklin and his son took shelter in a small shed near the trees. There they stood in the open doorway, allowing the hemp line to unspool and the kite to wander wildly in the gulfs of darkening sky.

For a long while nothing happened. The rain was falling more heavily. The iron key remained dead to the touch. Franklin decided that the experiment was a washout. He got ready to take the kite down and to pack away the Leyden jar he'd brought with him to collect the charge. Then he noticed that a few strands of hemp in the line, now thoroughly wet with rain, were slowly rising up and sinuously undulating like snakes. He reached out cautiously to touch the key, and a small bright crackle jumped the gap to the tip of his finger. Quickly he held out the Leyden jar to the key and charged it.

That was all. He and his son reeled the kite in and rode back into town. Franklin didn't even bother to tell anybody what he had done. The story of the kite didn't become known for several years afterward. For once he was content with the private knowledge that he was right.

Franklin's letters to the Royal Society about the proposed electricity experiment were immediately published as a pamphlet and circulated among the natural philosophers of Europe. In France, one group of noblemen at the court of Louis XV (a famous patron of electrical research, mainly because he liked electricians' shows) decided to be the first to try it. They didn't bother with the platform on the cathedral. Instead, they simply erected a forty-foot metal pole in a village green outside Paris and waited for a thunderstorm. It didn't take long for the blustery summer weather to oblige. The pole was struck one afternoon with a dazzling, deafening bolt. The noblemen dealt with it cautiously; they were mindful of Franklin's advice about insulating themselves from the charge. But they resorted to a more traditional and aristocratic form of insulation. They paid a local citizen to make the final approach for them. He held out a copper wire to the pole. Immediately there was a flash and a bang that knocked him flat. The noblemen paid him off (he was shaken up but otherwise appeared unharmed), and they rode back in triumph to Versailles.

In Russia, a Swedish natural philosopher named Georg Richmann, a professor at the prestigious Academy of St. Petersburg, devised yet another and more elaborate version of Franklin's experiment. He set up his metal pole on the roof of his house—an incongruous glint among the peaked stone of St. Petersburg's skyline. He attached it to a brass chain that ran down the exterior wall and through his study window. In the study the chain was connected to an iron rod suspended by wires from the ceiling. Below the rod was a large compass needle on a spike. Below the spike was a bowl of water in which Richmann sprinkled iron filings.

He did all this in the summer of 1753, which happened to be unusually dry, with only a few fleeting rainstorms. For weeks the whole apparatus remained silent. But Richmann was gratified to notice that the iron filings did mysteriously shift and rearrange themselves slightly in the bowl of water whenever threatening clouds glided overhead.

St. Petersburg didn't see a big storm until August. Richmann was attending a lecture at the academy when he heard the thunder. He hurried home, accompanied by a colleague named Sokolaw—an engraver at the academy who had been hired by Richmann to illustrate the book he was writing about his experiments. Richmann wanted him there to document the moment of his triumph. They reached Richmann's house before the storm broke. The apparatus was still motionless; the iron filings hadn't stirred. Richmann told Sokolaw there was no danger yet—although, he said, he wouldn't swear to how safe it would remain when the storm hit.

As Richmann was talking, he was leaning toward the bowl of iron filings. The compass needle twitched slightly. Then Sokolaw saw something strange: the air around the iron rod began to shimmer. A little sphere of dazzling light congealed in midair. Sokolaw described it as "a globe of blue and whitish fire, about four inches in diameter." It floated up from the iron rod, hovered for a moment, and then arrowed directly into Richmann's forehead.

There was a deafening thunderclap. The room imploded: papers and books and glass jars on Richmann's shelves were hurled to the floor; the door to the study was blown inward off its hinges; Sokolaw ended up flat on his face with charred debris and shards of glass pummeling his back. Then there was silence. Sokolaw roused himself cautiously and surveyed the room. Scraps of hot metal from the wrecked apparatus were scattered everywhere. Everything made of glass was shattered, and everything made of paper or fabric was singed—even Sokolaw's clothes were singed.

Richmann's body was lying beneath an overturned table. His hair had been burned off, his skin scorched a deep ruddy red, and one shoe had been blown apart—marking the place on the sole of his foot where the brilliant blue and white globe, after tearing through his flesh, had burst out into the air again and melted away in the universal ocean of electrical fire.

When Franklin heard the news of Richmann's death, he was inspired to create a new prop for an electrical show. It was a wooden toy house, about the size of a doll's house. There was a metal rod fixed to its chimney and a wire running down to the ground. The electrician would stand on the other side of the stage and direct a static discharge toward it; the charge drained away harmlessly. He then removed the rod and wire and repeated the display. The house (which had been secretly filled with gunpowder before the show) promptly exploded. Franklin called it the Thunder House. The electrician would conclude the show by urging audience members to install lightning rods on their houses. The lightning rod was Franklin's invention—his first success at finding something useful to do with electricity.

Meanwhile, the death of Richmann made Franklin world famous. It was taken as a spectacular confirmation of what the natural philosophers of Europe were calling, in honor of Franklin's hometown, the "Philadelphia experiment." After that, they were all rushing to try the experiment for themselves. From everywhere came reports of success; one group in England independently had the idea of using a kite, and they, too, returned with a charged Leyden jar. Franklin himself, in a somber account of Richmann's death written for *The Pennsylvania Gazette,* couldn't help but add that, tragic as it was, it did prove the theory correct.

Franklin was now a universally respected natural philosopher, the world's authority on all things electrical. But he was soon discomfited to realize that because of the Philadelphia experiment, everybody also thought of him now as something more—the great authority on a subject he knew almost nothing about: the weather.

2

A Little More of the Marvelous

One night in the summer of 1749, a waterspout appeared in the Mediterranean Sea just off the coast of Italy. This wasn't an unprecedented event. Waterspouts had always been seen in the Mediterranean. The Roman writer Pliny the Elder, in his *Natural History,* mentioned the mysterious pillars of water that sometimes materialized out of nowhere in the open sea and overturned boats. But for the most part, these waterspouts were remote and vague apparitions—white writhing snakes that danced in the heat of a blue afternoon and vanished before anyone got too close. The 1749 waterspout was a pitch-black monster crowned with lightning that came roaring from the dark sea after midnight and crashed its way onshore.

Its landfall was in the port town of Ostia. It swept through the ancient clutter of stone docks and warehouses that swarmed the harbor and then moved inland, roughly along the track of the old imperial road toward Rome. As it thundered across the countryside, it tore the trestled roofs off farmhouses, stampeded flocks out of their straggling pens, and hurled debris against the crumbling stone arches of antique tenements. The trail of damage went on for nearly twenty miles. Hundreds of buildings were wrecked—some had been standing for more than a thousand years—dozens of people were injured, and three were reported killed. The spout finally collapsed on the outskirts of the old Roman suburbs.

The news of this strange visitation caused a panic throughout the region. The spout was almost universally believed to be a sign of the apocalypse. The pope was one of the few skeptics, but he kept his opinion to himself. In order to calm the populace, he announced that he was calling upon a well-regarded expert to investigate the incident and issue a public report. The expert was the most famous natural philosopher in Italy, Father Ruder Boscovich.

Father Ruder was a Croatian raised by the Jesuits of Rome. His specialty was astronomy, a subject in which he had made several major discoveries. But the pope thought of him more as an all-purpose authority on anything scientific or technical. He had once consulted him on a project to drain the Pontine Marshes. When there was an uproar in Rome because cracks had been discovered in the dome of St. Peter's and its collapse appeared to be imminent—this, too, had been regarded as a sign of the apocalypse—Father Ruder had been called in to solve that crisis as well. He designed a set of concentric iron rings to brace the dome. The solution worked, and the father demanded and got an unusual form of payment: the pope had to agree to remove Copernicus from the Vatican's Index of banned books.

Summoned to investigate the waterspout, Father Ruder set to work at once. He inspected the trail of ruin. He interviewed survivors and eyewitnesses. He did some research among the records of unusual meteorological events in the vast Vatican library. Then he wrote a detailed monograph laying out his investigations and conclusions. The work only took him a few months, and his monograph was printed and on sale by the end of the year—a fast turnaround time in those days for a two-hundred-page book.

The title was *On the Whirlwind During the Night of June 11–12 (Sopra il turbine che la notte tra gli XI e XII giugno)*. Because of the speed of its composition, it was a fairly slapdash piece of work. Much of it was taken up with what anxious readers would have regarded as an irrelevant side issue: the father's speculations on the general nature of the atmosphere. The father was highly intrigued by a recent suggestion made by the British philosopher Stephen Hales that the atmosphere wasn't one uniform substance but a combination of many gases and particles; many pages of the book were spent exploring the idea. But at last he came to the point: his analysis of the great waterspout. Here the father was both concrete and specific. While people tended to believe that waterspouts were phenomena of the deep waters of the Mediterranean, the historical records were clear that they did sometimes appear in the shallows off the coasts, and there had been a few documented cases of waterspouts coming ashore. His conclusion was that this was a rare but not unprecedented natural occurrence, and certainly not a sign of the apocalypse.

The book was widely read in Italy, and a Latin translation was soon published for the benefit of the scientific community in Europe. (Latin was losing its dominance by then as the lingua franca of intellectual discussion, but it still had more readers than Italian.) In the summer of 1750, a year after the spout, an extended English-language synopsis and review of the book ran in the London magazine *The Monthly Review.* It stirred up a lot of interest. Over the next few years, several philosophers became intrigued about the nature of waterspouts. But there was clearly only one person whose opinion mattered. Copies of the *Review* began arriving in Benjamin Franklin's mail, with cover letters asking what he made of it.

In his haphazard way, Franklin had come up with a few ideas about weather over the years. He had realized, for instance, that in North America large storms tended to move from southwest to northeast; this was an obvious truth that no one else in the colonies seems to have noticed. He had also grasped that in large storm systems the prevailing winds at the surface don't necessarily reflect the direction the storm is moving in—a subtle principle that wouldn't be fully accepted by meteorologists for another century. But none of this made him an expert on storms. His great discovery about the nature of lightning happened only because of his speculations about static electricity; thunderstorms had entered into the picture almost by accident.

But he, too, found himself fascinated by the story of the great spout. He immediately threw himself into an investigation of the nature of waterspouts. He had never seen one himself, and he wasn't about to mount an expedition to find them; this was strictly a paper chase. He and his friends and correspondents ransacked old histories and travelers' tales for stories of waterspouts. There wasn't much to go on. The richest vein of material was in the back issues of the *Philosophical Transactions,* where there were detailed accounts sent in by explorers and ships' officers who had long experience of the perils of waterspouts in the Mediterranean and the tropics. Some of them had even conducted their own science experiments: they had fired cannonballs at the spouts to see if that would break them up. (It didn't work.)

As Franklin read through these stories, he very rapidly fashioned a theory; he tended to arrive at his theories in a great rush or not at all. The prevailing belief then was that a waterspout was a hollow pillar of water, rising up out of the sea or descending like a waterfall from the clouds. (The Hebrew word for "waterspout," as used in the book of Psalms, could also be translated as "waterfall.") Franklin immediately realized that this was physically impossible. The tube of the waterspout simply couldn't be made out of water. Water is extremely heavy—so heavy that no force known in nature could raise or sustain such a large body of it in midair. So this meant that the solid appearance of the spout had to be an illusion. The spout, Franklin believed, was in fact an ascending column of air, and it only appeared to be made of water because a fog of water vapor was condensing around it as it rose.

Franklin then had a second and odder realization. If the spout was air and not water, then there was no necessary reason for it to be confined to seas and oceans. It could, at least in principle, appear over land as easily as it did over water. The track of the Italian waterspout already suggested as much. But where were all these native landspouts? In the Bible there were many references to mysterious whirlwinds and columns of smoke (one of them had led Israel to the promised land). But Franklin wanted evidence that was modern and unequivocal.

He found his first piece of evidence deep within the archives of the *Philosophical Transactions*. In the volume for the year 1703, there had appeared an account by an English minister named Abraham De la Pryme of something he had witnessed over the Yorkshire countryside. De la Pryme called it "one of those strange works of nature called spouts, or rather hurricanes." He described it as "a great circumgyration or whirling, which made a noise somewhat like the motion of a millstone. Ever and anon it darted down out of itself a long spout, in which I observed a motion like that of a screw." This spout had swept through the countryside, doing minor damage to village rooftops, and had vanished as mysteriously as it had come.

This was clearly a whirlwind over land, just what Franklin was looking for. He was encouraged to go on searching. And that was how, deeper in the archives, he came across Increase Mather's old, forgotten story of the illustrious providence—the strange cloud that had passed over Cambridge.

Franklin read through Mather's story with minute care. (The author's name was certain to have caught his eye anyway, because in his early childhood the Franklins and the Mathers had been family friends.) Its similarity to De la Pryme's account of the "circumgyration" was striking. Both clouds had made strange noises, one singing and one grinding; in both there had been a curious screwlike revolving motion. They were obviously the same type of storm.

Franklin then found another story. This was a report to the Royal Society made by a British naval physician named Alexander Stuart. On an August afternoon in 1702, Stuart had witnessed a cluster of waterspouts in the Atlantic off the Barbary Coast. One passage in particular made a great impression on Franklin. "It was observable of all of them," Stuart had written, "but chiefly of the large pillar, that towards the end it began to appear like a hollow canal, only black in the borders, but white in the middle; and though at first it was altogether black and opaque, yet one could very distinctly perceive the sea-water to fly up along the middle of this canal, as smoke does up a chimney, and that with great swiftness, and very perceptible motion."

Franklin saw at once the resemblance to the Cambridge cloud. He compared Stuart's description of the white column of the waterspout with Mather's of the revolving pillar of light at the heart of the storm. "These accounts," Franklin wrote, "the one of water-spouts, the other of a whirlwind, seem in this particular to agree; what one gentleman describes as a tube, black in the borders, and white in the middle, the other calls a black cloud with a pillar of light in it; the latter expression has only a little more of the *marvellous,* but the thing is the same."

Franklin could even think of a possible explanation. He thought both witnesses were seeing sunlight illuminating the hollow column of rising air hidden within the cloud. If so, then the Cambridge cloud was the same type of cloud as the tropical waterspout. And both were like the screwlike spout that the English minister had seen in Yorkshire.

Maybe it was an extraordinarily rare phenomenon, but here was plain evidence that there existed a violent whirlwind on land identical to a waterspout at sea.

What caused it? What sustained it? Where was it to be found? Franklin couldn't begin to imagine the answers to any of these questions. He didn't even know what the thing should be named. Sometimes he referred to his quarry as a landspout. Other times he simply called it a whirlwind.

One word he never used for it was "tornado."

The word did exist. It had been coined sometime in the late sixteenth century. It was a mashup of two Spanish words: *tronada,* which means thunderstorm, and *tornar,* to turn, to twist, to return. It seems to have been used first by British sailors, and they may have originally meant it as a joke—a way of scoring off the tendency of Spanish and Portuguese mariners to have overly precise technical terms for the weather. *Tornar* plus *tronada* became "tornado," because ending with an *o* is how English speakers have always made up words of mock Spanish.

Its actual meaning, to the extent that it had ever acquired one, was vague. Generally, it was used to describe a bad storm at sea, particularly one where the wind direction kept changing. One seventeenth-century traveler remarked that the tropics were "wonderful unwholesome . . . for we had nothing but tornadoes, with such thunder, lightning and rain, that we could not keep our men dry 3 hours together, which was an occasion of the infection among them." Another wrote that his ship had been becalmed for eighteen days, "having now and then contrary winds and some tornadoes."

But then, most of the words used for storms and tempests had indefinite meanings, or no meaning at all. "Tornado," "hurricane," "gale," "whirlwind," "windstorm," "cyclone"—well into the nineteenth century, all these words in popular usage meant little more than "a bad storm with strong winds." They were used interchangeably, sometimes in the same sentence: news accounts talked about "a remarkable hurricane," "a terrible whirlwind," "a tremendous gust of wind," "a tremendous tornado," "the most violent tornado or hurricane ever known in the memory of the oldest person living in this part of the country." In only a few cases is it possible to tell what type of storm was meant. In fact most people didn't grasp that storms even had distinct types. A storm was simply a vast outbreak of anarchy, a shapeless chaos of rain, lightning, and destructive wind.

Franklin and his circle appear to be the first natural philosophers to try to sort out storms into distinct categories. In his writings, Franklin himself seems to have used the word "tornado" only once, in order to refer to tropical storms at sea, and he meant it to indicate the kinds of storms he was specifically not interested in. One of his correspondents, the philosopher John Perkins, may have been the first person to use it in the modern sense. In a paper submitted to the Royal Society in the late 1750s, he complained about the confusing terminology being used for windstorms and how hard that made it to establish what exactly the storms were. He suggested that "tornado," despite its original meaning, be reserved for the kind of storm that Franklin was talking about. "By the term tornado, or wind-spout," he wrote, "I mean a violent wind which has been observed in these northern colonies a few times since they were discovered and settled by our people."

Franklin's first rush of forward progress was quickly stymied by the elusiveness of the subject. None of his correspondents had ever seen a landspout, and not many believed it existed. But then, they weren't impressed with his theory of spouts generally. He composed a formal monograph laying out his best guess as to the waterspout's internal workings, and he submitted it to the fellows of the Royal Society; not only did they fail to read it aloud to their membership, as they had with his letters on electricity, but they declined to bump it up for immediate publication. Instead, it languished with the rest of their backlog for years.

Franklin circulated the monograph among his friends and correspondents. None of them were enthusiastic. In fact their general tone was niggling, critical, and dismissive. The particular point of contention was the thing that Franklin considered the core of his whole theory: the waterspout was an ascending column of air. Nobody believed this. It was obvious that waterspouts were made of water. Nor did they accept that waterspouts rose up rather than descended. From the testimonies collected in Franklin's own investigation, most witnesses were absolutely clear that the column of the spout reached down from the clouds to the ocean. So how could anything about Franklin's theory be true?

Franklin's correspondents tried to be helpful. One of them wrote condescendingly, as though correcting a clever child, that he himself had seen a waterspout and obviously knew better than Franklin did. The base of the waterspout had writhed in the ocean like the snout of an elephant, and it had distinctly emitted a loud hissing noise: this was proof that the spout was exhaling air rather than taking it in. Clearly Franklin needed to reexamine his theory and would then doubtless arrive at a correct explanation. To another correspondent, Franklin was obliged to write politely, "At present I would only say, that the opinion of winds being generated in clouds by fermentation is new to me, and I am unacquainted with the facts on which it is founded."

The real problem—as Franklin himself realized—was that the theory didn't work. It foundered on one essential point: how waterspouts and other whirlwinds formed. Franklin believed that there had to be some sort of near vacuum in the heart of the storm that was drawing the winds into it at great speed. But with no evidence to suggest how this vacuum might come into existence and no theory of how it could sustain itself, Franklin was at a loss to explain the hows and whys of spouts on land or sea. He was at a dead end. In 1754, he wrote to John Perkins (one of those who'd originally sent him the magazine article about the Rome waterspout): "I am now not much nearer a conclusion in the matter of the spout than when I first read your letter."

3

To Treat Master Franklin

In those years, the main road through the American colonies was known as the King's Highway. Franklin spent a lot of time traveling on it during the early 1750s. He had three great projects he was engaged upon then—the same era when he was consumed by his research into the mystery of the landspout. He had founded a teaching academy in Philadelphia; he'd accepted an appointment as assistant postmaster for the colonies; and he'd become the quartermaster for an ambitious military expedition to conquer and colonize the richly fertile land of the Ohio River valley—he believed it was both inevitable and desirable that the colonists would ultimately take the entire forest from the Native Americans, and he thought it would take a major war to accomplish this. He needed money, he needed political support, and he needed influential contacts to accomplish the three tasks, and to find all these things, he needed to be on the road.

That wasn't easy. The King's Highway was an abysmal way of traveling. It was named not for the current king (George II) but for a much earlier one, Charles II, who had ordered the road built eighty years earlier. It still wasn't finished. The highway threaded down through the colonies from New England to South Carolina, and everywhere it was erratic, fragmentary, and dangerous. It trailed off unpredictably in the depths of forests, or dead-ended within impassable valleys, or melted away on the outskirts of vast, gloomy bird-haunted marshes. The journey from one colony to the next could take weeks. Despite Franklin's best efforts as postmaster, it was often said to be far quicker to get a letter from Paris to New York than it was to forward it on from New York to Massachusetts.

The highway was a perfect example of what frustrated Franklin about the American colonies. After more than a century, they were still nothing more than a rickety agglomeration of disparate settlements. Franklin envied the Native Americans of the Iroquois Federation, who had put aside their tribal differences and forged a military empire in the northern forests. It dismayed him that the colonists of a putatively superior civilization couldn't do what the primitive natives had succeeded at so brilliantly.

Did he know what he wanted to do about it? If he did, he was still keeping it to himself. From the outside, he appeared to be nothing more than a public-spirited rich man who was making virtuous use of his leisure by involving himself with socially responsible projects. The convivial round of his days continued: the meetings with prominent men, the stays at country houses, the charming horseplay, the indiscreet talk about politics after too much drinking. But, deliberately or not, these were his first forays into the dangerous world of politics and practical diplomacy, and the first stirrings of the idea of independence from Great Britain—the grand venture that would occupy him for the rest of his life.

In the spring of 1754, Franklin was in Maryland. He was visiting a friend named Tasker; in his letters he usually called him "the excellent Colonel Tasker." Tasker was a gambler and a breeder of thoroughbred horses, which was not necessarily Franklin's usual company, but Tasker was also one of the most well-connected men in the state. The Taskers were considered the cream of the Maryland aristocracy.

Tasker invited Franklin and his son William to stay with him at Belair House, his great family estate in the hilly depths of the countryside. On their way, in the middle of a wide, richly flowing landscape of valleys and forested hills, one of the men in the party called a halt. He gestured for everyone to look down into a little vale that opened up to the side of their path. Below was a dusty road winding through the meadowlands. Moving along the road like a bustling traveler was a tight little commotion of air: a newly forming whirlwind.

The whirlwind looked, Franklin later wrote, like "a sugar-loaf"—by which he meant it resembled a funnel (that was the shape that sugarloaves were commonly spun into). The funnel swerved off the road and came sweeping up the hillside toward them. It swelled as it approached; by the time it crested the hill, Franklin guessed, it was around forty or fifty feet high, twenty or thirty feet across at its height, "no bigger than a common barrel" at its base. It moved past them at a walking pace, with an odd, irregular bob and swerve like a spinning top.

Everyone in the party reared back—except for Franklin. He later said that he just couldn't help himself. He had to urge his horse to a trot, and he went tagging alongside the funnel to see what it would do. He thought of how sailors were supposed to have broken up waterspouts by firing cannons at them, so he tried lashing at the whirlwind with his whip—"without any effect," he admitted.

Then the whirlwind turned again and meandered off into the trees. Franklin followed it. He lost sight of the road. The wind was getting louder; the countless rotted leaves of the forest floor were being sucked up into the funnel in a rushing whisper. All around the funnel, the treetops in the woodland interior were bending and snapping in frantic circles. "The progressive motion of the whirl was not so swift but that a man on foot might have kept pace with it," he later wrote, "but the circular motion was amazingly rapid." By then, the funnel had turned into a swirling column that appeared to be made entirely out of dead leaves, which were soaring up out of sight in widening spirals. And it was still gathering strength. Franklin saw that it was now sucking up large dead boughs along with the leaves. That was when he wondered for the first time about his own safety.

By that point, Franklin guessed, he'd followed the whirl into the forest for about three-quarters of a mile. His son William, who had been trailing along behind him the whole way, came up alongside. When William saw that Franklin was hanging back, he urged his own horse forward. The funnel was roaring in the depths of the woods; William boldly pursued it for another half mile. The chase ended when the funnel emerged into the open air of an old cultivated tobacco field, and there unexpectedly melted away into nothingness.

Franklin and William, covered in sweat, their clothes spangled with countless leaves, made their bedraggled way back to the road. The air all around them was filled with a storm of leaves, billowing and drifting and soaring in the gusts. Franklin later noted that the leaves kept falling on them for miles afterward. One of the company then turned to Colonel Tasker and asked if these kinds of whirlwinds were common in Maryland.

"No, not at all common," Tasker said. "We got this on purpose to treat Master Franklin."

After the Revolution, the great push into the American forest began, just as Franklin had wanted. But the vast war he had envisioned never materialized. Even though there were constant skirmishes, horrific massacres, and a scattering of pitched battles, the full-scale war proved superfluous. It had in a sense already happened, out of sight of the invading colonists. Plagues had done the work of the military. Wave after wave of epidemic disease had swept over the nations of the woodlands—smallpox, measles, yellow fever—and their populations had been devastated. Many of the nations had been reduced to a tenth of the numbers they'd had a century before; some had vanished entirely.

The colonists and settlers found that endless reaches of the forest interior were deserted. Silent glades stood where there had been thriving villages, and there were empty rivers with overgrown margins of reeds that had once been heavily trafficked trading lines. The depths of the forest had returned to the pristine bird-chattering aloofness they'd had before human beings had first arrived in North America.

The hush of the landscape seemed unimaginably deep. One traveler recorded finding, in the forested hills of western Ohio, an ancient spring; from the spring was slowly trickling, drop by drop, a line of brick-red sediment that trailed down a rill to the base of a steep grassy slope. The deposit of sediment at the bottom was at least thirty feet thick. For how many undisturbed years had it been accumulating? Thousands; maybe millions. The sight left the traveler profoundly shaken. He wrote that the chronology of the world in the Bible must not have been "rightly computed."

But there were also, here and there, signs of something currently abroad and active in the deep forest. Nobody knew what it was. Any

traveler came across the tracks sooner or later. The shrouded tree canopies would be broken by a wide patch of golden sunlight; from close
up it proved to be not some peaceful glade but a swath of downed and
shattered trees. The settlers called them windfalls. Sometimes a windfall
area would be enormous: tens of thousands of trees were downed in a
band a few hundred yards wide and a couple of miles long. These trails
the settlers called windroads.

Where did they come from? There were few reports from eyewitnesses. Sometimes a trapper or a trader would claim to have seen something: an impression of faraway trouble, a vague echoing roar in the
distance, a black cloudy shape rampaging somewhere within the recesses
of green gloom.

Did anybody make the connection between the windroads and
Franklin's landspout? Apparently not. Since Franklin's time, there had
been a few strange storms seen in the settled areas of the East Coast. But
they had popped up at rare intervals and usually in remote places—one
in the wilderness of upstate New York, a few years later another in the
swamps of South Carolina, a third in rural New Jersey. Local newspapers and travelers' journals contained baffled accounts of them. One
storm cloud, it was said, "burst upon the earth and began with breaking
limbs from trees and scattering fences . . . Buildings were unroofed or
prostrated in the dust, while their fragments were borne with violence
before the wind." Another "came in sight over the western hills like a
body of thick dark smoke or fog, wreathing and whirling in the most
furious forms . . . Those who were directly before it saw the appearance
of fire." Another was described as "a black column from the earth to
the cloud, of about thirty rods diameter, so thick that the eye could not
pervade it. It whirled with amazing velocity and a most tremendous
roar—it appeared luminous and ignited, and was charged with broken
pieces of fences, and huge limbs of trees, which were continually crashing against each other in the air, or tumbling to the ground."

But these reports went publicly unconnected and unexamined. The
problem was that few people were really all that interested in natural
philosophy, and nobody was making any systematic study of meteorology in America. Farmers and plantation owners kept weather logs for

their own benefit (George Washington and Thomas Jefferson both did), but nobody had the idea of compiling them. It was true that Franklin's writings on waterspouts and landspouts were available; he was a revered figure, and his papers and letters were already being published in imposing collected editions. But the volumes devoted to his scientific writings tended, just as they do now, to go unread.

The windroads were more easily explained by folklore. Their unknown maker gradually acquired a name: the Storm King. In the literary magazines of the Republic, there were poems and prose rhapsodies about this mysterious figure. He was imagined as a furious rider through the wilderness, an immortal dweller in the grandeur of his cloud castles—normally hidden from human eyes, but occasionally glimpsed at the heart of his traveling retinue of storm and lightning bolt.

The work of the Storm King could be seen all throughout the eastern forests, to the edge of the great expanse of empty grassland in the center of the continent. Lewis and Clark saw a long, very recent windroad as they ascended the Missouri River; they concluded it had been cut by a "hurricane." But the most extensive windroad in America was in southern Illinois. It was one of the few that had witnesses to its creation, and so can be dated precisely: to the afternoon of June 8, 1805, when a gigantic black cloud came out of the steep hilly country of southern Missouri and crossed the Mississippi River.

On the Illinois shore was an area known as the American Bottom. This was an extraordinarily lush lowland zone. One anonymous magazine writer, twenty-five years later, described it as "the most charming alternation of prairie and woodland" that he had ever seen; he remembered "forests of grass, or cane, and of stupendous oaks and cotton woods." But on June 8, it became what he called "a scene of unequalled grandeur and horror" as "whole forests in a moment twisted from the ground." Trees were ripped from their roots, smashed together in mid-air, and pummeled into splinters. The skies were black; a weird howling, "a sound of universal distress," came from all directions; it was a vast confusion of sky and earth in which "cattle, horses, lake, trees, houses and whatever was in the way" were carried off and dropped as wreckage.

This was, a historian wrote late in the nineteenth century, "the most violent tempest that ever visited Illinois." He called it a hurricane and helpfully classified it as "one of those tempests of the whirlwind order." The landscape it crossed was so densely forested and so sparsely occupied that only two or three people were reported to have been killed. But the windroad it left behind was like nothing anyone had ever seen. It was two miles wide and hundreds of miles long. It stretched from the Mississippi River across southern Illinois and into Indiana. (One account claimed it didn't peter out until it reached Ohio.) The rule of thumb among the settlers was that a windroad lasted for about twenty years before the forest erased it. But this one blocked land passage through southern Illinois for half a century—an interminable, impassable barrier of heaped-up and rotting trees like the ancient defensive wall of an abandoned forest kingdom. Its traces could still be found in the woodlands long after the Civil War.

PART II

THE STORM WAR

4

The So-Called Tornado

In the late afternoon of June 19, 1835, an unusually violent thunderstorm came up over the farm country of New Jersey. The storm was spotted by the passengers on the steamboat *Napoleon,* just then descending the Raritan River. One of the passengers, a college professor named Lewis Beck, later recalled that they were about six miles from the town of New Brunswick when a friend of his tugged his sleeve and pointed out the strange shape the storm clouds were taking in the northwestern sky. Beck described the clouds there as exceptionally dense and hanging very low; they were stretched out in a straight line near the horizon like a black curtain. About midway across, Beck said, one part of the cloud line "was dipping towards the earth in the form of a funnel or inverted cone, and was gradually uniting with another cone whose basis apparently rested on the surface." Beck had never seen anything like it before, but he was a man of wide education and he knew it for the "remarkable occurrence" it was. This must be, he later wrote, "the so-called tornado."

It was a spellbinding sight. Beck and the other passengers watched in fascination as the cloud churned across the landscape. It writhed and twisted around itself, continually breaking up and re-forming. By the time it had passed along the river—Beck estimated that it came within around a mile of the steamboat—it had assumed the appearance of "a large black column spreading wide at the top," which reminded Beck of a volcanic explosion. This was the form it took when it struck New Brunswick.

Its appearance over the rooflines caused a panic. None of the people on the streets had any idea what it was. Many of the eyewitnesses later said that they believed it was the smoke from an enormous fire. The fire alarms were sounded. The rumor immediately spread that there were inexplicable explosions and small fires breaking out all over town. Everybody rushed into the streets to see what was happening. They were even more confused and panicked by what they found. The sky was turning black, and there were gigantic, extraordinary rushes of wind sweeping down every street of the commercial district. Entire houses were being torn apart and sent flying; heavy rafters were soaring in midair and crashing through windows; the crowds in the streets were stampeding toward shelter as an enormous wall of smoke and fume roared through the heart of town.

Then the cloud was gone; it had crossed to the far bank of the river. In New Brunswick there were dozens of serious injuries, but only four people were reported killed. The fire alarms rousing everybody into the open had doubtless saved hundreds of lives; otherwise they would have been crushed in the collapsing buildings. One eight-year-old boy was found dead, nearly decapitated by a rafter in a wrecked dry-goods store. Meanwhile, the cloud was roaring through the woodlands on the Atlantic shore, shedding the debris of the town behind it. As the tornado crossed out over the Atlantic, it scattered into a shower of hail, and the entire suspended cloud of wreckage collapsed into the ocean. Splintered planks, roof shingles, bedding, and glassware were reported to have rained down as far away as Staten Island.

The assorted gales and windstorms and hurricanes and tornadoes reported in the early days of the Republic had almost all taken place in rural and remote locations, but the New Brunswick storm had struck in the most heavily populated zone of the nation. New Brunswick stood right on the old King's Highway, which was still, as it had been in Franklin's time, the main thoroughfare through the Atlantic states (although since the Revolution the New Jersey stretch was generally referred to by the unroyalist name of Straight Turnpike Road). This meant that the news of the storm quickly gained a wide circulation. There were stories in the big newspapers of Philadelphia, Boston, and New York City, and within a few days the news had drawn to New Brunswick an unusual crowd of tourists.

They were the nation's leading natural philosophers—the ones who were just then inventing a new science, which they called "meteorology."

The word had actually been around since the ancient Greeks. It's the title of a text by Aristotle, and it roughly means "knowledge of the upper air." But the word had preceded any actual knowledge by more than two thousand years. Aristotle had been perfectly ignorant of the upper air; his text was nothing but a compendium of Greek weather folklore mingled with some nonsensical quasi-scientific mysticism. But such was the state of scientific knowledge in the West that Aristotle had remained the standard authority on meteorology ever since. Not until the beginning of the nineteenth century did philosophers begin a fresh and systematic study of the forms and appearances of the atmosphere. (Their inspiration wasn't Aristotle but Franklin, who was already revered as one of the great names in the history of science.) Their starting point was a new system for classifying clouds that had been proposed in 1802 by a British amateur philosopher named Luke Howard. The terms Howard invented—"cirrus," "cumulus," "stratus"—had been immediately adopted all over the world; the most famous poet of the age, Goethe, had even written a poem in praise of them. (They are still the standard terms today and are vaguely believed to go back to ancient Greece.)

The New Brunswick tornado was an opportunity for all students of meteorology to see the effects of a mysterious phenomenon of the upper air firsthand, and they took full advantage of it. Professors came from Yale, from Princeton, and from the prestigious Franklin Institute in Philadelphia. For weeks after the disaster they were on the scene. As the town was burying its dead, and caring for its injured, and repairing its acres of damaged buildings, the citizens were dogged by these clusters of formally vested and hatted out-of-towners. The philosophers poked at the rubble with their walking sticks, and pulled out compasses and measuring tapes to record the patterns of fallen trees, and obliviously held conversations while blocking the work crews who were clearing away the wreckage. They interrupted the murmured condolences among mourners to ask after eyewitnesses; they triumphantly emerged from the underbrush with trinkets that had been blown miles from some lady's private washstand. "Probably in no other instance," wrote one of the philosophers, "have the effects of a tornado been so faithfully and skillfully traced, ascertained, and registered."

In the evenings they gathered in taverns and hotel lobbies and dining rooms, and they drank and they argued over what they'd seen. They were all evolving their own theories as to what the tornado had been and whether the evidence in the wrecked town proved them right. But one debater stood out—the most impassioned, the most eager to convince, the most certain he was right. To no one's surprise, this was one of the visitors from the Franklin Institute, James Espy.

James Espy wasn't a professor but a former schoolmaster and a passionate amateur meteorologist. It was the goal of his life, in fact, to become America's first professional meteorologist—a job that did not then exist. He was attempting to invent it any way he could, principally by lecturing on meteorology at the Franklin Institute and writing reviews for the leading journals on natural philosophy. He was fifty years old at the time of his visit to New Brunswick; he was known among his colleagues for his boundless enthusiasm for his subject and the remarkable originality of his thinking. As it happened, he believed he had discovered a new and fundamental theory of meteorology, and he had come to New Brunswick to look for evidence to support it.

Espy had stumbled across this theory while reading a book called *Meteorological Observations and Essays* by a British natural philosopher named John Dalton. In one passage Dalton considered one of the puzzles that had recently arisen in the study of the atmosphere. It had been known since Franklin's time that the atmosphere wasn't one uniform substance but a kind of soup where several distinct elements were blended. Chemists had managed to isolate them: air was made up of nitrogen, oxygen, and hydrogen in fixed proportions. But there was something else—a small quantity of water vapor, in a proportion that seemed to be different each time it was measured. Its presence was clearly significant and necessary (people did understand that clouds and rain were formed out of water vapor), but where did it come from and why did its proportion keep changing?

Dalton suggested an answer. The molecules of water vapor were circulating freely, suspended among the other elements in the atmosphere, and their quantity varied at any particular time according to the temperature and air pressure. The hotter the temperature and the higher the pressure, the larger the number of water molecules the atmosphere could support. The lower the temperature and pressure, the more likely it was that the water molecules would lose their buoyancy and descend back to earth.

Dalton imagined the process mathematically. There were three numbers that could be used to quantify any body of air. One was temperature; the second was barometric pressure; the third was a new one Dalton invented. He called it the dew point. It defined the amount of water vapor the air could hold. The dew point was continually floating and shifting in relation to the other two numbers. If the temperature and pressure of a body of air declined, the air would eventually reach its dew point. The water vapor would then condense out. Close to the ground, the vapor would appear as dew or frost; in the upper air, it would fall as rain or snow or hail.

The dew point was what gave James Espy his inspiration. He was led to it because he was fascinated by a problem about clouds that nobody had solved yet: how the various types of clouds were formed. In particular, he wanted to explain the origin and dynamics of the most extreme and dramatic cloud, the cumulonimbus, the thunderstorm cloud.

The way most students of meteorology pictured it, the atmosphere was made up of diffuse domains of air, circulating and mingling randomly, and it was their haphazard collisions that produced clouds and rain. But Espy had a different idea. He pictured humid air near the surface of the earth being warmed by the sun and beginning to rise. Only in his version, it didn't ascend in a shapeless, dissolving mass; it formed a distinct column moving upward, essentially untouched by the surrounding mass of cooler air. At a certain point the column would reach a zone of colder, drier air aloft that had much lower pressure. That was when the column would begin to spread out and cool. As it lost its heat and pressure, it would reach its dew point, and its water vapor would condense out to form a cloud.

But now Espy's mental image ran into an obstacle. This could not be all there was to the process. If the column dissolved at one particular altitude and stopped ascending, then the resulting cloud would simply spread out horizontally there like a pancake. Some clouds did in fact look that way, the ones Luke Howard called stratus clouds. So Espy's model could account for them. But what about the towering cumulonimbus thunderheads? Where did the energy come from to form them?

Espy was stymied. That was when he began to consider more closely the idea of how the water vapor condensed—in particular, its relationship to temperature.

At that time, heat was still a mysterious concept. It was generally believed to be a physical substance contained and released by matter; that is, it was a subtle fluid, like electricity. The subtle fluid of heat was generally called caloric. (The concept survives now in the word "calorie.") It was known that caloric had a curious property: it could be hidden. There was more heat contained within certain phenomena than could be perceived or detected with instruments. The detectable heat was known as sensible caloric (because it could be known to the senses); the hidden heat was called latent caloric. Some physical processes were known to release latent caloric, and one of them was condensation. When water vapor condensed, the surrounding air warmed up. This could only mean that its latent caloric had been freed.

That idea was what led Espy through to his goal. He went back to his image of the rising column of air. When the column cooled and lost its water vapor to condensation, its latent caloric was released. As a result, the column would warm up, and, necessarily, it would begin to rise again. It would go up into higher and colder air; its dew point would once again be reached; more water vapor would condense; the column would continue to rise. At the most extreme, the end would be a monstrous column towering up to the upper atmosphere, shedding vast torrents of rain: a cumulonimbus thunderstorm.

In other words, the atmosphere was a kind of universal steam engine, spontaneously creating columns of rising air that pumped warmth and humidity into the cold air aloft like pistons. Espy called this process "caloric rarefaction." (This was the common term then for what is now called convection.) Then the clouds formed and the rain fell according to the simple and lucid principle of the dew point. Caloric rarefaction and the dew point fit together in a beautiful self-contained, self-sustaining process.

That was the secret of the storm cloud, Espy declared: "steam power." The idea hit him, he later said, like "an instantaneous transition from darkness to light." He wrote: "A thousand contradictions vanished, and the numerous facts, a rude and undigested mass, which had been stowed away in the secret recesses of my memory, presented themselves spontaneously to my delighted mind, as a harmonious system of fair proportion." Steam power, he wrote, "was the lever with which the meteorologist was to move the world."

Espy spent the summer in New Brunswick in a state of enthusiasm bordering on the manic. As he and Professor Alexander Bache, his friend from the Franklin Institute, walked the trail the tornado had left through the woodlands and into the town, he kept seizing upon curious windfalls and pointing out freaks of damage—fence posts driven into tree trunks, houses that had been upended, bedsheets off a laundry line that had been wadded up into the cracks in a crumbling brick wall. He seemed to grow more ebullient the more of the wreckage he saw. Everywhere he looked, he could discern a lucid pattern. The fallen trees, the ruined houses, the seemingly random dispersal of debris: they all suggested a single underlying process. The tremendous winds that had destroyed the town had all been rushing straight into the tornado funnel, and they had been drawn up through the funnel to staggering heights in the upper air. From the way the debris had rained back downward onto the landscape, Espy guessed the draw of the tornado had to be at least a mile high, maybe more. There could be no doubt about what this meant. Within the mysterious black funnel of the tornado, there was a rapidly rising column of air, exactly as his theory of steam power had predicted.

But as he considered the scene, he became convinced of something else. The eyewitnesses in the town were mistaken on one crucial point.

They were all agreed that the tornado funnel had been spinning or rotating. Espy was sure this could not be correct. The tornado was not a spout or a whirlwind, as Franklin had thought it was. The winds were drawn into the central column from all sides in perfectly straight lines, like the spokes of a wagon wheel, and from there they rose up in perfectly straight lines through the clouds to the sky.

His friend Bache heard him out as they wandered through the town and the surrounding countryside. Then he pointed out an obvious objection. Here and there, the tracks of damage clearly showed circular or spiral patterns. Espy dismissed this at once. The visible evidence was simply accidental. The movement of the tornado funnel would doubtless leave a confused and contradictory wake behind. It was clear to Espy that, viewed correctly, the underlying simplicity would shine through. Bache then brought up the problem of the sheer number of eyewitnesses—not only here, but in other accounts of the storm going back to Franklin and before. They all reported the cloud had rotated: How could they all be wrong? That didn't faze Espy, either. Tornadoes were so rare, they appeared so suddenly and moved so quickly that nobody could be expected to provide a reliable description of what they'd seen.

Bache, caught up in Espy's enthusiasm, withdrew his objections and became a convert to the theory on the spot. Adding up all the evidence they saw in New Brunswick, he later wrote, "I think it made out that there was a rush of air from all directions, at the surface of the ground, toward the moving meteor, this rush of air carrying objects with it. The effects all indicate a moving column of rarefied air, without any whirling motion near the surface of the earth."

But Bache thought they needed another opinion, so they wrote to the Franklin Institute and invited another colleague to join them. This was the celebrated chemist Robert Hare. He was a notorious contrarian and would be, Bache thought, the perfect counterbalance for Espy's fervor. There were few things that Hare liked to do better than argue with Espy; his highest satisfaction was the complete annihilation of some new idea of Espy's that he found exasperatingly absurd.

Hare arrived in New Brunswick in July. He followed the same paths that Espy and Bache had taken around town, through the ruined blocks of houses and the debris-strewn public squares and along the windroad cut through the forest. He examined the damage thoroughly and—he believed—objectively. He conceded that there was a lot of evidence for an inward rush of winds. And he accepted that the wide scattering of debris around the town and the countryside could probably be explained only by assuming that it had all been carried upward high into the cloud and then dispersed. His conclusion was that about many aspects of the tornado, Espy was probably right.

But about Espy's larger theory Hare was unconvinced. He was particularly skeptical about Espy's claim that the tornado funnel didn't spin. Some of the damage in New Brunswick, he wrote, "cannot be explained without supposing a gyratory force." But he conceded that the spin might not be an essential element of the tornado's behavior; it could be a local effect caused by chance variations in the inrushing winds.

What was more serious for Hare was Espy's belief that the updraft in the tornado funnel was caused by differences in temperature and pressure between the surface and the upper air—that is, the whole notion of steam power. He had already fought with Espy over steam power; it was obvious to Hare that caloric rarefaction simply wasn't a powerful enough force to generate anything as large as a thunderstorm. He was beginning to work out a theory of his own, which was based on a new model of atmospheric electricity. Hare had found one piece of evidence extremely significant. On the far bank of the river was an area of downed trees where the leaves and the underbrush were all withered, as though they'd been flash heated by a swiftly moving flame. To Hare it strongly resembled the kind of scorching that one of his own electrical devices would have caused. He had always believed—and had frequently told Espy so—that electricity was the motive power of violent storms. This appeared to be proof. He left New Brunswick with the conviction that he had found the cause of tornadoes: the tornado funnel was a kind of conduit through which an extraordinarily powerful electrical current was flowing.

"I conceive," he wrote, "that the inevitable effect of such a current would be to counteract within its sphere the pressure of the atmosphere, and thus enable this fluid, in obedience to its elasticity, to rush into the rare medium above." In other words, Hare thought the electrical current flowing up the tornado funnel would be surrounded by a vacuum, which would draw a violent inflow of air from the surrounding atmosphere up with it into the higher altitudes. "After maturely considering all the facts," he concluded, "I am led to suggest that a tornado is the effect of an electrified current of air, superseding the more usual means of discharge between the earth and clouds in those sparks or flashes which are called lightning."

There was another investigator at New Brunswick. His name was William Redfield. He was another amateur enthusiast of the weather, with no scientific training; he was a successful businessman who ran a steamship company. He was uncomfortable around the other, more philosophically inclined tourists and stayed aloof from them. During his days in New Brunswick, he and his son made their own way along the debris trail and through the forest, taking their own measurements of the wrecked buildings and fallen trees, and they said nothing to anyone about their results.

Redfield was looking for evidence for his own pet theory about the tornado. This was a notion that he'd been investigating now for almost fifteen years. He'd come upon it not through speculation and book learning, as Espy had done, but through a fluke occurrence during the greatest tragedy of his life.

In 1821, Redfield had been a storekeeper in the small town of Cromwell, Connecticut. He had recently remarried, after losing his first wife to a prolonged illness. His new bride, Lucy, had almost immediately become pregnant; the birth had been a calamity, the child had died after two days, and Lucy had gone into a steep and irreversible decline.

One day that September, a few weeks after the loss of the baby, as Redfield was sitting with the bedridden Lucy, a gigantic storm had come over their town. Redfield had never experienced anything like it: his misery over his wife's deteriorating health was temporarily dwarfed by terror at the fury that was engulfing them. It was hour after hour of banshee winds, torrential rains, and cannonading thunder. Afternoon gave way to the evening, and the storm, to Redfield's disbelief and horror, kept getting stronger. It didn't peter out till after midnight, when it left a disconcertingly placid starlit sky in its wake. For decades afterward, people in Connecticut called it "the Great September Gale."

Lucy died two weeks later. A few days afterward, Redfield traveled to the town of Stockbridge, Massachusetts, to visit her parents. He wanted to return to them some of her belongings and tell them the story of her last illness. Stockbridge was seventy miles away, which was a two-day trip. Redfield took his oldest son, John, with him; John in his memoirs would describe it as the strangest journey of his life. The signs of the gale's passage were everywhere. Farmhouses were wrecked and fields were sodden ruins; the roads were washed out for long stretches and were blocked every few hundred feet by downed trees. But what John found most memorable was his father's behavior. Redfield slowly stirred out of his melancholy as they rode. He became curious about the ruined scenes around them; then he was fascinated; by the end of the journey he was obsessed.

What exactly had been the nature of the gale? The more of its aftermath Redfield saw, the odder it all seemed. In the immediate neighborhood of their home, the trees appeared to have been knocked down by a gigantic wind blowing from the southeast, off the Atlantic. But inland, they could see that the trees had been downed by an equally strong wind blowing in the opposite direction, out of the wilderness country to the northwest. How was that possible? Did the windstorm come ashore, push inland, and turn around and come back?

At each stop they made, Redfield interrogated the locals. He heard the same thing everywhere: no matter which direction the wind had been blowing, the storm that night had hit its peak at around nine o'clock. That was Redfield's memory as well: he had passed that evening watching helplessly over Lucy and listening to the clock tick in the rare lulls in the storm, and he had noticed that the wind had reached its most demonic fury exactly at nine.

But this seemed impossible. It required believing that there had been two storms, equally strong, passing each other in opposite directions, each reaching its peak at the exact same hour. He kept turning this mystery over and over in his mind, and he couldn't make the slightest sense of it. The whole way home from Stockbridge he kept remarking to John how strange it was. John listened to him with only the dimmest sense of what he was talking about. But John did remember quite vividly how it ended. Just as they were approaching their house in Cromwell, his father abruptly fell silent.

He remained silent the rest of the way home. He said nothing more to John about it after they arrived. He didn't talk about it to his friends. He said nothing about it to anyone for the next nine years. But he had just had the most startling idea of his life.

He didn't unburden himself until a summer day in 1830, when he happened to be riding a steamboat on its regular shuttle from New York City to New Haven. He learned that one of the other passengers was someone whose name he recognized: Denison Olmsted, professor of mathematics and natural philosophy at Yale University. He immediately sought Olmsted out, introduced himself, and launched into an impassioned speech about hailstorms. It was an unusual opening for a conversation, but Olmsted was perfectly delighted to talk about hailstorms. He had just published a paper in the *American Journal of Science* outlining his theory about how hail was formed. He believed that hailstones were raindrops that passed randomly from domains of warm air to domains of cold air, until they froze in flight and fell to the earth. Redfield had read the paper and wanted to know if such pockets of cold air really existed throughout the atmosphere. Olmsted pointed out that the high mountains in India had snowcapped peaks. Redfield quoted some obscure travelers' tales he'd read about unusual weather in the tropics. And so, as the steamboat glided on, the two men became more engrossed in talk and speculation about hail, clouds, lightning, and storms.

Redfield was a man who perpetually kept his own counsel; he rarely unburdened himself to either friends or family. But encouraged by Olmsted, he began talking for the first time about the Great September Gale. He had spent years looking for evidence about the gale and other severe Atlantic storms—in newspaper stories, explorers' accounts, and ship logs. All of them confirmed his suspicion. There was only one way of explaining the damage the gale had left behind. There hadn't been two identical storms passing each other in opposite directions. The gale had been a gigantic whirlwind, spinning around a moving center like a top.

Olmsted was stunned. He had no idea if Redfield was right, but the audacity of it took his breath away. He told Redfield that he had to publish it at once. Redfield immediately demurred. He wasn't a philosopher; he was an amateur, a practical man of business who dabbled in natural philosophy. He would have no idea how to write up such a thing, and anyway he would have no standing among the real authorities on the subject. Olmsted brushed all these objections aside. It was true that science was becoming a professional field (perhaps most clearly marked by the increasing use of the word "science" instead of "natural philosophy"). But major contributions were still being made by the amateurs and the self-taught. After all, one of the most respected natural philosophers in America was Joseph Henry of Princeton University, who hadn't spent a day attending college.

By the time the steamboat arrived at New Haven, Olmsted had won Redfield over. The two men arranged a deal: Redfield would write out his ideas, and Olmsted would vet them and send them on to the *American Journal of Science*. It was the beginning of a professional association and friendship that would last for the rest of their lives. Redfield wrote out his theories of the Great September Gale; he followed it by many more papers about Atlantic storms, about steamboat design, and about the fossil record of New Jersey. By the time of the New Brunswick tornado, he was already gathering a reputation for his unusual ideas.

This had not turned out to be a blessing for him. Most of the reputation was negative, due to the hostile reviews his papers had received from one particular critic—James Espy. Espy was scornful of the notion that any of the very large Atlantic storms, the ones generally known as hurricanes (in those days a vague catchall term, like "tornado" or "windstorm"), displayed signs of circular rotation around a moving center. Where would the energy come from to power and sustain this gigantic whirlwind? The storm, Espy wrote, "would soon be destroyed by its outward motion, unless some mighty cause exists, of which we have no knowledge, to generate new motion in the air."

Redfield presented himself as a humble amateur who had no stake in higher theoretical questions. As his son John remembered: "My father would never permit his views to be called a theory; he used to say, Theory had he none, his work was simply to record and map out the *facts* that had been observed, to show not how storms were produced, but what storms *are*. If these recorded observations could not be reconciled to the theories of others, so much the worse for the theories."

But that said, he was outraged and hurt by Espy's criticisms, and he wrote letter after letter to the scientific journals disputing them. He also began mocking Espy's theory of steam power, which he said was self-evidently nonsensical, and he soon grew so belligerent that he refused to acknowledge some of his own gross errors in basic science (he didn't appear to grasp, for instance, how the moon's gravity affected the tides); the most he would concede was that he had been "too aggressive" in putting forward his unconventional views.

Espy was taken aback at the vehemence of Redfield's response and immediately wrote him a private conciliatory letter. He invited Redfield to come to Philadelphia and take part in a club he'd recently started at the institute, which he called the Franklin Kite Club. It was intended as a tribute to Benjamin Franklin, but Espy had his own serious purpose as well: he was fitting thermometers and barometers to his kites and guiding them into the convection columns beneath the clouds in order to track how their temperature and pressure fell off with altitude. (This calculation is now called the saturated adiabatic lapse rate and is an essential part of modern meteorology.) But Espy didn't stress this lofty goal. The drift of his letter was more relaxed: join me, maybe we can settle our differences, at least we can indulge ourselves in the sheer pleasure of playing hooky by spending a sunny spring afternoon doing nothing more momentous than flying kites.

Redfield immediately wrote back to decline the invitation. He considered it unforgivably frivolous. He wanted nothing to do with Espy and even less to do with his theories. This was why, when he learned that Espy was in New Brunswick studying the tornado, he took care to stay as far away as possible.

Besides, he wanted to accumulate evidence to prove his own notion about the tornado—that it was a whirlwind like the hurricane. His son John would remember that July as a long solitary trudge through a succession of hot sunlit afternoons. Redfield wasn't much interested in inspecting the damage track that cut through the town; most of the wreckage had been carted off already. He was focused instead on the downed trees in the woodlands. He brought along a compass and chain to measure the width of the storm track, and he had surveyor's charts that he used to note the position and direction of each tree. The surface whirlwind pattern was perfectly obvious to him. Nor did he see any evidence at all of a rising column of air, as Espy believed. But he had no intention of engaging in any more debates about that. This was all just for his private satisfaction. He managed to collect his evidence and get out of New Brunswick without once running into Espy, and he would go on avoiding him for years.

5

The Philosophy of Storms

There was a story about James Espy and his youth on the Kentucky frontier—that he hadn't learned to read or write until he'd almost turned eighteen. He'd only been inspired to learn when a friend took him to hear the celebrated politician Henry Clay. Clay was just at the beginning of his long career then, but he was already making a huge impression as an orator; Espy heard him at a large outdoor gathering, where he stood on a makeshift platform and held the crowd spellbound with his electrifying, impassioned praise of Federalism, of American identity, and of the necessity of holding the nation aloof from foreign wars. He spoke for an hour in a grand booming voice that surged and lulled and thundered again like the ocean. Afterward, descending from the platform, he was immediately mobbed by admirers. Espy pushed his way through to the inner circle but then found himself too tongue-tied to speak. One of Espy's friends yelled out to Clay, "He wants to be like you, even though he can't read." Clay immediately plucked up one of his advertising posters from the platform, pointed to the big letter *A* in "CLAY," and said to Espy, "You see that, boy? That's an *A*. You've only got twenty-five more letters to go." Espy was so inspired that he set out to learn to read at once. A year later, he was admitted to college.

Espy's family didn't much like this story. One of his nieces described it in her memoirs as a scurrilous lie invented by Espy's enemies. But that's unlikely. Espy did make a lot of enemies, but this wasn't the sort of rumor that would have hurt him. Illiteracy was common on the early frontier, and there was no social stigma attached to it then (that came later, after the Civil War); besides, if he really had taught himself to read so quickly, it would have only made his admission to college that much more impressive. The most likely source for the story, true or not, was Espy himself. It goes along well with his lifelong sense that he was destined to accomplish great things—and also with something he was less comfortable acknowledging: that his inspiration was always basically oratorical.

Transylvania Academy, in the wilds of western Kentucky, was despite its remote location one of the best colleges in America. It had been founded as part of a widespread movement of teachers and educators who, fired up by the values of the Revolution, had come out like missionaries to spread learning to the frontier. Espy gained a solid education in mathematics up through calculus and a good grounding in both Greek and Latin. He was always a strong student. "He shows an ardent desire for knowledge," his older brother wrote of him in those years, "and promises to be both intelligent and useful." But he also had something wayward and theatrical about him. He organized a debating society on campus that earnestly discussed the issues of the day—the rapid spread of statehood, for instance, or the American attacks on the Barbary States of Africa. But he also invented for it a secret hand signal; whenever one of the debaters flashed the signal, everybody had to switch sides and keep on arguing with exactly the same passion, just to see how long it took the audience to catch on.

After graduating, he went east and became a schoolmaster at a small academy in Pennsylvania. He lived in Bedford—a small and decorous town, where the people boasted about their close family ties to the Founding Fathers. Espy didn't have those kinds of connections, but he was personable, self-confident, eloquent, and strikingly handsome; he met and courted a highborn local girl named Margaret Pollard and charmed not only her but her whole aloof family. After he and Margaret were married in 1809, he took her family name and signed himself James Pollard Espy.

Margaret was tall, slim, graceful, and well educated; she was at least as smart as he was, as he always admitted, and knew much more about literature and art than he had ever bothered to learn. But she was also in chronically poor health—so much so that the family considered her unmarriageable—and after she and Espy were married, she remained a lifelong invalid. But she proved to be a devoted and endlessly supportive spouse. "Having no children to occupy her care," one friend wrote, "and being of high mental endowment and of enthusiastic temperament, she found a never-failing source of interest and gratification in watching the development of Mr. Espy's scientific ideas." She remained steadfast even after Espy's ideas led him to give up his secure position with the academy and begin his fitful and ill-paid career with the Franklin Institute.

The institute was a curious establishment. It was one of several public-spirited organizations known as mechanics' institutes that sprang up in the early Republic and were intended for the education of the working poor. The institute's full name was the Franklin Institute of the State of Pennsylvania for the Promotion of the Mechanic Arts, and it was open to mechanics, craftsmen, and artisans. For a nominal membership fee they could hear lectures and attend classes. They could also make use of the libraries, which had large collections of both classic literature and the latest scientific and technical books. There was also a public museum, which staged exhibitions of practical crafts. These exhibitions tended to be loud, exuberant, and delightful shows, where steam engines thundered, lumbering metal arms clacked, and big electrical toys sizzled and banged and flashed. Its blend of gaudy entertainment and educational uplift would be the model for P. T. Barnum's notoriously raucous American Museum and for the great World's Fairs later in the nineteenth century (as well as for institutions like Chicago's Museum of Science and Industry today).

The institute proved to be a congenial home for Espy. He made friends there—in particular, Alexander Bache, who volunteered there apart from his duties as professor of natural philosophy and chemistry at the University of Pennsylvania. Bache was brilliant, intellectually open-minded, and easygoing. He was also one of the best-connected men in America and the great-grandson of none other than Benjamin Franklin. He and Espy got on well; his essential amiableness was a good contrast to Espy, who was characteristically boastful and extravagant. "Mr. Espy," Bache later remembered, "was eminently social in his mental habits, full of bonhomie and of enthusiasm, easily kindling into a glow." This made him a good fit for the institute: that was where, Bache wrote, "Mr. Espy found the mental stimulus that he needed, and the criticism which he courted, the best aids and checks on his observations, speculations, and experiments."

Espy's other close friend was Robert Hare—also a volunteer at the institute and like Bache a professor at the University of Pennsylvania. He was teaching not from necessity but from love: he happened to be an enormously wealthy man, the scion of the Republic's most famous brewing family; Hare's American Porter was a brand known all throughout New England. But when Hare was young, he had decided to leave the family business; he'd taken a medical degree, but his real love was chemistry and what would now be called electrical engineering. He had invented the oxyhydrogen blowpipe, an electrical device that allowed metalwork to be done at extremely high temperatures. He had also invented the galvanic deflagrator, a complex array of metal plates that formed a powerful voltaic battery (it was strong enough to ignite charcoal). Conclusively and several times over, he had refuted Benjamin Franklin's old fear that electricity would prove to have no practical value.

Hare was a choleric and ferociously contentious man, known for shouting down anybody who disagreed with him. But he found a strong opponent in Espy, who was almost impossible to defeat in an argument. Espy had the exasperating knack of appearing at all times to be amused rather than enraged by opposition; he conveyed a sense that he simply couldn't believe he was being disagreed with. "His views were positive and his conclusions absolute," Alexander Bache later wrote, "and so was the expression of them. He was not prone to examine and re-examine premises and conclusions, but considered what had once been passed up by his judgment as finally settled."

But the three friends still managed to work together, sometimes harmoniously, on several scientific projects the institute was conducting. In the late 1820s and early 1830s they collaborated on a project to discover the causes of steamboat explosions. They found the mathematics extremely difficult to work out and resorted instead to practical experimentation: they set out arrays of boilers in a deserted quarry and tried all the different ways they could think of to get them to blow up.

Later, after they got a federal grant, they bought a corner plot on the outskirts of Philadelphia and commissioned a house to be built there according to their peculiar specifications: it had a bricked furnace with an observation window of thick glass; inside it they would set their custom-designed boilers of brass and iron and rig them to explode. The whole neighborhood was jarred by the bangs and crashes and explosions within the mysterious little corner building—like a life-size version of Ben Franklin's old Thunder House.

Espy often came home with pieces he'd salvaged from the exploded boilers. He had turned the enclosed backyard of his and Margaret's house in Bedford into his own private open-air experimental laboratory. He was attempting to construct what he called a nepheloscope (*nephele* is "cloud" in ancient Greek)—a device that would create clouds and mist in a glass chamber. The yard was jammed with copper vessels, piping, ceramic vases, tubs of water, and a battalion of thermometers and barometers that allowed Espy to calculate and record minute variations in the dew point. The whitewashed back fence was covered over with Espy's scribbles; he used it to keep track of his results. His niece remembered that the fence was "so covered with figures and calculations that not a spot remained for another sum or column."

The New Brunswick tornado turned out to be the making of Espy as a public figure. Soon after his visit to the disaster zone in 1835, he started including descriptions of what he'd seen in New Brunswick in his lectures on the theory of steam power. He noticed an immediate jump in the attentiveness of his audience, and soon, as he devoted more time to the subject of tornadoes and how they demonstrated his theory, he noticed a jump in the size of the audiences as well. He continued to give his lectures for free at the institute, but he branched out to another and more lucrative form of speaking engagement—the new American lyceums.

The lyceums were the major cultural movement of the era. They had grown out of the mechanics' institutes like the Franklin: they were places where ordinary citizens could learn about and argue through the issues of the day. In the 1830s, there were lyceums in cities and small towns all over America—in old wooden meeting houses and in great stone-pillared downtown buildings, in barns and in open fields. There were celebrated and well-compensated speakers who traveled the lyceum circuit full-time, lecturing on their pet subjects, and there were regular open debates when anyone could speak out on whatever controversial subject was then raging. The flimsy and precarious economy of the country was always a hot topic, particularly after the latest bank crashes and the catastrophic panics in the financial markets. The morality of slavery and the treatment of the Native Americans were widely and bitterly debated. But passions could run furiously hot on almost any topic—American stage actors versus the British, for instance, an issue so controversial that it caused a riot in New York City in 1849, during which twenty-five people were killed.

Everyone was welcome to attend a lyceum. Even unescorted women were admitted, which in the early years was almost unprecedented. Lyceums printed up special admission tickets for women that had a space labeled "Introduced by ____," to be filled in with a male name—any name would do. (Later, this whole charade was dropped, and women not only attended freely but took part in the public debates; several women became famous as lyceum speakers.)

The lyceum movement was a lifesaver for Espy. He began lecturing at Philadelphia lyceums in 1837 and within a year was traveling to lyceums all over the country. "He took the bold resolution," his friend Bache wrote, "though past middle age, to throw himself into a new career, laying aside all ordinary employments, and devoting himself to the diffusion of the knowledge which he had collected and increased, by lecturing in the towns, villages, and cities of the United States."

He was a masterful, electrifying speaker. "He showed remarkable power in explaining his ideas," Bache remembered. "His simplicity and clearness enabled his hearers to follow him without too great effort, and the earnestness with which he spoke out his convictions carried them away in favor of his theory." He also excelled at dramatic storytelling; he spent a lot of his time at the podium describing the weird appearance of the New Brunswick tornado and the catastrophic destruction it had caused. He was particularly adept at the give-and-take with audience members in open debates afterward. He was never fazed, never flummoxed, always courteous even with the rudest interlocutor.

He grew used to the hostile question he inevitably got—even from polite and attentive audiences—after the spell of his tornado story wore off: What earthly difference did it make which theory of storms was the correct one? After a year on the lyceum circuit, he had worked out a startling answer.

He always began by acknowledging the problem. At that time, the leading theories were his own theory of steam power and Redfield's theory of whirlwinds, but which was the true one mattered only to natural philosophers. Nor would he offer that feeble old rationale that the answer was worth knowing merely for the abstract good of possessing knowledge. His audiences were practical people, and so he had a practical notion to offer them. Suppose, he said, that his theory of steam power had a great consequence, an almost unimaginable consequence. He was prepared to let his audience in on the secret. Steam power, he said, would allow mankind to control the weather.

"Mankind for thousands of years has been vainly endeavoring to discover the laws which regulate the weather," read his advertising poster for a lyceum appearance in Philadelphia. "Professor Espy (a native of Pennsylvania and a citizen of Philadelphia) *has made the great discovery* which mankind have been seeking ever since the flood, and is now giving a course of lectures on that subject, at the northeast corner of Eighth and Chestnut streets." This was, he promised, the most significant scientific breakthrough of modern times—"not excepting the law of gravitation—Dr. Franklin's discovery of atmospheric electricity—the cotton gin—the spinning jenny—or the application of the paddlewheel to the steamboat." With his theory firmly recognized and put into practice worldwide, people could cause rain to fall wherever they needed it. Canals and rivers would be navigable year-round; droughts would be a thing of the past. Most amazing of all, it would make a reality something that nobody had even imagined would be possible before: accurate weather prediction. "It will enable farmers, mechanics, manufacturers and travellers to anticipate the weather for a day or two, and sometimes for a longer period in advance." The poster concluded, "Let those who doubt come to the lecture this evening and hear for themselves."

The essence of his theory, as he explained it, was simple. If a storm was caused by a rising column of hot air, then, logically, we should be able to create a storm whenever we wanted to by artificial means. All we had to do was create a huge source of heat, and this would cause rain to fall wherever we needed it. The simplest way of creating this heat was by building a fire.

There was an obvious objection at this point: fires did not cause rain. Espy had an answer for that, too: they did, but we didn't realize it. An ordinary fire might not result in observable rainfall, but a really big fire would. He had discovered several documented cases where cumulonimbus clouds had formed over volcanic eruptions. His conclusion was that an extremely intense, hot fire set in a region of severe drought would create a thunderstorm large enough to break the drought and restore normal weather.

The idea struck many listeners—perhaps most—as sheer foolishness. The typical response was one he got from an editorialist at his hometown of Philadelphia: "The thing is too absurd for rational consideration." He didn't help his case with his exuberant, theatrical manner; as one newspaper noted, it all too obviously resembled "the charlatanry of a quack—a really scientific man never went to work in this way." But Espy was imperturbable. He even published an open letter in Philadelphia conceding that the public ridicule of his proposal was "proper enough," because he hadn't had a chance to prove that it would work. That was a shrewd move. It forced some people to reconsider what he was saying. Quacks and cranks, some of the press observed, generally lacked the ability to laugh at themselves. "We surely wish him success," one of the most openly derisory of the editorialists now wrote, "though we do smile sometimes at his enthusiasm."

By the end of the 1830s he had become one of the most popular and successful figures on the lyceum circuit. He sometimes found himself in direct competition with other lecturers: once in Boston, it was with the celebrated preacher William Miller, who had conclusively established from biblical prophecy that God would destroy the world on March 23, 1843. The joke went around that Miller was on one side of town announcing that God was about to burn down the world while Espy was on the other side arguing that people should do it themselves.

But Espy knew he would need something fresh to keep the audiences coming. That was when he hit upon the idea of finding a regular debating partner to take the opposite side. He thought the logical candidate was William Redfield. He decided to coax Redfield into touring with him so that they could debate their respective theories at every stop on the circuit. He issued a series of public challenges to Redfield from the lyceum platforms, and he wrote more reviews ridiculing his theory of whirlwind storms.

Redfield didn't take the bait. Since his initial controversies with Espy, he had returned to his old life, which was dignified and prosperous enough for anyone. His steamboat company, the Swiftsure Line, had offices and a large warehouse on the New York City docks and a large fleet of boats, some of them extremely lavish, running on the rivers and canals of New York and New England. For relaxation he took long and strenuous camping trips; he'd participated in one expedition into the unexplored reaches of the Adirondacks, which had found the source of the Hudson River. He was a respected member of New York City society; he sat on the board of New York's Lyceum of Natural History, which ultimately became the New York Academy of Sciences. Through the lyceum, he'd become acquainted with many of the leading figures in American science, including some of the experts in meteorology he'd avoided in New Brunswick. But even though his relations with them now were perfectly cordial, he'd take no part in their scientific debates. When he was asked about New Brunswick, he'd say that he was certain that Espy was wrong and the tornado was a whirlwind but he had no intention of publishing his views on the subject—a remark that caused several of his new friends to chide him for being "unphilosophical."

But while Redfield left Espy's taunts and challenges unanswered, somebody else accepted the challenge: Redfield's old mentor Denison Olmsted. He agreed to a single debate, which was held at the Mercantile Library in New York City. The event drew a big crowd and a lot of press coverage. The two men were in fine form. Espy played the noble, commonsensical man of the people standing up to the hidebound professor; Olmsted was the distinguished authority who was going to teach an impertinent upstart his manners. They clashed and tussled over Espy's steam power and his ideas about artificial rain; they even squabbled about Olmsted's theories of the formation of hailstones and the origin of comets and shooting stars: Olmsted believed that comets had an extraterrestrial origin; Espy thought that was absurd and that they were obviously optical tricks caused by humidity in the lower atmosphere.

Espy gradually got the upper hand. Olmsted, even after his years in a university lecture hall, simply wasn't as skilled a public performer. Espy later described Olmsted's manner as "sneering." Toward the end, after an hour of Espy's relentless goading, Olmsted made the fatal mistake of losing his temper. He said, as Espy remembered it, that "I had failed to convince men of science of the truth of my theory, and that I had appealed to the people, who were incapable of judging."

That settled the debate as far as the audience was concerned. The next day the New York City newspapers were unanimous in proclaiming Espy the winner. From then on he was regarded in the press as a major authority on American science. That was when he acquired a nickname: wherever he went, reporters covering his appearances called him the Storm King.

Espy's celebrity gradually drew the whole of the meteorological community into the question about the nature of tornadoes. Everybody felt obliged to take a side—either with Espy, that a tornado was a swiftly rising column of air, or with Redfield, that it was a whirlwind on the ground. In 1840 the general consensus was probably still with Espy. But his support was growing shaky; the problem was his theory of rainmaking, which was making it increasingly impossible for his partisans to discuss the idea of steam power objectively. Joseph Henry, the professor of natural philosophy at Princeton, politely said that Espy's public posturing and feuding were increasingly displaying "a want of prudence." Alexander Bache admitted a kind of sorrowful concern over "the strange direction my friend's career is taking." Robert Hare wrote an essay for the *National Gazette* saying that Espy's theories about storms and rain-making were "demonstrably incorrect" and his ceaseless propagandizing for them was "a perversion of the public mind."

Meanwhile, Espy had at last managed to goad Redfield into publishing angry rebuttals to his attacks. But he seems never to have realized just how much Redfield had come to despise him. Redfield saved his real venom for his letters to his friends. There he denounced Espy as a fraud. Espy was no longer even pretending to do serious science; he was merely saying whatever came into his head to draw more fame to himself. His new career, Redfield wrote, was only about his "yearning for immortality." At the same time, Redfield couldn't help following Espy's career obsessively; he noted with great satisfaction every time there was a news report of an Espy lecture that was poorly attended. Favorable news coverage, on the other hand, was simply proof of how skilled Espy had become at manipulating the press. "In order to account for the present tone of our newspaper press relating to him," Redfield wrote in one letter, "you must understand that he lays regular siege to the corps editorial, and plies them with as many of his puffing missives as their credulity or good nature will endure."

By then Espy's tornado lectures were also becoming sufficiently famous to draw public criticism from another, wholly unexpected quarter: the growing number of tornado survivors and eyewitnesses. There was near-universal agreement among them that the distinguishing quality of a tornado was its violent rotation, and they were angered to hear such a prominent figure as Espy so blithely dismiss the evidence of their own eyes as mistaken. One of the strongest denunciations came from Professor Lewis Beck, the man who had watched the New Brunswick tornado of 1835 from the deck of the steamboat *Napoleon*. Beck wrote a long paper for the *American Journal of Science* in 1839 describing his experiences that day. He presented it as a personal memoir; its real purpose was a point-blank attack on Espy's analysis of the storm. He granted that Espy was right about one thing: the tornado funnel was an ascending column of air. "The upward movement," he wrote, "was distinctly visible at a distance." But the rest of Espy's ideas were absurdly wrong. The funnel had absolutely and indisputably displayed a strong, swift, and continuous rotation. In fact, Beck believed it was precisely the spiraling winds that had done all the damage: "There was also undoubtedly a *whirling* motion, to which the destruction produced by the tornado is to be chiefly ascribed. This motion, as I have already said, appeared to us from on board the Napoleon, to succeed the upward movement and characterized the progress of the tornado until it passed from our view. That the tornado possessed this whirling character, was also abundantly demonstrated by the appearances presented in New Brunswick and its vicinity."

Beck's conclusion was unequivocal. "I must confess," he wrote, "that I was greatly surprised when I saw it subsequently stated that there was no evidence of a whirling motion . . . I am constrained to believe that had the facts been carefully examined without reference to a previously adopted theory, such an inference would not have been drawn from them." In other words, Espy was so in love with his theory of steam power that he was deliberately suppressing or falsifying evidence that didn't fit.

Espy didn't respond to Beck directly. But a clue to his attitude around that time was caught by a physician and university professor named Usher Parsons. Parsons happened to accompany Espy on a tour of a tornado damage track in New Jersey. Parsons raised the question of why so many eyewitnesses described the tornado as spinning. Espy shrugged. He said he had originally believed that all those eyewitness reports were mistaken; now he had heard so many of them that he supposed they were true. But according to Parsons, Espy "attaches less importance to the gyratory motion than Redfield and others have done, and believes it to be accidental." All that mattered to Espy about the tornado was the mechanism of steam power; the rotation of the funnel was a minor detail.

In 1838, at the annual meeting of the new British Association for the Advancement of Science, there was a public debate on the nature of tornadoes. Espy's steam-power theory was defended by his friend Alex-

ander Bache, who happened to be traveling in Europe that season; Redfield was championed by a British admirer, Lieutenant Colonel William
Reid of the British Engineering Service. The two men met in a furious
intellectual clash before a packed house. In attendance was the most
celebrated man of science in England, the astronomer Sir John Herschel. Herschel, like most of the audience, ended up favoring Redfield
and Reid. Herschel said in the public discussion that he couldn't see
how Espy's theory could work: the tornado vortex would require an
area of low pressure inside the funnel to create suction, but the straight-
line inflowing winds imagined by Espy would make the pressure in
the funnel higher than the surrounding air. Herschel went on to say,
though, that whichever view was correct, he'd found the debate profoundly illuminating. It had even given him a strange and radically new
idea about one of the deepest mysteries of his own field: the nature of
sunspots. What if, he asked the startled audience, sunspots were really
tornadoes—unimaginably vast tornadoes, tornadoes larger than the
earth itself? On that dizzying note the discussion ended. Redfield's and
Espy's two champions then shook hands; Bache even complimented
Reid for being so unselfish an advocate for an American scientist, an
unusual act for a Briton in those days. They parted friends. They were
like seconds at a duel who wouldn't allow the dispute between their
principals to get in the way of their own sense of courtesy.

The news of the debate soon made its way back to America. When
Espy heard about it, he was incensed. Herschel's objections particularly
galled him; he was certain that if he had only been there, he could have
shown Herschel how he was mistaken. He was determined to correct
this injustice at the earliest opportunity—which is how, two years later,
he was himself in England, to present his views at that year's meeting
of the BAAS.

It was held in Glasgow that year; more than a thousand people
attended. Most of the prominent scientists of Britain were there—
almost all of them, in fact, but John Herschel, who (to Espy's bitter
disappointment) had decided to skip that meeting. Espy began his lecture with a clever hook he'd invented in his years on the lyceum circuit:
when speaking in a strange town, he'd bone up beforehand on some

famous local storm that everybody in the audience was likely to remember, and he would discuss it in so much detail he might have been an eyewitness; then he would proceed to show how it was a perfect demonstration of his theory. For the BAAS, he picked a violent gale that had cut across Great Britain the previous year. He put up a large map of the British Isles on which he'd drawn arrows indicating the prevailing winds during the gale and showed how they all converged in straight lines at the storm's center. From there he went on to the views of Redfield. He had prepared diagrams of several hurricanes Redfield had described, and showed that in each case the winds had not displayed any rotation but had all blown inward in straight lines. Then he went on to speak in great technical detail of his theory. He described the process of caloric rarefaction, and he illustrated it with a detailed demonstration of his nepheloscope (which he'd brought with him from America). His talk was a long one, but he meant it to be long; he was always certain that if only he was given sufficient time, he could win over any audience. It was with the greatest reluctance, with the creeping feeling that his triumph was still slightly out of reach, that he at last opened up the floor to debate.

The questions came at him fast, and few of them were friendly. Was he aware that the numbers for his theory of caloric rarefaction didn't add up? Weren't the patterns of fallen trees he had mapped too haphazard for the conclusions he wanted to draw from them? Why hadn't Espy considered the possibility that the tornado's rotation was caused by the centrifugal force of the inflowing winds? The objections grew more detailed and technical. "The small funnel at the centre of the tornado, through which Mr. Espy supposed the air to rise, would be insufficient to vent all the air which would rush during a tornado, with the frightful velocity we know it to attain." "All the vapor in the air would be condensed into cloud much sooner than Mr. Espy supposed . . . the violent ascending vortex calculated upon by Mr. Espy would not exist."

Espy was taken aback by the barrage. He argued back heatedly but ineffectually. It was a rare thing for him to be at a loss in a public forum, but the truth was that at the lyceums he'd mostly been debating people who didn't know that much about science; he was out of the habit of responding to detailed and substantial criticisms of his ideas. So he simply tried to talk the objections down without refuting them, and then he would explain himself over again more patiently. He answered all the questioners "at considerable length," one observer wrote: "Mr. Espy seemed to think that he had been misunderstood."

Espy was left crushed. He was enough of an objective judge of his performances to know that this had been a disaster. He also knew that he was going to have to do something very dramatic very quickly to repair his reputation. He'd booked an extended lecture tour through the British Isles that summer and fall, but in the wake of Glasgow he abruptly canceled his remaining dates. Instead, he left for Paris, where he would try presenting his theory to the French Academy of Sciences.

It was a bold move, but a shrewd one: French intellectuals in those years were known to be much more hospitable to Americans than the British traditionally were. The academy did agree to hear him out. A panel of respected natural philosophers listened to him courteously as he explained his views at great length. When he was finished, they congratulated him on the originality of his ideas. They promised to consider them in depth and issue a statement. But they made no promises about when.

By then the news of the Glasgow meeting had reached America; several newspapers had reported that he'd been thoroughly humiliated. That, together with the growing disdain of the American scientific community, induced in him a sudden wave of despair—maybe even of self-doubt. He simply couldn't see any point in going back to America with nothing to show for his trip. So he decided to stay on. He spent the rest of that autumn, and the whole of a clammy Parisian winter, waiting for word from the French Academy of Sciences.

It took the academy six months to issue its report. But when Espy at last received a copy, he was elated. The panel members had concluded that Espy's theory of steam power was convincing and that caloric rarefaction must be the correct mechanism for the creation of thunderstorms. They also accepted his description of straight-line movement in tornadoes and dismissed Redfield's whirlwinds: "Mr. Espy's theory, which is based upon facts, refutes the idea of a whirling motion of the air in the tornado." They had only one demur: they believed that Espy didn't give sufficient weight to the influence of atmospheric electricity on tornadoes. (This was in fact a general bias in the thinking of French meteorologists of the time.) They told Espy that he needed to include more about "the action of electricity." Then, they concluded, his theory "will leave nothing to be desired."

The report included a recommendation: "Mr. Espy should be placed by the government of the United States in a position to continue his important investigations and to complete his theory." They considered this to be particularly important given that America was, "as it were, the home of these fearful meteors."

Espy thanked the members of the panel graciously for their helpful suggestions. He promised them that he would think over the question of the relationship between tornadoes and lightning, and immediately forgot all about it.

Espy returned to America in the late spring of 1841. The news of his great triumph in Paris had preceded him. This was at a time when many Americans still acutely felt their cultural inferiority to the Europeans; an American scientist winning the approval of the French academy was a major event. He found his new lectures enormously well attended and the press coverage rapturous. He immediately decided to put together a book to cash in on his fame. He called it *The Philosophy of Storms*. It was a hasty piece of work: a jumble of his old drafts and papers, plus a stop-the-presses account of his adventures in Glasgow and Paris. But it sold very well and solidified his fame. It also earned him his most distinguished and objective praise, from the celebrated mathematician Benjamin Peirce, who wrote a long notice for *The Yale Review*. It wasn't an unqualified rave; Peirce began by mocking Espy's public persona in debate:

> I shall attempt to examine Professor Espy's theory in a spirit of perfect candor and impartiality, but, I fear, without success; for there is an air of self-satisfaction and contempt for the views of other observers in his statements, which irresistibly arouses the demon of obstinacy. Even storm-kings are intolerable in a republic; and not the "infinite

utility" of this new theory, nor the singular modesty with which its author affects to be merely the Newton of Meteorology, can lull the hardened democrat into submission to the tyranny with which he acts the sole monarch of the winds, the veritable cloud-compeller, the modern Zeus nepheligepetis, and treats other observers as invaders of his domains. [*Nepheligepetis* is classical Greek for "begetter of clouds."]

But about the theory of steam power, Peirce was generous in his praise. He did note, as others had done, that the mathematics of caloric rarefaction didn't add up, but he didn't consider this a fatal flaw; the data could have been sloppily collected or incorrectly analyzed (both of these things were in fact true). What mattered was the elegance and explanatory power of the theory itself. "Its simplicity attracts and delights," Peirce wrote, "and it seems to be demonstrated at a glance, by the most direct and necessary connexion of cause and effect . . . This beautiful mechanism, whether it has been adopted by Nature or not, is most worthy of her; and Mr. Espy may honorably be proud of its conception."

Back on the lyceum circuit, Espy found his celebrity status solidly in place. He was introduced to Ralph Waldo Emerson, who recorded in his journal that Espy "amused me with storms and metaphysics." A widely read satire on current American celebrities included "Professor Espy . . . with a tremendous storm in a gum-elasticbag"; the author was Nathaniel Hawthorne. The popular *Godey's Lady's Book* ran a story called "The Rain King," set in Philadelphia a century in the future, when "the theory of a certain ingenious and highly scientific philosopher, who flourished towards the middle of the nineteenth century, had now been brought to practical perfection." The story described a procession of citizens petitioning the Rain King for their own favorite weather: children wanted school rained out, a woman required fair skies so she could flee her husband, umbrella makers demanded unexpected downpours, and parasol makers paid for permanent sunshine. "With the agency of steam power," the author explained, rain could now be generated on demand; the artificial clouds had turned out to be just as good as real ones, "except that they could not promise to rain frogs."

6

Under the Map

Robert Hare's laboratory was as elaborate and mysterious as an alchemist's den. It took up most of a wing at the University of Pennsylvania. There was an enormous hearth and a forge room. There were two fireproof workrooms with groined arches. There was an enclosed study above a scullery; the scullery had sinks and a large boiler and river water piped in from the city's public works. There was an air furnace, and evaporating ovens, and several sand baths, and an alembic. The walls were heavily bricked and reinforced in case one of his large electrical experiments went wrong, and there was an elaborate ventilation system with a flue and fifteen vents, because the experiments, even when they worked perfectly, were so often toxic.

Prominently displayed around the main room were the famous inventions of Hare's early days—the oxyhydrogen blowpipe, the deflagrator, the electrical plating machine. All manner of gear testified to work in progress: piping, tubing, plates, and rods. The stone pillars of the room were wound up in yard after yard of copper wire as though they were cocooned—Hare wouldn't explain why. At the far end of the room were rows of wooden seats on risers, where his students would sit for his lectures. He was a ferocious lecturer. He had written a standard handbook on electricity and electrical research, and he expected his students to know it by heart. He also expected them to ignore any book on chemistry by another hand. Hare had had fallings-out with almost all of his colleagues, either because he considered them idiots or because he was convinced they had stolen his ideas. If any student had the gall to mention work by any other chemist—up to and including the greatest chemist of that era, Michael Faraday—he would be met with an incinerating glare of hate, and sometimes permanent banishment from his lectures.

Many people blamed Hare's perpetual foul mood on his lack of progress in his work. Hare's major inventions had all been made when he was young; his current work consisted of refinements to the devices for electrical heating and electroplating that he'd first constructed decades earlier. He was always extremely touchy about his professional standing. He was driven to a rage whenever he felt as though his achievements were not being given proper acknowledgment. His professional correspondence was filled with fantastic tirades directed at the leading scientists of the age, because in Hare's view they were all hacks, incompetents, thieves, or intellectual swindlers. One colleague said that it was dangerous to write to Hare about anything personal, because he would immediately publish it together with a furious point-by-point refutation.

Part of the reason his progress had stalled is that his worldview had never budged from his earliest days. His ideas about the physical universe were essentially those of an earlier generation—Benjamin Franklin's generation, in fact. He still believed in the theory of subtle fluids. The new theory that heat was the product of molecular motion he dismissed as pernicious nonsense. He thought the only problem with Franklin's original work on electricity was that it hadn't pushed the idea of the subtle fluid far enough. Hare believed that all the strange phenomena of the atmosphere, from comets to tornadoes, were really forms or by-products of lightning.

It happened that he had witnessed a tornado in Philadelphia in 1840 and had written up a report of his own perceptions of it for the Franklin Institute's journal. He could not see any evidence of a whirlwind; on the other hand, he said, he "could not reconcile the relative situation of the clouds, or their evident reaction and diversity of movement, with the theory of Mr. Espy." In the tornado funnel, he wrote, he "had distinguished two clouds, one much above the other, between which there appeared to be an electrical reaction, tending to keep them at a distance." He concluded that "this could not but demonstrate that electricity was the principal agent in the production of such phenomena."

Through all those years of controversy, Hare and Espy had managed to remain friends—at least until Espy's endorsement by the French academy. This was a particularly galling blow to Hare. He considered it a betrayal—not so much by Espy as by the members of the academy. He had himself appeared before them a few years earlier, and they had been extremely enthusiastic about his electrical theories. He was not mollified to learn of the committee's advice to Espy that he needed to reconsider the importance of electricity to his model of tornadoes. That seemed to him to be a fig leaf covering up a despicable intellectual compromise.

Ordinarily, he would have fired off a volley of furious letters to both Espy and the academy. But this time he had a more cunning idea. He wrote to William Redfield instead and expressed his sympathy over how the academy had slighted Redfield's whirlwind model. He suggested that Redfield complain to the academy about this injustice.

Redfield obliged; by then he was enraged whenever anything good happened to Espy. But not one of his letters was answered. That was only what he had expected. He was thoroughly disenchanted with the scientific establishments of America and Europe for tolerating such an obvious charlatan as Espy. He was content to let the matter drop.

But that didn't prove to be so simple. When Hare realized that Redfield wasn't going to keep pressing the case against Espy, he flew into one of the largest, most rancorous, most extravagant rages of his life. From then on, he was certain that Espy wasn't the real enemy; Redfield was. What followed was the greatest sustained barrage of printed matter in the whole long controversy. Hare wrote pamphlet after pamphlet over the next few years, including *Objections to Mr. Redfield's Theory of Storms, Additional Objections to Redfield's Theory of Storms, Further Objections and Strictures*. Their tone never varied. A surface of brittle courtesy covered over a seethe of sarcasm, building each time to a triumphant, haughty, absolute dismissal. Redfield was a buffoon dispensing self-evident nonsense: Redfield's idea of rotating storms was a physical impossibility, and all the evidence that Redfield had collected was meaningless tripe.

Once again, under the savage goading of public criticism, Redfield roused himself for a counter-barrage. He dismissed Hare's criticisms wholesale. Hare had no "reliable facts and observations" to offer in opposition to what Redfield described as "the established character of storms." And if Hare absolutely required a theory, there were any number of possibilities. The rotation of storms could be the result of gravity, of the rotation of the earth, or of a natural tendency of water and wind to form spirals. These ideas were so obvious that Redfield didn't see why the scientific community was so reluctant to accept them. But then, he thought that "the whole modern meteorological school," from John Herschel on down, had fallen into what he called "a grand error," by allowing itself to be seduced by the absurd theorizing of the likes of Espy and Hare.

Hare's counter-counter-replies duly followed. The notion that the rotation of storms, even granting it existed, could have anything to do with the rotation of the earth was the most preposterous idea he'd ever heard. Didn't Redfield realize that as the earth turned, the atmosphere turned with it, and therefore the net effect would logically be zero? If Hare himself, along with the rest of the scientific community, rejected such absurdities, it was with good reason. Redfield knew nothing about science and had no business proposing his ideas in the first place. "I cannot give to this alleged theory the smallest importance," Hare wrote; the scientific principles it relied on "exist only in the imagination of the author."

Redfield was so stung by Hare's onslaught that he was moved to something like humor. In his next reply he asked why, if his ideas were so worthless, Hare was taking so many pains to refute them. Hare's reply ricocheted back: the issue was the sinister fact of Redfield's growing influence. "I admit," Hare wrote, "that his essays have met with an attention which may have justified him in pluming himself on their success." But that was the danger: "Some men of science of the present time are prone to lend a favorable ear to any hypothesis, however in itself absurd, provided it be *associated with observations.*"

Redfield replied to that pamphlet, too, of course, and the one after, but exhaustion had finally set in. He told a friend that he never would have replied in the first place if he'd known Hare better. Hare was, he said, the sort of man who simply went on arguing until he was the last one left.

In the 1840s, the capital of the country—it was then known as Washington City—was still more of an idea than a real place. The great stone constructions like the Washington Monument and the Capitol Dome were unfinished; the existing government buildings were scattered along a maze of mud tracks; the street grid was cut through by a half-finished canal that overflowed with sewage. It had a reputation for being little more than a disease-ridden swamp—not unlike its reputation as a seat of power. But it was still the only practical option Espy had left, if he was going to be America's meteorologist.

He had already approached the Pennsylvania legislature for a grant to mount a pilot program in weather control. He'd even managed to get the idea heard by the Pennsylvania House of Representatives. But the result had been a fiasco. The debate had quickly degenerated into whimsy. Speaker after speaker took turns indulging in mock-alarmist oratory denouncing the idea of allowing any one man to control the weather. Think of the power he'd have over the state economy, to say nothing of his political clout; they all agreed this would be a calamity for Pennsylvania, and they unanimously voted the proposal down.

Espy was undaunted. He went to Washington City and paid a call on the U.S. House of Representatives. In January 1842 he met with John Quincy Adams. Adams was an influential man. But more important for Espy's purpose, he was known to be an eccentric man, with a tolerance for unusual ideas. He had even at one point endorsed the theories of a strange itinerant lecturer named John Cleves Symmes, who believed the earth was hollow and that the interior could be accessed at the North Pole. During his presidency, Adams had been prepared to back an expedition to search for the polar entrance and make contact with the interior's inhabitants, but he'd left office and returned to Congress before the expedition could be mounted.

Adams proved to be far less hospitable to Espy's ideas. "Mr. Espy, the storm-breeder," Adams wrote in his diary, "left me with a paper exposing his three wishes of appropriations by Congress for his benefit—about as rational as those of Hans Carvel and his wife." (This was a reference to a dirty story in Rabelais: Carvel has a dream in which he begs the devil to make his wife faithful; the devil shows him a ring and tells him that his wife can never betray him while he wears it; he wakes to find his hand between his wife's legs while his wife is telling him to pull out his finger.) "The man is methodically monomaniac," Adams wrote, "and the dimensions of his organ of self-esteem have been swollen to the size of a goitre by a report from a committee of the National Institute of France, endorsing all his crack-brained discoveries in meteorology. I told him, with all possible civility, that it would be of no use to memorialize the House of Representatives in behalf of his three wishes."

But Espy wasn't done. In fact, he explained, a memo from Adams to the House wouldn't serve at all. He had a grander goal: he wanted to address the Senate. He knew that he could sway its members to his cause just as he had the French academy. Adams wrote that Espy asked him "if they should pass a bill in his favor, whether I would support it in the House. I said if the Senate should pass such a bill I would do all that I could for him in the House."

Then he excused himself from further discussion, pleading urgent House business.

At that time, Adams and the rest of Congress did happen to be contending with a particularly complex piece of business. A British scientist and investor named James Smithson, inspired by the ideals of the American Revolution, had willed his considerable estate to the people of the United States, with the direction that the money be used to fund an establishment "for the increase and diffusion of knowledge among men." Adams sat on a House select committee that was trying to decide what to do with this bequest. The committee members had been arguing about it for several years and still hadn't arrived at a plan.

Espy, though, had an idea. He brought it to Adams a few weeks after their first meeting. Espy proposed, Adams recorded in his diary, "that a portion of the fund should be appropriated for simultaneous meteorological observations all over the Union, with him for a central meteorologist, stationed at Washington with a comfortable salary." That idea pleased Adams no more than any of Espy's other talk.

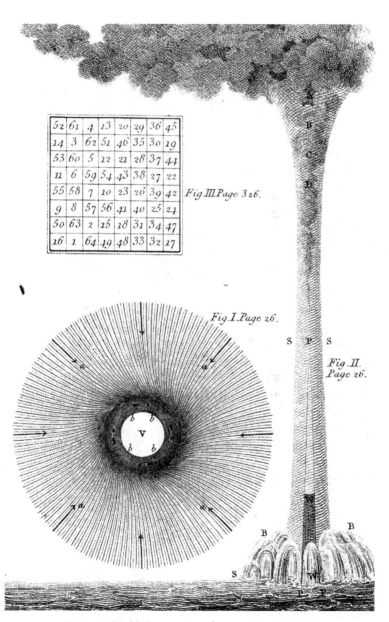

52	61	4	13	20	29	36	45
14	3	62	51	46	35	30	19
53	60	5	12	21	28	37	44
11	6	59	54	43	38	27	22
55	58	7	10	23	26	39	42
9	8	57	56	41	40	25	24
50	63	2	15	18	31	34	47
16	1	64	49	48	33	32	17

Fig.III.Page 326.

Fig.I.Page 26.

Fig.II.
Page 26.

Benjamin Franklin's conception of a waterspout. (NOAA)

An unusually accurate depiction of Franklin and the kite,
from an 1877 book on meteorology. (NOAA)

James Pollard Espy,
the Storm King. (NOAA)

William Redfield, Espy's great
antagonist in the storm war.
(*Popular Science Monthly*/Wikimedia Commons)

Robert Hare, chemist
and tornado enthusiast.
(*Popular Science Monthly*/
Wikimedia Commons)

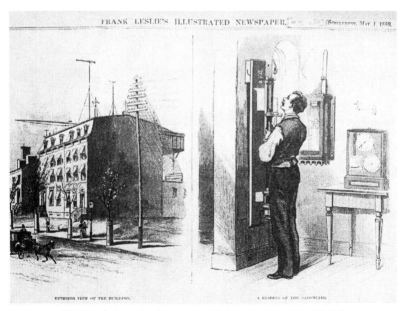

The Signal Corps headquarters in Washington City, 1880. (NOAA)

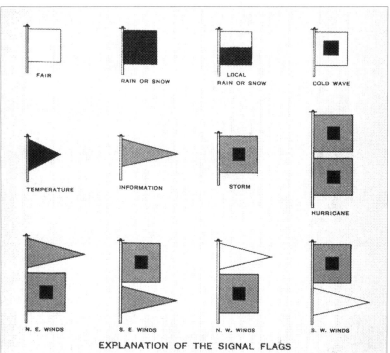

EXPLANATION OF THE SIGNAL FLAGS
USED AT
WEATHER BUREAU DISPLAY STATIONS.

FAIR SIGNAL. The White Flag alone indicates fair weather, stationary temperature.

RAIN OR SNOW SIGNAL. The Blue Flag alone indicates rain or snow, stationary temperature.

LOCAL RAIN OR SNOW SIGNAL The White and Blue Flag indicates local rain or snow, stationary temperature.

COLD WAVE SIGNAL. The White Flag with Black Center indicates sudden fall in temperature, usually accompanied by stormy weather.

TEMPERATURE SIGNAL. The Black Pennant above indicates warmer weather of the type represented by the lower flag; below, cooler weather of the type represented by the upper flag.

INFORMATION SIGNAL. The Red Pennant indicates that the local displayman has received information of a storm covering a limited area, dangerous only for vessels bound for certain points.

STORM SIGNAL. The Red Flag with Black Center indicates that a storm of marked violence is expected.

HURRICANE SIGNAL. Two Storm Signals one above the other indicate the expected approach of a tropical hurricane or a severe and dangerous storm from the interior.

WIND SIGNAL. Pennants with the Storm Signal indicate the direction of the wind; red, easterly, from northeast to south; white, westerly, from southwest to north. The Pennant above the flag indicates that the wind is expected to blow from the northerly quadrants; below, from the southerly quadrants.

Forecast flags of the Signal Corps, a common sight
in America until the 1920s. (NOAA)

Whirlwind. A *trombe,* or spout, from
Camille Flammarion's *L'Atmosphère,* 1888. (NOAA)

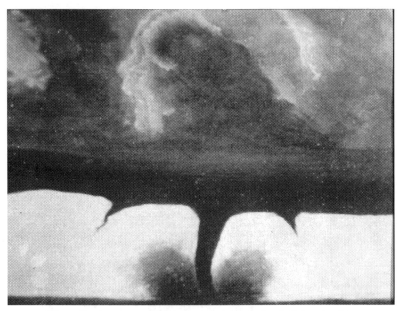

The earliest known tornado photograph, taken in South Dakota in 1884,
heavily retouched for sale as a postcard. (NOAA)

Cleveland Abbe, "Acting Probabilities,"
in his office. (NOAA)

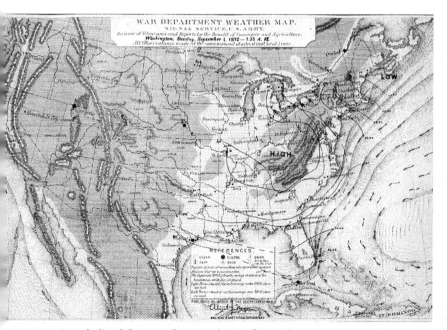

An early Signal Corps weather map, showing fair weather over the country's
midsection and a major storm in the Atlantic. (NOAA)

Photograph of the havoc wrought by a Louisville, Kentucky,
tornado circa 1913. (Library of Congress)

The great cyclone, tornado, and fire at Louisville, Kentucky.
Newspaper panorama of the great Louisville tornado of 1890. (Library of Congress)

But Espy stayed on in Washington City and continued to press whatever political contacts he could find. (He did have several well-connected friends at the Franklin Institute.) By the middle of that summer, one of them came through: he was appointed a consulting mathematician to the secretary of the navy. Whether or not the job was supposed to have any real duties Espy wasn't entirely clear. But he decided to seize the opportunity anyway. He rented rooms in Washington City (his wife, Margaret, remained back home, away from the foul night fogs and swamp gases of the capital) and declared himself to be the War Department's official meteorologist.

It was not an implausible position. The War Department had been accumulating meteorological records for decades. Army doctors were supposed to keep detailed logs of the weather, because it was believed then that most illness was caused by the fogs and fumes of the atmosphere. As it happened, nobody had ever done anything with these logs, but Espy had a use for them: he wanted to make them the baseline for a new nationwide system of meteorological observation.

It was one of his most audacious ideas, but he went about it with admirable practicality. He knew that he couldn't pry funding for any such system out of the government, but he believed he could attract volunteers. That had been, after all, one of the continual surprises of his lecture tours: how many people in America were interested in the weather. So he wrote a circular letter addressed "To the Friends of Science in the United States, Canada, West Indies, Bermuda, etc.," and he mailed it to hundreds of universities, newspapers, government agencies, and scientific associations. (One of the perks of his official position was free postage.) The request was simple: send in any and all meteorological observations, records, diaries, and journals, past and present, and "enclose to the Navy Department, Washington City, Care of J. P. Espy."

Within a year he was drawing the first national weather maps. He also began assembling specialized data concerning tornadoes and thunderstorms. He sent out more circulars, this time pushing his own theories: he declared that he was particularly interested in patterns of fallen trees in the wake of tornadoes and also any evidence of rainfall after large fires.

In the meantime, he became practiced at working the government bureaucracy. This was a practical necessity, because he had to wheedle the annual reauthorization of his salary in the federal budget. John Quincy Adams recorded another visit from Espy in 1844; he was startled to learn that Espy had never left Washington City. "Mr. Espy, the storm-breeder, came with a complaint that the Committee of Ways and Means were about to retrench the appropriation for some small interloping office under the War Department with which he has been allowed for the last two years to pursue his study of storms." Espy was prepared with a sales pitch about the importance of his work: "He said that he had contemporaneous observations made at a hundred and fifty military stations, the results of which he had reported to the Secretary of War, and his report had been communicated with that of the Secretary, accompanying the President's annual message to Congress, and he showed me ninety engraved maps, on which was marked the direction of all the storms at the several stations of observation, all confirmative of his theory."

Espy got his salary approved that time. But the next year it was more difficult. By then his superiors in the War Department had finally caught up with what he was doing and informed him that they had no use for a professional meteorologist. What they wanted was the actual job description: a mathematician. They expected him to do mathematical analyses of their countless engineering projects.

Espy made a few attempts to appease them. He offered the department a practical project of his own: a design for a new ventilator, based on his theory of steam power. It was a conical metal cap that could be fitted to a chimney, which created a convective effect that resulted in a stronger draw. Espy later claimed that this design was such a success that it was installed on every chimney in the White House.

But most of the assignments he was given he simply ignored. In 1843, the secretary of the navy ordered him to break off his storm studies and report for duty at the Depot of Charts and Nautical Instruments; Espy refused. In 1845, he was assigned to a naval vessel in order to carry out a long-term mission involving military engineering and mathematics. He declared it would interfere too much with his real work, and he resigned.

He didn't stay unemployed for long. Congress had at last disgorged the Smithson bequest, and an institution was being duly created for the increase and diffusion of knowledge among men.

The Smithsonian Institution was officially founded in 1846. Its director (the official job title was first secretary) was Espy's old friend and colleague Joseph Henry of Princeton. Henry's brief was open-ended: find some way of fulfilling Smithson's intentions. He took it as an invitation to be ambitious. From the beginning, he wanted to put the Smithsonian at the heart of American science. He ordered the construction of a library and public museum in Washington City—something along the lines of the Franklin Institute but much more imposing. He put out a general call for scientific archives and collections. He wanted anything and everything: exotic butterflies, whale teeth, Native American artifacts, antique scientific equipment, fossilized prehistoric fish. He determined that the institution should start a printing house and become the leading publisher of scientific books. He began by acquiring a major work in manuscript: the first substantial archaeological study of the mysterious Mound Builder culture of the ancient Mississippi valley.

Henry most wanted to make the Smithsonian a home for the latest and most daring research. He was especially interested in research on American weather. James Espy was one of his first hires.

Henry was impressed with the weather records that Espy had been collecting through the War Department. He had the political capital to make Espy's project into something much grander. He persuaded the federal government to give him priority access to the lines of the new telegraph companies then being strung around the country. Each morning, volunteer weather spotters would be given first rights to send their messages to the Smithsonian in Washington City, and for the first time there would be current weather information available for the whole country.

Espy had managed in the end to attain his impossible goal. He was now America's official meteorologist. But it rapidly became obvious that this wasn't enough for him. He wasn't prepared to sit in an office in the Smithsonian and do nothing but review streams of incoming weather data. He wanted immediate federal authorization for his rainmaking scheme; he intended to remake the entire climate of the nation at a single stroke.

Soon after he began working at the institution, he wrote up a formal summary of his plan, and he began another series of public lectures around the country to promote it. He wanted enormous fires set along a series of longitudinal lines throughout the western region of the country. Each line was to run for at least seven hundred miles. He calculated it would take about a week of continuous burning for the rain clouds to form. The rain would fall in moderate amounts beginning in the fire zone and then spread eastward across the whole country. "It will rain enough and not too much in any one place," he said—only a few hours per fire. He promised that the rain "will not be attended with violent wind either on land or on the Atlantic ocean; that there will be no hail nor tornado at the time of the rain, nor intermediate; that there will be no destructive floods, or injuriously low waters; that there will be no oppressively hot nor injuriously cold weather."

The larger benefits would come as soon as the rainmaking system was fully in place and in continuous operation: "Farmers and mariners will always know, in advance, when the rains will commence, or nearly so, and when they will terminate; all epidemic diseases originating from floods and droughts, will cease; the proceeds of agriculture will be greatly increased, and the health and happiness of the citizens much promoted."

If federal backing wasn't immediately forthcoming, he believed that the citizenry shouldn't wait but should start setting the fires themselves. They should save up all combustible materials until the first dry spell of summer. Then the fires should be set weekly, in stages along lines of longitude, according to a schedule he had devised: "Let all west of 87 degrees of west longitude set fire to their materials only on a Thursday, those west of 90 degrees in the morning at ten o'clock, and those east of 90 degrees at six in the evening," and so on. He hoped that all citizens would participate, "not only because all are interested in the probable result, but because it will be attended with no expense."

He thought the project would be so cheap because of the ongoing and rapid deforestation taking place in the American interior. As he wrote: "There is at present, and will be for many years to come, a vast amount of timber cut down in clearing lands, and burnt every summer, in the western parts of the United States; enough, perhaps, to produce the wide extended rains so much desired." He estimated that the total cost would add up to "a sum not amounting to a half a cent a year to each individual in the United States."

After William Redfield had given up on his debates with Robert Hare, he retreated to his study and occupied his idle hours (more and more of them, as he gradually turned over his business to his partners and his son) in amateur research. Over the years he built up an immense private library on ocean navigation in general and on the Atlantic in particular. He became the leading expert on the Atlantic in all its peculiarities. For one maritime publisher he wrote a detailed guide for navigating the most treacherous coastal waters of northern Europe and the British Isles. For another, he provided a meticulous catalog of the North Atlantic ice fields. He did all of this from his desk; he never once in his life sailed the Atlantic out of sight of the American coast.

His most sustained work was an exhaustive study of three major Atlantic hurricanes. The project took him years. For just one of the hurricanes—his son estimated—he accumulated and analyzed logbooks from 164 ships: "How well do I remember the hours which my father spent extended upon the floor over a large chart of the Atlantic Ocean, on which he was plotting the facts recorded in the log-books of the ships, which at various points over an extent of thousands of miles had encountered the various phases of that terrific hurricane." The work met with the expected response from the scientific community. "A writer in one of the English scientific journals," his son wrote, "had the effrontery to say that not one of the contenders for the rotary movement of storms had ever collected a sufficient number of observations from both sides of a storm-track to prove the rotation!"

Redfield continued his collaborations with Lieutenant Colonel Reid; it remained the closest and most harmonious friendship of his life. They shared a passion for pure research with no thought of theory. One time Reid delighted Redfield with a gift: observational records from lighthouses on the European coast of the Atlantic. Redfield responded with copies of American ships' logs, for presentation to the British Admiralty. Reid tirelessly recommended Redfield's pamphlets to British scientists; Redfield pressed on his American friends copies of Reid's monograph *An Attempt to Develop the Law of Storms.* Their fondness for each other never flagged, even though—or perhaps because—it was strictly a postal relationship; the two men never met in person.

Their most significant project was a set of navigation guidelines for mariners in hurricanes. Their advice was simple, practical, easy to follow, and extraordinarily effective. Ships' captains and navigators who didn't have the slightest idea whether or not hurricanes were rotational could testify that the guidelines worked. By the mid-1840s, the standard navigation handbooks—books like Piddington's *Horn-Book,* a copy of which could be found in almost every ship on the high seas—routinely cited Redfield and Reid.

Redfield also found himself an accepted member of the American scientific community—somebody who could be counted on to organize committees, write letters of recommendation, find potential donors, and sit on advisory boards. When the American Association for the Advancement of Science was founded at the end of the 1840s, the organizers' first thought for a chairman was Redfield.

Robert Hare retired from his professorship at the University of Pennsylvania in 1847. He then made what he believed to be the greatest possible gesture of support for the Smithsonian: he donated to it his laboratory. All his intricate gear, his historic oxyhydrogen blowpipe, his custom-made vials and ceramic pestles and electric plates, his furnaces and sand baths and alembics and evaporating ovens, were crated up with exquisite care and shipped to Washington City. Hare intended it to be of some use to the Smithsonian's younger researchers, but he was also expecting it to be appreciated at its true worth: as the invaluable archive of one of America's greatest scientists.

Retirement didn't mellow him. He had even more time for his relent-less correspondence: time to quarrel, to pick out flaws in the published work of his rivals, to chide authorities in the field for succumbing to dubious new theories, and to claim credit for ideas that he thought were being stolen from him without attribution. He hated idleness. He was a rich man who had no pressing need to work, but he was driven to find a new career anyway. So he decided to make a go of authorship.

He had always written—not just his professional papers and his con-troversial pamphlets, but reviews and essays of opinion for newspapers and journals on economics, history, and politics. Now he set out to master a new field: historical romance. It proved much harder than he expected. The composition of his first novel was a tough slog. He had no easy way with plot or character. He was helpless to move the story forward without the heavy use of coincidence, and his powers of inven-tion were such that he was obliged to have all the major dramatic events take place offstage. Still, he managed to drag his novel through to the end. The title was *Standish the Puritan: A Tale of the American Revolu-tion,* by "Eldred Grayson, Esq."

As a literary experience, the novel serves mainly to demonstrate the total stranglehold that Sir Walter Scott had over American fiction in that era; without the examples of *Rob Roy* and *The Tale of Old Mortality* in front of him, Hare would have been unable to write the novel at all. But what may be even more striking is the emotional iciness of its lead characters. The plot ostensibly concerns the lifelong friendship among three men (George De l'Eur, the scion of an aristocratic British family; William Standish, a stalwart representative of the new American upper classes; and Julius Caesar Snifling, a rapacious mercantile dealer and speculator on the make), but they regard each other with contempt, indifference, and at best an aloof respect. If Hare didn't keep insisting they are friends, one would have taken for granted that they are enemies.

The first time Espy, Hare, and Redfield are known to have been in the same room together was at a meeting of the American Association for the Advancement of Science in 1849. Espy was there to give a technical talk on one of the Smithsonian's ongoing projects, the correct calibration of barometers. Hare was attending only as an interested spectator. Redfield was there to give the keynote address; he had agreed to be the association's chairman.

When Redfield came to the podium, he began by acknowledging Espy's and Hare's presence in the audience. Then he immediately launched into a long, copiously detailed, and blistering attack on how both Espy and Hare had wrecked America's progress in science through their overreliance on theory. Since 1830, he said, when he had first described his model of whirlwind storms to Professor Olmsted, there had essentially been no progress at all in the study of meteorology, and he blamed Espy and Hare for the stalemate. This was nothing he hadn't said in print many times before, but this was the first time he'd ever made the claim in a public forum, when his antagonists were there and could reply to his face.

Hare rose to accept the challenge. He wasn't a scheduled speaker; he addressed the gathering from his seat in the audience. He said he wanted to have on record his own complete disgust with what had happened to American science over the course of his career. He need look no further than Redfield's presence on the podium as chairman; in itself that demonstrated the decline in scientific standards. Redfield's ideas about storms, as he had repeatedly shown, weren't science at all; they were simply nonsense. Large bodies of turning air couldn't cohere or sustain themselves, because they had neither "a restraining vessel" nor a "stirrer." He denounced Redfield's current campaign to get his directives for navigation in hurricanes accepted by maritime reference books. All Redfield was doing, Hare said, was "spreading poison."

Then Hare turned to Espy. Hare declared that he had done everything he could for the past twenty years to explain to Espy that his theory of caloric rarefaction (or convection, as he himself preferred to call it) simply didn't work. But it had done no good. Espy was incapable of acknowledging his mistakes. It was a defect of his character, compounded by the undeserved praise he'd received from allegedly authoritative institutions like the French academy. Hare said it was fundamentally dishonorable and unpatriotic for Espy to keep bringing up the French academy anyway; Espy would never be a good American or a true scientist until he freed himself from the "intellectual tyranny" of the Europeans.

Redfield refused to say anything in response to Hare. Espy likewise remained silent. When it came time for Espy to give his scheduled lecture, the whole audience was expecting one of his most dazzling extempore flights of denunciatory and self-dramatizing rhetoric. But Espy simply read his prepared remarks on the technical difficulties of calibrating barometers and left the hall without another word.

Back in Washington City, Espy and Joseph Henry had a large cloth map of the Republic hung in the main hall of the Smithsonian's new building. Each day Espy compiled the latest weather information from his spotters network and had the major cities and towns on the map marked with their current conditions. It almost immediately became a landmark. All over Washington City, people would say casually to each other, "Let's meet under the map." Many visitors read a political message into it: its daily display of information from all over the country was a symbol of the way America was growing from a scattering of isolated communities into a single interconnected nation. Students of meteorology were impressed to see, each day, proof of a truth first put forward by Benjamin Franklin: that weather systems in America weren't random, but moved in grand sweeps from southwest to northeast. Others simply liked to come by each day and watch the information change. Even if they couldn't have explained why, they found a curious sort of satisfaction in knowing that yesterday it had rained in Charlotte, North Carolina, and today it was sunny.

7

One Dead, One Exhausted, One Converted

In his last years, whenever James Espy considered—as he often did—the question of where things had gone irretrievably wrong for him, he would go back to 1850, when his wife passed away. His friends agreed: he was never the same after he lost Margaret. Alexander Bache wrote: "Mrs. Espy's mind was essentially literary, and she could not aid her husband in his scientific inquiries or experiments; her health was delicate, and she could not assist him in his outdoor observations; but she supplied what was of more importance than these aids—a genial and loving interest ever manifested in his pursuits and successes, and in his very failures."

His personal loss was shortly followed by a professional defeat. Joseph Henry of the Smithsonian had been growing increasingly concerned about the rainmaking project. He wanted the ongoing support of Congress and the public, but the fantastic nature of the scheme, and Espy's increasingly grandiose claims for its prospects, were beginning to make the Smithsonian look like a refuge for cranks. He told Espy that if he wanted to keep his job, he had to drop the rainmaking talk and find something more practical to work on.

Espy was devastated. Earlier, when he still had his old brashness, he probably would have made a grand gesture of departure and appealed to the public for support. But now he lacked the strength. He gave up talking publicly about rainmaking and looked for a new project.

He quickly found one. He announced that he was going to devise and promulgate a series of precise guidelines for mariners in hurricanes. This would immediately replace Redfield and Reid's nonsensical rules, because it would be based on a true understanding of the wind patterns of large Atlantic storms.

Redfield may never have been more angry in his life than he was when he heard what Espy proposed. In practical terms, whether it was right or wrong, it would be a disaster: Redfield himself had been trying for years to get the Naval Department to adopt his guidelines as official policy; so if he succeeded, and if the Smithsonian published Espy's counterproposal, the federal government would in effect be endorsing two mutually contradictory sets of rules.

But the real issue was Espy himself. Redfield's letters to Reid and his other correspondents reached new heights of vindictive rage. Espy was a liar and a manipulator whose entire career had been a sham. All the endorsements he'd received from the scientific establishment, Redfield believed, were fraudulent: Espy had somehow contrived to ghostwrite the praise himself. (Redfield thought better of sending some of these letters, and they turned up in his papers after his death.)

Redfield found himself with an unexpected ally: Robert Hare. Hare didn't actually have the slightest interest in giving advice to mariners. But his brittle, continually repatched friendship with Espy had just come definitively apart. Hare had gone to the Smithsonian to see how his irreplaceable laboratory instruments were being treated. He had perhaps gotten the idea that they would be displayed in one of the exhibition halls, as a shrine to his decades of scientific accomplishment. Instead, they had been unceremoniously warehoused, except for those that Espy had rooted out to use for the construction of his newest nepheleoscope. One of Hare's beautiful custom-fired ceramic pestles was sitting on Espy's desk; Espy was using it to hold table salt for his lunches.

Hare returned to his home with a draft copy of Espy's proposal. He subjected it to his most detailed, withering, and relentless scrutiny. He wrote up the results as another of his "strictures," which he immediately had printed at his own expense. He then sent copies to the president, the vice president, the cabinet, and every member of Congress.

But it went for nothing; Espy still had Joseph Henry's public backing at the Smithsonian, and Hare's attack was ignored. Espy's guidelines for mariners were duly approved, published by the Smithsonian, and distributed to interested parties in America's naval industry. Whether they were ever used isn't clear. They were extremely complicated and impractical; they required, for instance, a series of careful barometric readings, which it's unlikely any mariner would bother to take in the middle of a hurricane. (Redfield and Reid offered simple instructions based on incoming winds.) They were also phenomenally dangerous, based as they were on Espy's disastrously mistaken notions of surface wind patterns in hurricanes: anyone who followed them would be led directly into the most dangerous region of the storm. If there were no recorded complaints among the users of the guidelines, it may be because there were no survivors.

That proved to be the last great flare-up of the storm war. By then the public at large had lost interest; after two decades of the warriors slogging out their battles in lyceums and lecture halls and newspaper interviews and hot-from-the-presses pamphlets, nothing had changed, nothing had been resolved, and the entertainment value of the whole affair had long since dwindled away. Within the scientific community, the controversy had turned to frustration and indifference. Little was being published in those years on the subject of whirlwinds and other forms of violent weather; promising approaches were being immediately shot down. A natural philosopher named Elias Loomis, for instance, who had taught at Western Reserve and New York University, was attempting to draw attention to a new, and (as it proved) absolutely essential, idea: that storms could not be understood as static events but needed to be analyzed as evolving systems. Loomis spent years accumulating records and eyewitness testimony in order to reconstruct a complete narrative history of what he called "my favorite storm," a single severe thunderstorm that he had once observed passing over the Ohio River valley. It was a brilliantly original approach to thinking about weather— the first instance on record of what's now called synoptic analysis. But Loomis was ignored. If he'd been heard out, the progress of American meteorology might have jumped forward at least a generation.

In the meantime, at the meetings of the American Association for the Advancement of Science and other scientific associations, people had begun changing the subject and drifting away if they saw any of the principal warriors come within earshot. Even James Espy's oldest friend and advocate, Alexander Bache, was heard to say that they weren't making the slightest progress and there was simply no point in discussing the issue until something new happened.

Joseph Henry did ultimately find Espy a noncontroversial job. He assigned Espy on missions to travel around America and the Caribbean basin in order to take barometric readings. This was in fact necessary work: little could be done with the data being sent in by weather spotters until the Smithsonian had a way of standardizing its instruments and establishing a reliable baseline of conditions around the country. Espy performed this job conscientiously and thoroughly. There were parts of it he greatly enjoyed: he had always been a good traveler. But he still knew the score: Henry had come to think of him as a liability and was just trying to keep him out of trouble.

In the summer of 1853, Espy was in Louisville, Kentucky. This was the region where he'd spent his childhood, and he was pleased to see how thoroughly it had been tamed: hills and meadows of bluegrass had supplanted the primeval forest; there were railway corridors where before there had only been windroads.

At breakfast one morning on the veranda of his hotel, he happened to meet up with a married couple, a physician named Samuel Gross and his wife, who had known his wife's family back east, and he gladly spent the morning in civilized talk. In his memoirs, Dr. Gross remembered the scene vividly. Espy, who was then nearing seventy, was "a remarkably handsome man, tall, erect, well-proportioned, with a large head and a fine face, expressive of intelligence, and he had about him all the magnetism and characteristics of a well-bred gentleman." On the other hand, by that point Espy had come to think of conversation as synonymous with monologue. As Gross wrote, "Mr. Espy was an enthusiast. Whatever had possession of his mind was not easily dislodged by outside considerations." He spent two hours lecturing the couple on his theory of storms. The longer Espy talked, the harder it was to tell the enthusiasm apart from anger. He spat venom at a succession of enemies—particularly those who had thwarted his rainmaking project. "This disappointment was a great, if not a constant, source of annoyance to him," Gross concluded, "serving to embitter the evening of his life."

The bitterness also came to dominate his writings and correspondence. He could not stop going over old grievances. Sir John Herschel's incomprehensible failure to accept the self-evident truth of his tornado model, for instance. "I think if Sir John Herschel examines this subject," he wrote in a letter, "he will retract what he said nearly twenty years ago, before the British Association . . . He shall find, as I think he will on examination, that the theory explains more than a hundred phenomena never explained before, many of which were not known before, but predicted by the theory." Espy still held out hope that someday Herschel would "cheerfully acknowledge" that steam power was "a magnificent specimen of inductive philosophy."

"I am now nearly seventy-three years of age," he wrote in another letter, "and it would gratify me much to see my theory universally received before I die; but my gratification is a small matter compared with the interest in all mankind in adopting the true, instead of a false system. It is painful to me to see the whole meteorological world groping in the dark, for more than twenty years after the true system has been developed."

He made one last effort to explain the system, in a series of lectures he gave at the Smithsonian. The lectures didn't attract much attention— except from Robert Hare, who had still not forgiven the business with the table salt. Hare wrote to Henry to protest that Espy was once again spreading his nonsense with official backing. He threatened to produce another pamphlet for the benefit of Congress, recommending that Espy's salary be eliminated from the Smithsonian's budget.

Henry wrote back and told him not to bother. Espy's salary was already being eliminated; Espy had decided to retire from the Smithsonian and move to his parents' old home in Ohio.

After William Redfield lost his fight over Espy's rules for mariners, he retired at last from scientific controversy. He would have been content to vanish from public notice altogether, if something wholly unexpected hadn't happened. In 1855, Admiral Matthew Perry returned from his great expedition to Japan, and he declared in newspaper interviews that the voyage would have been impossible without the guidelines of Redfield and Reid. Shortly afterward, Perry contacted Redfield directly. He was writing a book about the expedition, and he wanted Redfield to contribute a chapter about the typhoons of the Pacific.

Redfield immediately agreed. Over the next several months he built up a new reference collection of books, charts, and ships' logs about the Pacific. John Redfield recalled how happy his father was to hunker down on the floor of his study one more time with big maps and stacks of books scattered all around him and become wholly absorbed in working out the characteristic behavior of typhoons.

Redfield had finished the chapter for Perry's book by the end of 1856. Shortly after the New Year, he fell ill with pneumonia. He was immediately confined to bed. He passed the time by reading a new book about a polar expedition. As his condition worsened and he faded in and out of delirium, he was increasingly tormented by images from the book. In his worst days before his death on February 12, 1857, he saw himself as navigating a ship through endless ice fields toward an unknown goal.

Robert Hare also mostly withdrew from meteorological work in those years. But he continued his researches into new terrain, and in 1854 he began demanding that the American Association for the Advancement of Science allow him to present his results. He was repeatedly rebuffed, once the association members had a glimmer of what he intended to talk about, but his public eminence and his long-standing record of scientific accomplishment forced them at last to give in. He gave a formal lecture on his new research at the annual AAAS meeting in 1855.

He began the lecture by unveiling his newest and most daring invention. It consisted of a large disk with an attached pointer on an elaborately constructed pulley and spring. The pointer ranged freely over the disk, which had been imprinted with letters, musical notes, and a handful of phrases: "Yes," "Doubtful," "No," "Don't know," "I think so," "A mistake," "I'll spell it over," "A message," "Done," "I'll come again," "Good-bye," "I must leave." Hare called the device a spiritoscope, and he informed the crowd that he had used it successfully to contact the dead.

He had been attending séances for about a year now. At first he had been wholly skeptical, but once he had seen with his own eyes the tables moving and heard the spirits rapping, he'd begun to wonder. He could see no evidence that he was being fooled. It was unquestionably obvious to him that the characters of the mediums he visited were above reproach. He wasn't fully convinced until a séance in which he made contact with his father and his sister on the other side.

Hare's father had explained the afterlife to him in considerable detail. The spirit world consisted of seven concentric spheres enclosing the earth, beginning about sixty miles up. Each level was progressively more beautiful than the one below it. By the third sphere, the vistas of mountains and forest, white-domed city skylines and pillared parks, were lovelier than anything that could be imagined on earth. The spirit world was a republic, with the government of the spheres "exercising legislative, judicial, and executive powers." The laws, Hare's father explained, "are realized in simultaneous and homogeneous opinions awakened in the minds of the ruling spirits, as truth takes hold of the minds of mathematicians." Otherwise the republic was a strict meritocracy. The ruling spirits were for the most part rich men who'd used their wealth wisely.

Hare declared that his father's message was more convincing than the whole of the Bible, which he considered "pernicious." It was also more satisfying to him than anything he had learned in science. Science was a dead end, he told his audiences: a lifetime of his labors had finally proved to him "our utter incapacity to comprehend the powers and properties of material atoms." The physical world, he had concluded, was simply "beyond our comprehension."

His presentation went over poorly. But he was prepared for that, he told his listeners. Their criticisms were of no matter to him. A spirit had recently visited him whom they all knew; this spirit had endorsed his work and had urged him to go on with it for the benefit of mankind: Benjamin Franklin.

Franklin had recently arranged for Hare to attend a great séance where all of his most abstract and scientific questions about the afterlife could be answered. Attending this "Convocation of Spirits," along with Franklin himself, were George Washington, Martha Washington, John Quincy Adams, Andrew Jackson, Henry Clay, Isaac Newton, the poet Lord Byron, and assorted "relatives and friends." The answers provided by the convocation were recorded by the spiritoscope. Typical of the exchanges was this one, concerning the issue of why ghosts glow in the dark:

Question from Hare: "Is it not luminiferous matter which causes the effulgence of spirits, analogous in its effects to that of luminiferous insects, though consisting of a spiritual material entirely different from those which enter into the luminiferous matter of insects?"

Answer from the convocation: "Yes."

From his vantage at the Smithsonian, Joseph Henry remarked on the curious way the war among his three great friends and colleagues had ended—"one dead, one exhausted, one converted to Spiritualism." Nothing had ever been resolved, and there were still no answers to any of the basic questions of the war. Neither Espy nor Hare made any attempts to reconcile in the last few years of their lives, and neither had anything further to say in public about hurricanes and tornadoes.

In May 1858, Hare announced that he had made a new breakthrough in his spiritualist researches, which had led him to the greatest secret of the alchemists: he had created the philosopher's stone and could now transmute base metals into gold. A few days later, before he had a chance to reveal the stone to the world, he died in his sleep. He was survived by a wife and three adult children; none of them, then or later, would admit to knowing where the stone was.

Espy returned to his family home in Ohio. He did no more work on meteorology and instead took up a new subject: moral philosophy. He had always been a devout Christian, but he had long ago concluded that many aspects of traditional Christian theology were absurd and unconscionable—chief among them the idea of eternal damnation. He set out to write a book that would explain the absolute goodness of God and his creation. Its thesis was that any apparent evil in the world—even the destructive chaos of the tornado—was a surface illusion; behind it was a simple, lucid, and radiantly harmonious pattern in the mind of the Almighty.

Espy died on January 24, 1860. His book on moral philosophy was left unfinished; from the posthumous publication of the surviving manuscript, he appears to have gotten no further than the preface.

The last of the storm controversy was buried with Espy. America was consumed then by the run-up to the Civil War, and almost all scientific research was grinding to a halt anyway. When work resumed after the war, the issues of the controversy already looked as quaint as something from the Middle Ages. The community had moved on, because in the intervening years the long stalemate had been broken. Somebody had finally had a new idea.

This was a theory proposed by a self-taught Kentucky schoolteacher named William Ferrel and vigorously promoted by Henry at the Smithsonian. Ferrel had begun his amateur education with a close reading of the works of Isaac Newton, which some passing scholar had accidentally left behind in a dry-goods store where Ferrel shopped. From there he had rapidly progressed through the whole of meteorological theory all the way up to the storm war, and in its course he had discovered a way that the views of Espy and Redfield could be reconciled.

Ferrel's proposal was a radical reenvisioning of the large-scale mechanisms of the atmosphere, based on the then-little-known ideas of a French mathematician named Gaspard-Gustave Coriolis. The essential idea in Coriolis's work was that the rotation of the earth causes a slight but continuous drag and deflection in the atmosphere. Ferrel demonstrated that the Coriolis effect could explain the behavior of global prevailing winds like the trade winds at the equator and the southwest winds that dominate the middle latitudes. It also explained—or so Ferrel believed—the rotation of hurricanes and tornadoes. According to Ferrel, Espy had been right that these storms are powered by convection; but as the convection columns rise, they are deformed by the Coriolis effect from the straight-line inflowing winds that Espy imagined into the spiraling whirlwinds described by Redfield. The theories of Espy and Redfield weren't irreconcilable opposites but two halves of the same process.

The effect of Ferrel's ideas on the meteorological community was galvanic. More than two decades earlier, Espy had argued that Redfield's theory of whirlwinds had to be false, unless there was "some mighty cause . . . of which we have no knowledge, to generate new motion in the air." Ferrel had identified this mighty cause. The reaction among meteorologists was so strong, so immediate, and so positive that it retroactively rewrote the history of the storm war. Ferrel became the reigning genius, and Espy, Redfield, and Hare were now simply his forebears. In popular histories of American science written in the later decades of the nineteenth century, when the three combatants were mentioned at all, they were most often described as amiable colleagues working together for the common good of scientific knowledge. Any differences they may have had were too petty to be worth remembering.

Today Ferrel is generally seen as the progenitor of modern meteorology. Hare and Redfield are forgotten. Espy, if he's remembered, is just a theatrical charlatan who got brief fame with a nonsensical theory of rainmaking. This is surely unjust—especially to Espy. After all, about the main thing, the theory of steam power, he was right. His model became the basis of the modern understanding of severe storms. Nobody talks now about "latent caloric," but the term people do use, "convective available potential energy," or CAPE, essentially means the same thing. And as for his theory of rainmaking: he was universally mocked for it in his lifetime, but it turned out that he was right about that, too.

8

The Finger of God

There were always fires in the northern hardwood forests. The Native Americans of that country had traditionally been careless about extinguishing their fires because they took for granted that any fire not constantly fed and tended would quickly be snuffed out by the forest itself. White hunters and trappers followed their lead and routinely built big bonfires in their camps for safety. They could sleep through the night in the deep forest knowing that the blaze and smoke would cause the innumerable predatory animals to shy away, but in the mornings they could leave their camps with the fires still smoldering and trust that the clammy dawn mists would smother the last embers.

It was a rich, green, humid country. In the late summer, when the land and the air were at their hottest and driest, the fires did sometimes burn for hours or days, but these served only to clear out the chokingly dense underbrush from beneath the tree canopy and free up the soil for fresh growth the next spring. As the farmers began arriving and cutting down the forests, they learned to appreciate the value of an extended drought, because that was the only time that they could burn off the felled trees and the pulled stumps they'd hauled away from their fields.

This is why the serious drought in the summer of 1871 at first excited no alarm. The hottest months passed with little or no rain: the forests were becoming dry and airless, and the underbrush was turning brown—for the settlers this was a great opportunity. The farmers began setting small fires along the margins of the cleared land in order to enlarge their property as painlessly as possible. In eastern Wisconsin near Green Bay, hundreds of laborers were cutting through the forest to lay tracks for a railroad, and they, too, began setting fires to save themselves work. The big logging camps scattered through the forest were accumulating huge hills of waste wood and slag, which they were sometimes torching just to gain themselves a bit of elbow room.

Everyone assumed—if they gave the question any thought at all—that the drought was bound to break as droughts always did, with the great drenching rains of autumn. But by summer's end, with still no rain, the settlers were becoming aware that their situation was growing precarious. The scatterings of ordinary small short-lived fires—the smoldering ash pile left behind in a camp, the smoky fire in a dead tree trunk, the lightning-set flash fire through the browned underbrush in a remote glen—weren't being extinguished as they usually were but were persisting and growing. By September most towns had formed fire patrols. The railroads assigned crews to make regular inspections of the woodlands on either side of the rail corridors: every train that passed was spewing out sparks that were setting off fires. Travelers through the Wisconsin wilderness on September nights were reporting countless small glimmers and glows in the forest depths. One resident, Father Peter Pernin of the town of Peshtigo near Green Bay, wrote in a memoir that one night at the end of September he and a young guide got lost and wandered through the woodlands. Only two sounds were audible in the darkness. One was the creaking of the treetops in the wind; the other was a strange low crackling that was coming from what Pernin described as "a tiny tongue of fire that ran along the ground, in and out, among the trunks of the trees, leaving them unscathed but devouring the dry leaves that came in its way."

For the better part of an hour Pernin and his guide stumbled through the forest, all the while calling for help. Then Pernin began firing his rifle as a distress signal. They heard people hallooing for them in the distance. But they faced a more serious problem by the time their rescuers reached them. The tongues of fire in the underbrush, fanned by the hot dry winds, were running together and spurting up in sudden flares. "We soon found ourselves," Pernin wrote, "in the center of a circle of fire." But it was still small enough for the rescue party to find a way, by taking big branches and beating down one of the thinner patches of blazing brush, until Pernin and the boy could dash across.

Peshtigo was an industrial town of around fifteen hundred people. It was on the Peshtigo River, a couple of miles up from the river mouth at Green Bay. The river was about five hundred feet wide at that point, and the two sides of the town were connected by a bridge. On the northern side were the lumber mill, a woodenware factory (it made churns, tubs, and pails), a machine shop, and a sash and door factory. The southern side was mostly houses and a scattering of general stores and shops. Father Pernin's church was on the southern side, on a dirt street around a thousand yards down from the bridge. There were a handful of Catholics in town, but his parish also included a number of smaller villages along the shores of Green Bay and throughout the Wisconsin wilderness. He spent many days away from the Peshtigo church, riding through the forest or taking steamboats up and down the bay.

Pernin was fascinated by the landscape: "Trees, trees everywhere, nothing else but trees as far as you can travel from the bay, either towards the north or west . . . The face of the country is in general undulating, diversified by valleys overgrown with cedars and spruce trees, sandy hills covered with evergreens, and large tracts of rich land filled with the different varieties of hardwood—oak, maple, beech, ash, elm, and birch." It was all, he called it, "a wild but majestic forest."

At the beginning of autumn, his church at Peshtigo was in the middle of a major refurbishment. The weekend of October 7–8 he had emptied it out for the plasterers, who were supposed to start that Monday; the altar, the hangings, the tables, and the pews had been dragged into the back lot beside the cemetery grounds, while the sacks of lime and marble dust were waiting by the front steps. Pernin told the parishioners that there would be no service that weekend, and instead he'd spend it up the bay at his church in the village of Cedar River to the north. But his parishioners were nervous about his leaving and several of them urged him not to go. "There seemed to be a vague fear of some impending though unknown evil haunting the minds of many," he wrote. He admitted that he was feeling uneasy himself. "It was rather an impression than a conviction, for, on reflecting, I saw that things looked much as usual, and arrived at the conclusion that our fears were groundless, without, however, feeling much reassured thereby."

He certainly saw no reason to change his plans. On the afternoon of Saturday, October 7, he rode from Peshtigo to Menomonie on the river mouth, where he waited for the *Dunlap,* the regular steamboat making stops along the bay. The day was hot, dry, windless, and cloudless—one more in the string of the drought season. The smoke from the countless small fires along the forest margin came drifting out over the water of the bay in thick shrouds. As Pernin waited on the wharf, he heard the foghorns sounding all up and down the shore. The afternoon passed; the *Dunlap* was late. "It was the only time that year," Pernin wrote, "she failed in the regularity of her trips." Then the word spread toward sunset that the *Dunlap* wasn't coming at all. It had made its usual rounds, but when it came to the river mouth, the smoke was so thick the captain decided not to risk getting any closer to land. Pernin rode back to Peshtigo.

Sunday morning he said Mass for his parishioners in his own house, before a temporary altar that he'd set up in his sitting room. Then, he later recalled, "the afternoon passed in complete inactivity." His sense of foreboding had grown to a mood of overpowering dread. He tried to talk himself out of it: the situation, he reasoned, was really no worse than it had been over the preceding couple of weeks. It was better, in fact, since the townspeople were alive to the danger of a catastrophic fire and had already organized patrols and brigades in the event of an outbreak. And yet he couldn't shake the conviction that nothing would work and disaster was at hand. "These two opposite sentiments," he wrote, "plunged my faculties into a species of mental torpor."

Around 7:00 p.m., he roused himself. He decided to take a quick ride around town. The streets were crowded; everybody was too restless to stay in. Their mood was nervous but festive; the laughter and the singing of the young people in particular, Pernin wrote, "was sufficient to make me think that I alone was a prey to anxiety, and to render me ashamed of manifesting the feeling." But everywhere was the hanging smoke of the fires, the hot windless air, and a solemn hush seeming to thicken in the late-afternoon light.

Pernin went first to the home of a Mrs. Dress, a widow who lived on the outskirts of town. The two took a stroll around her fields. She was just as tense as he was; she'd been urging her children to take precautions, she told him, and they'd simply laughed her off. As they walked, a wind suddenly sprang up and began to buffet them in hot puffs, then it dwindled back into stillness. They were at the far edge of her property when a very strong gust swept across them and a small huddle of old dead tree trunks suddenly burst into dazzling light; it was, Pernin said, "just as if the wind had been a breath of fire, capable of kindling them into a flame by its mere contact."

On his way home he saw that something strange was happening in the west. Above the dense low-hanging smoke that shrouded the sunset was a vast domain of clear air that was glowing a brilliant red. The silent air was becoming troubled; from the direction of the red sky there could be heard a faint muffled roar, the sound of a remote continuous tumult.

Pernin suddenly felt galvanized. He was inspired with a plan: he would dig a trench outside his house, load it with the church valuables and his own few possessions, cover it over, and then take refuge in the river. "Henceforth this became my ruling thought," he said, "and it was entirely unaccompanied by anything like fear or perplexity. My mind seemed all at once to become perfectly tranquil." It was then around 8:30. He set to work excavating his garden, where the soil was loose and sandy. The trench went quickly at first. But gradually the work became horribly taxing. Pernin was a vigorous man in excellent shape; he was being worn down by the heat and the gathering smoke. The atmosphere seemed to be growing heavier moment by moment. The night sky was getting brighter as the zone of bright red spread up to the zenith. The mysterious sound in the west was becoming louder, too. In between the thuds of his pickax and the shuffle of dirt in the shovel, he could hear it: "It resembled the confused noise of a number of cars and locomotives approaching a railroad station." Meanwhile, the townspeople were passing by, as though taking in the evening air and admiring a particularly garish afterglow of sunset, barely pausing to remark that the town priest was out in front of his church, digging what looked like a grave.

The way meteorologists later reconstructed it, there was an unusually pronounced low-pressure system moving across the Great Lakes and the northern forests on October 8. It kicked up strong southwest winds across the entire region—sustained winds of thirty miles per hour, with gusts up to fifty. They were hot dry winds that could rapidly fan a small fire into a much larger one and turn a large fire into a catastrophe.

Throughout the evening of the eighth, enormous fires began springing up throughout the drought region. There were several major fires in the forests of upper Michigan, where almost no measurable rain had fallen since midsummer. In Chicago, 250 miles south of Peshtigo, there had already been one very large fire on October 7, which had destroyed several blocks of the downtown commercial district, and a number of smaller fires scattered throughout the city. Sometime during the evening of the eighth, a small fire broke out in the enormous tenement district southwest of the city core. The district was a wooden labyrinth of apartment blocks, factories, and warehouses, heaped together in gigantic, randomly interconnected edifices; the single-family houses and cottages all had livestock barns stacked to the rafters with hay and coal bins loaded for the winter. One small barn fire wasn't seen as particularly alarming, and it went unreported for at least an hour. By the time the city fire department was aware of it, it was already burning out of control. The winds blew its sparks and flames and embers northeast toward the heart of the city. The winds were so fierce that the fire was soon leaping ahead of its main strength, where the firefighters were attempting to block it, and fresh fires were being kindled faster than they could be spotted or reported. Within hours, fire engulfed the city core and stampeded the population in a frantic race to the waters of Lake Michigan. Three hundred people died, and four square miles of the city burned.

In eastern Wisconsin, the winds by evening were intensifying to gale force. The countless small fires scattered through the woods were being fanned into a fury. They began drawing toward each other and leaping together to form large areas of sustained burning of extraordinary intensity. The worst of them was in the dense forest southwest of

Peshtigo. At some point during the mid-evening this fire underwent a catastrophic transformation.

After Pernin was satisfied with his work on the trench, he began loading it with his books and his trunks of papers and clothes. He carried over the valuables that had been taken from the church interior, the hangings and candlesticks and ornaments, and gently laid them down over his possessions, then he covered the pile up with the sandy soil. By then the sky was almost bright enough to read by, and the noise was a continuous thunder. But he couldn't seek shelter yet; he still had to deal with the Blessed Sacrament, which he had no intention of leaving behind. (It was, after all, "object of all objects, precious, priceless, especially in the eyes of a priest.") It was still in the temporary altar he'd arranged in his sitting room. He was so nervous and in such haste that he dropped the tabernacle, but he managed to get the Eucharist out to his wagon. Then he decided to cut his horse loose, assuming he'd have a better chance on his own.

He went back inside for the chalice. That was when he realized he had lingered too long. Something strange was happening in the interior of his house. Clouds of dazzling sparks began bursting up out of nowhere and disappearing, flashing from vases and lamps and the mantelpiece, darting from room to room like a sprite. Pernin had no idea what was happening; he had the vague thought that the air was becoming saturated by "some special gas." He was terrified that contact with an actual fire, rather than with these spectral lights, would cause everything to explode.

He heard the wind rising and knew he was out of time. He called to his dog, who refused to budge from under the bed (where he died a few minutes later). He ran back outside to the wagon. When he went to open the gate, the wind tore it out of his hand and then tore the fence away as well. The air was swarming with debris, with fierce streamers of sparks and embers, with furious trails of smoke and dust, with swift stinging clouds of burning-hot cinders. Everyone on the street was in a panic. They were hurrying in all directions, on foot and on horseback and riding wagons. Nobody could see where they were going, and they were all colliding with each other; the air was black and was so thick with smoke that it was impossible for people to keep their eyes open. The noise was deafening; Pernin remembered "the neighing of horses, falling of chimneys, crashing of uprooted trees, roaring and whistling of the wind, crackling of fire as it ran with lightning-like rapidity from house to house—all sounds were there save that of the human voice. People seemed stricken dumb by terror. They jostled each other without exchanging look, word, or counsel."

Pernin's idea was to drag his wagon down to the riverbank and take shelter in the water with the Eucharist. The wind was so strong then that he found it almost impossible to keep on his feet. It was also becoming almost impossible to breathe. He stumbled and collapsed, rose and stumbled again; once he tripped over something and fell on his face; he found that the obstacle was a dead woman cradling her dead child. A few hundred yards down from his house he found his horse standing frozen with terror in the middle of the street. The horse put his head on Pernin's shoulder; he was violently trembling. Pernin tried to coax him into coming with him, but he wouldn't move, and his half-burned corpse was found there the next morning.

By the time Pernin managed to drag his wagon down to the river, the buildings on either side were all on fire. The wind was growing so fierce that a storm of flame and cinders was raking across the river's surface. Pernin had the idea of crossing the bridge to the far side to look for shelter there, but the bridge was, he later recalled, "a scene of indescribable and awful confusion." People on both ends were trying desperately to get across to the opposite side, and the result was a frantic pileup in mid-span of crowds, wagons, and cattle. The flames were already spreading to the wooden trestles, and many people were jumping into the river. Pernin turned to the right of the bridge and looked downriver, where he knew there were shallows he might be able to wade across, but there the sawmill on his side and a company warehouse on the far side were both roaring with fire, and the river between them was being swept by the flames. He turned to the left, where the river above the dam ran deeper. That was where he shoved the wagon into the water and jumped in after it.

He emerged from the water long enough to see that the great disaster was on them. The roaring was suddenly hushed; the smoke and cinders were sucked away, and the air around the river was clear. Along the riverbanks were crowds of people standing motionless, oblivious to the flames around them, indifferent to their own safety. Their eyes were staring, their mouths open, their tongues hanging out, their heads turned toward the sky. Pernin followed their gaze and witnessed the inconceivable.

James Espy had been too close to the problem. He had correctly analyzed the core phenomenon: intense heat events like forest fires and volcanic eruptions do create powerful convection columns, and these can, under certain circumstances, generate rain clouds. The clouds are now known as pyrocumulus (one of the few fundamental additions to Luke Howard's original scheme of cloud classification). Pyrocumulus clouds have been extensively documented since Espy's time. In fact they ultimately became one of the most recognizable symbols of the modern world: the mushroom cloud of a nuclear explosion is a pyrocumulus cloud.

But Espy had been unable to think through the consequences. As his friend Bache wrote in his memorial, this was his fatal limitation, particularly in his later years. "The earnest and deep convictions of the truth of his theory in all its parts, and his glowing enthusiasm in regard to it; perhaps, also, the age which he had reached, prevented Mr. Espy from passing beyond a certain point." That "certain point" was critical. Espy had seen into the mechanism of storms with a profundity no one had ever attained before. But it never occurred to him that his beautiful mechanism of steam power could have unpredictable side effects. The heat of the strongest fires, as it turns out, can cause catastrophic instabilities in the pyrocumulus clouds they create. The intensity of the Peshtigo fire led to a series of runaway chain reactions that turned what was already a disaster into a situation of almost unearthly calamity.

At some point during that evening, the temperature in the hottest zone outside Peshtigo spiked upward to at least fifteen hundred degrees Fahrenheit. That was hot enough to make the surrounding forest erupt by spontaneous combustion. A gigantic convection column swept upward and began drawing the surrounding air toward the heart of the fire at speeds approaching two hundred miles an hour. As the flames and heat roared up the convection column, the pyrocumulus cloud formed just as Espy had predicted. But the heat was so intense and destabilizing that the cloud immediately evolved into a monstrous new form: a pyrocumulonimbus. Torrential rains began falling from the cloud, most of which immediately flashed away as steam. But their downdrafts were sufficiently stable and powerful to cause a self-sustaining thunderstorm to form, and in the midst of this storm a tornado appeared.

The tornado roared through the heart of the fire zone to the northwest. It sucked in flames from the surrounding air and drew them up through the funnel so that by the time it reached Peshtigo, it appeared as a gigantic funnel cloud of fire extending up from the burning forests to the sky. Its heat was so intense that everything around it instantly exploded. In the town, every house was whirled upward into a spiral of sparkling fire; grain elevators vanished as though they'd been made of paper; steam locomotives in the rail yard levitated off their tracks and smashed together in midair. Around the tornado funnel there was a swirling swarm of burning debris that came raining down in firebombs and avalanches of scalding rubble. There was also something else. The survivors called them fire balloons. These were strange black spheres, each about ten feet across, that came floating out of the upper reaches of the funnel. They descended randomly on the surrounding countryside, where they exploded into fire. One witness saw a fire balloon land on a family fleeing in a horse-drawn wagon; the balloon touched down on them, burst like a soap bubble, and engulfed the wagon in flames. No one survived.

On the riverbanks, as the funnel passed directly overhead, many people were consumed where they stood and were instantly reduced to ash. Others were found dead, apparently untouched, but with every coin in their pockets melted. Amid the thrashing chaos of people and animals in the river, those who kept their heads above water were scalded to death or suffocated, and those who went too far under drowned or succumbed to hypothermia. Pernin somehow managed to stay alive. But he looked at the funnel too long, and his eyeballs were seared. He had no idea what he was seeing and was certain it was the end of the world. In his memoirs he called it "the finger of God."

The fire tornado calved into two smaller funnels northeast of Peshtigo. Two trails of complete destruction stretched out on divergent paths for several miles before blending into the general ruin of the fire. Around the trails were countless birds that had burned to death in flight and the bodies of forest animals that had suffocated as they ran, because the combustion of the fire tornadoes had been so intense it had consumed all the oxygen out of the surrounding atmosphere.

The paths of the tornadoes were easy to trace. Their heat was so intense that it melted the silicates out of the soil, fused them into molten glass in midair, and sent them raining down to the earth again. When the survivors and rescuers inspected the scene in the morning, after the worst of the fire had been doused (a gigantic rainstorm had sprung up in the wake of the tornadoes), they found that everything in the damage track—the stumps of trees, the charred foundations of houses, the seared ground—was all encased in glass.

The death toll at Peshtigo is unknown but is believed to be upwards of fifteen hundred people. More than a million acres of forest burned. The fire tornado was duly reported on in the press, but most scientists were skeptical: there simply was no record of such a gigantic, monstrous freak appearing anywhere else. Nor would there be any confirmed reports for decades to come—not until September 1, 1923, when a major earthquake struck Japan. Thousands of buildings instantly collapsed, a thirty-five-foot tsunami crashed ashore, and in Tokyo, a city built almost entirely out of wood, hundreds of fires broke out within the first hour. Tens of thousands of people escaping the burning wreckage of their city took refuge in an open field along the Sumida River as the fires around them joined and swelled and an immense pyrocumulonimbus cloud bloomed directly overhead. A fire tornado—some of the survivors named it "the twisting dragon"—congealed out of the air, crossed over the open field, and in the space of a few seconds killed more than forty thousand people.

PART III

RED WIND AND TORNADO GREEN

9

The Great American Desert

Every summer in the West, out past the most remote of the white settlements, caravans of travelers were abroad. The Native American nations of the plains had fallen into a tough routine of subsistence. They spent the spring coaxing crops out of the semiarid land where they had their villages; in the summer they left their crops to grow or to fail while they hunted bison in the short-grass country east of the Rocky Mountains.

Some of the caravans could be pretty raucous. There might be a couple hundred men, women, and children, along with horses, mules, dogs, wagons, sleds, and an ever-growing herd of buffalo. The women drove the wagons; the children hunted each other through the mazes of stinging grasses, while the men on horseback scattered out in wide orbits across the low undulating land. The men were scouting for bison, but they were also keeping watch for raiding parties from the other nations. This was not an especially peaceful time. The obvious focus of the hostility were the whites, but there was just as much tension among the nations themselves. Turf wars were raging between the original plains inhabitants and the waves of new exiles who had been forced from their ancestral homelands east of the Mississippi by the Indian Removal Act. Then, too, the exiles were arriving with their own issues—the Sioux, for instance, had never gotten along with the Miami—and they took occupation of their new domains with their old enmities intact.

In the summer of 1856, a Miami caravan was hunting in the vast empty terrain of the Kansas Territory. The Miami were viewed by the other nations as odd. Many of the nations traveled in gorgeous regalia, with florid dress and gaudily painted wagons; the Miami were known for their austerity. The men were in breechclouts—the flashiest among them would wear thin leather headbands—and the women had plain jerkins and very short skirts. The children usually wore nothing at all. The early white trappers and scouts often called the Miami "the naked people."

The Miami were dealing with the current tensions by keeping to themselves. But this particular company was unusual: there was a white person tagging along.

His name was Ely Moore. He was there, in effect, to learn the family business. His father was an Indian commissioner—a civil servant in the federal government responsible for the welfare of the Native Americans. Moore senior's particular brief was a group of nations originally from the Southeast: the Cherokee, Chickasaw, Choctaw, Creek, and Seminoles. These were the nations that had at one point been thought to be making the most successful assimilation to white culture (that is, until the whites decided to expel them anyway). They were still known as the Five Civilized Tribes.

Ely Moore, as it happened, wasn't much impressed with what his father considered civilized. This was one reason he took up with the Miami. Their dealings with whites were strictly practical: they wanted iron tools and farming implements, copper cookware, guns of all sorts, and rye whiskey. Toward the rest of white civilization they were indifferent. Like the majority of Native Americans, they thought the whites were insane. But they did get along with young Moore well enough. They had a reason: in those days it was said that scarcely a dozen whites west of the Mississippi could speak an Indian language, and Moore was one of them. He had gotten to be passable at the Miami tongue. He was never fluent, but the Miami appreciated his effort, and they came to consider him a friend. (This was a lucky thing for Moore, because the Miami were rumored to practice ritual cannibalism upon their enemies.)

Day after day, the caravan had the landscape to itself. This was an unpromising terrain: it was the sparse borderland that ran along the edge of the rain shadow of the Rockies, where the short grasses were beginning to thin out and give way to sagebrush and cacti. They did come across bison here and there, though it was nothing like the country of the central grasslands, where the bison congregated in astonishing horizonless herds. Some of the herds were made up of millions of bison grazing placidly over tens of thousands of square miles of mixed grasses, but here the Miami might go a whole day and see only one solitary bison nosing at a lone squat scrub tree. In Texas, the hunters would pick off the bison casually and relentlessly, take what they needed, and abandon the rest. Here they had to be careful. When they spotted one of those huge brown moving islets, they could take a whole day to hunt it down. But this was an art the Miami had become exceptionally good at. They were already admired and envied on the plains for their skill at setting up corrals within gullies and shallow valleys and driving the bison. Sometimes, especially in late summer when the grasses were drying, they would set fires in order to stampede the bison in the right direction. That was a deadly strategy (even though it grew to be almost universal among the nations of the plains): the fires could easily race out of control, and the bison—infamous anyway for their unpredictable surges of towering violence—might thunder straight toward the hunting party or trample on furiously through the heart of the caravan. But it had often saved Miami caravans from starvation.

There was little talking or chanting or singing during the daylight journeys, the way there tended to be with other traveling companies. But each evening after a successful hunt the Miami would set up camp and spend hours celebrating the day's adventures. They particularly liked to encourage and mock the younger hunters for puffing up their heroic deeds. Then they retold stories about their lost life in the forests of the East. The tale-teller might chant his way through a comic epic about Wisakatchekwa, the trickster-hero who took the form of a rabbit. The stories were often about times when Wisakatchekwa was tricked himself but eluded the trap at the last second. Later they'd move on to darker stories. The Miami, like most of the nations, believed that there was another world behind the surface of this one, a world inhabited by strange demons and shape-shifters. The Miami were always worried about these beings; they were notorious for appeasing them with midnight ritual orgies. They usually kept those ceremonies to themselves, though; no whites were on record as having witnessed one (Moore decorously kept silent about whether he did).

In a memoir written for a Kansas City newspaper fifty years afterward, Moore recalled how the languor of that summer was finally broken. The day that happened was like any other: hot, windy, and silent. Many of the scouts were surreptitiously nodding off on their horses. The land around them was a gulf of green grasses; the sky was a broken field of cumulus. The only sounds were the hiss of the wind, the drumming and creaking of the wagons, and the crunching sigh of the grasses going down beneath the wheels.

After noon the chief called a halt. He stood by himself for a long while, staring out to the west. Moore came up behind him. To Moore there was nothing but the grasses unfurling out toward the blue-hazed horizon. But the chief was so intent it was as though he were seeing into the landscape—his gaze reaching out for hundreds of miles, to where the last of the grasses dwindled and the sagebrush took over and the land began its slow broken rise toward the mountains.

Then the chief held up his hand. The hush seemed complete: Moore noticed that even the wind had died down. But Moore could hear a strange new sound. It was a pervasive rustling whisper like countless sheets of paper rubbing together. Something enormous and shapeless began to stir in the grasses before the caravan. The whisper turned into a roar. A black cloud reared up into the air and swept straight toward them. Everyone ducked down and covered their heads. Some of the children cried out in terror. The cloud was a swarm of grasshoppers. They surged harmlessly above the caravan and raced toward the east.

The chief gestured at the swarm as it receded. "They know," he said to Moore. "Storm coming."

Moore looked around again. The day was calm and the sky was clear. How bad a storm could it be?

"The devil wind," the chief said. "Will kill us all. Maybe."

Moore was skeptical, but he did suddenly become uncomfortably aware of their surroundings. This was a deadly place to be caught by a storm. There was no shelter anywhere within the ring of the horizon: no bluffs, no outcrops, no stands of trees. Moore looked out again to the southwest. Along the horizon was a line of white prominences that hadn't been there a few minutes earlier. They were the crests of storm clouds, still so remote their broken white towers seemed to be melting into the blue.

The caravan was already at work. The scouts located a shallow ravine that might serve for the bison herd. The men were hacking at the dirt with everything handy—poles, rakes, picks—and driving stakes into the ground to form a wide openmouthed corral. The women were methodically rummaging through the wagons, organizing and lashing down all the loose gear. They were also hanging up skeins of canvas, blankets, and gutta-percha sheets as catchments for the rainwater. Moore ran from one group to the next, trying ineffectually to help, but the Miami moved seamlessly, like a well-practiced theatrical company putting on an impromptu show.

By then the storm had swelled up to engulf the western horizon. The wind was surging and rushing all around them, in big grass-flattening sweeps. Soon the cliff wall of clouds blocked the sun, and the green landscape faded into shadow. Flickers of lightning were visible along the cliff base and around the cauliflower crests of the storm; it was still too far away for the individual strikes to be heard, but underneath the wind there was now a steady percussive grumble.

The Miami camp was ready. The bison had been herded into the corral, and a line of stakes closed off the entrance. The wagons had been drawn into a ring. The horses and ponies were huddled at its center. Beneath the wagons, the children cowered with the dogs. When the first curtains of rain swept across the grasses toward the camp, each man put his arms around his horse's neck to keep it calm.

Then there was a barrage of hail. The children cried out; the horses bucked and whinnied; the bison bumped against each other and grunted in pain. Rain came roaring down in vast gouts, as though being spilled from a tub directly overhead. The sky was black and the air was freezing cold. Moore kept staring out to the west, where the curtains of rain were thinning and falling aside. A zone of clear air opened up beneath the clouds and raced toward them. The rain stopped. In the lull the women at the wagons expertly tied off their bulging skeins of rainwater and stowed them in the wagons. But nobody in the company relaxed.

That was when Moore saw it: there was something strange in the under-hang of the clouds, a kind of upside-down whirlpool. It was a sickly color; Moore described it as "greenish purple." The swirl slowly extended into a bulging elongated shape that reminded Moore of a hot-air balloon. A billow of dust began circling and dancing directly beneath it. Then the balloon cloud reached through the dust to touch the ground. It churned forward and headed straight at the caravan.

It was enormous. Moore guessed that the base of the cloud was a half mile wide. As it approached, the air began to crackle with electricity: Moore could see phantasmal lightning, like St. Elmo's fire, darting and dancing all around the camp, ricocheting between the wagons and the corral. Then a new downpour fell on them, not rain, but wet sand and dirt and grass and dead weeds and small dead birds and stinging twigs. The air was filled with a continuous deafening roar. The women of the company wrapped their cloaks around the youngest children and bowed their heads; the men all threw themselves flat on the ground. Everything grew pitch-black. By one of the last starbursts of lightning, Moore saw that the entire company was praying.

Then something changed. The cloud was about a hundred yards away when it seemed to thin out; its base was suddenly growing bright and confused. Moore thought he saw sunlight shining behind it. The massed blackness above rose up as though it were skipping across the earth, and it soared over their heads, a hundred feet up, in a shrieking, whistling rush. And then it was gone.

They all turned to look behind them. A few hundred yards farther on, the base of the cloud re-formed, touched the ground again, and went roaring over the grasslands to the east. The western sky was already clearing. The late-afternoon sun lit up the receding cloud and shed a rainbow around it across the prairie.

The company quickly roused itself to move on. Nobody had been seriously hurt. Some of the horses were bleeding; their flanks had been gored by the hailstorm. A hailstone had also struck out the eye of one of the bison. On either side of their camp was a half-mile-wide swath of flattened grass and torn sod, like a vast road cut through the prairie. It was broken only where the cloud had taken its fluke hop over the camp. Moore was left staring at this track and wondering what on earth they had just been through.

All the nations of the plains told stories about tornadoes. Many nations said they were caused by the thunderbird, the storm god at the heart of the cloud who stirred up whirlwinds with the flapping of his great wings. The Comanche said the storm cloud itself was a sorcerer; the tornado funnel was his bag of winds and was so heavy that when he tired, he would sometimes drag it on the ground behind him. They all knew that tornadoes had strange habits and rituals: it was universally believed among the nations, for instance, that tornadoes would not go near rivers. They advised the whites—back when they were still willing to give advice to the whites—to build their settlements at river junctions. (It was only one more example of expert advice about tornadoes that turned out to be wrong.) But it was the Kiowa who spent the most time brooding about tornadoes, because they thought the tornadoes were their fault. There wouldn't be any tornadoes on the plains, they said, if only two Kiowa boys hadn't been so eager for horses.

There had once been horses in North America, back in the dawn world before the human beings arrived. But they had all died off with the other strange creatures of that age—the mammoths and saber-toothed tigers and dire wolves. The horses the Spanish brought with them at the beginning of the sixteenth century were the first seen in North America for more than ten thousand years.

The Native Americans were fascinated by them. They themselves mostly used dogs as pack animals, and some of the nations started calling the horses dogs—not that they thought they were the same species, but they were so impressed by the horse's doglike friendliness and adaptability. They were eager to get them for themselves.

There was one place they all looked. Each year the Pueblo Nation held large trading fairs. The other nations of the Southwest and the plains would come to barter over pottery and hunting gear and bison fat and livestock. Horses had started showing up for sale by the end of the sixteenth century. They were breeding pairs that had for the most part been stolen from the Spanish (by that point, the Spanish had several thousand horses in the New World). But they were tricky commodities: people had to learn how to keep them, how to provide grazing land for them, how to train them, and how to ride them. The negotiations for purchase often had to involve a deal for an instructor. (These instructors in the early years had acquired their knowledge mostly by trial and error, because the Spanish forbade Native Americans to have anything to do with their horses; later, as the horse population grew unmanageably large, the Spanish gave in and began hiring and training locals to work as horse herders.)

All this meant that the spread of horses through the plains happened slowly, over several generations. By the middle of the seventeenth century, horses had spread through Arizona, New Mexico, and Texas and were beginning to be traded by the Apache to the plains nations. By the beginning of the eighteenth century, the Kiowa of the southern plains had horses. But the northern Kiowa nation in the Black Hills still didn't. The way those Kiowa told it, two boys from the Black Hills saw horses for the first time while visiting their southern relations. They were too impatient to wait for their elders to barter for a breeding pair; they wanted a horse immediately. So when they came home, they went to their greatest sorcerer, the legendary Sindi, and they asked him to make a horse. They wanted the most powerful horse in the world, a horse that would leave all the other nations of the plains in awe. So Sindi set to work. He gave them exactly what they wanted. They watched in amazement as the horse took shape on the prairie in front of them. It was a great gray horse with flashing red eyes. But it quickly became apparent that they were never going to be able to ride it. The horse was filled with such powerful magic that it was in a perpetual fury. It at once reared up and let out a deafening whinny, and then it began kicking up and stamping the ground, over and over, spinning as its hooves thundered down, spinning till it was a whirling gray blur with its eyes glowing red within. This was why it was named Red Wind. It never stopped its furious spinning; it soared up into the clouds and became the heart of the storm; but afterward sometimes its rage was so great that its spin would carry it down again and its legs would reach from the cloud to stamp the earth beneath its hooves.

This was not a story the Kiowa always liked to tell. But they would sometimes use it to explain why only their charms and spells worked against the tornado. One Kiowa elder put it this way: When he was a young man, he was with a company that was caught out in the prairie by a roaring storm "that sounded like buffalo in the rutting season." The cloud dipped down a funnel with a red glow at its heart. Bolts of lightning came darting down through the funnel and set the dry prairie grass on fire. When the cloud came along the banks of the Washita River, it tore trees out by the roots and tossed them into the air. "We were terribly afraid," the elder remembered. "As it got near, it made our hair stand straight up." The group wanted to run. But the elders told them to take courage: "We understand about this," they said. "It is the horse that Sindi and the Boys made that is causing the big whirlwind." They had an urgent piece of advice: "Get out all the pipes and light them!" The chiefs produced their pipes. As soon as they had them lit, they turned their stems out and pointed them up at the funnel, crying out, "Smoke it! Smoke it!" They beseeched Red Wind to pass the group without harming anyone. "Don't come here!" they cried. "Pass on around us!" Red Wind heard them and swerved off to the side without touching them. "We were saved," the elder remembered. "But it was very close." Red Wind had understood them. Since they were the ones who had made him, he naturally spoke Kiowa.

On nineteenth-century maps of North America, the region of grasslands at the center of the continent was marked as "the Great American Desert." This might seem like an odd choice of words for such a lush landscape, but the mapmakers didn't necessarily mean "desert" to be taken in the modern sense—that is, an arid place with sand dunes and cacti. "Desert" still had some hint left of its original meaning, which now survives in the word "deserted." A desert was unpeopled terrain, waste ground. It's what Shakespeare meant when he called the Forest of Arden a "desert inaccessible." Any wilderness, no matter how tropically fertile, could plausibly be called a desert so long as nobody was living in it.

The grasslands of America were in this sense the biggest desert any of its white explorers had ever seen. Some of the explorers were so unnerved by the absence of trees that they thought the soil must be poisonous. They were all certain that it couldn't be farmed. Even if there was nothing unwholesome about the soil, the practical difficulties were insurmountable: the roots of the prairie grasses had been weaving and knotting and tangling together for thousands of years to form an unbroken mat that was in many places more than ten feet deep. The strongest wooden plow couldn't dent it (metal plows didn't come in till the middle of the nineteenth century), and the heaviest wagon wheel wouldn't leave a rut. This is one reason that many whites thought of the Indian Removal Act as fundamentally humane: since the Indians had demonstrated they could live in the Great American Desert, it was only fair to turn it over to them permanently, because it was land the whites would never want.

The early records of the whites on the prairie show that they had only one concern: getting across to the far side as quickly as possible. But that was an enormously difficult undertaking. From the western fringes of the forest, where the dense tree canopies opened up into parkland and meadow, all the way out to the shadow of the Rocky Mountains, where the true sagebrush desert began, the prairie unfolded in a serene and almost uniform sea of grasses. There were no peaks or promontories, no great valleys or canyons, barely any natural landmarks of any kind: just the grasses and wildflowers filling up the landscape out to every horizon.

In the eastern ranges, from Illinois to a few hundred miles west of the Mississippi, the dominant species of grass was big bluestem. This was a hardy and towering plant; it was why this zone came to be called the tallgrass prairie. At the peak of summer on the prairies big bluestem grew to six to eight feet high, and along the riverbanks, where the ground was wetter, it could get above ten feet. It was bright green on its upper leaf blade and dull milky green on the underside; when travelers were looking out onto a vast open expanse of big bluestem, they could see each gust of passing wind as a kind of racing footprint of paler color as the millions of grass blades bowed and yawed together. Big bluestem was also known on the prairie as ripgut grass, because the edges of its blades were razor sharp, sharp enough to draw blood. Anyone unwise enough to run unprotected through a stand of ripgut grass would emerge looking as though he'd been mauled by a panther.

Experienced leaders of wagon trains tried to stay out of the depths of the tallgrass zone. Big bluestem grew so high that people moving through its depths were hard-pressed to tell what direction they were heading in or whether they were going in circles. They were surrounded by the walls of yielding grass, endlessly shifting and rushing, closing up over their heads, briefly opening in the winds to show random scraps of the sky. Here and there, the grasses parted around their feet in what looked like trails, but they weren't human trails; they had been left by grazing bison and antelope (and by the wolf packs that hunted them), and they crisscrossed randomly in every direction. Any traveler foolish enough to follow one would simply end up deeper in a centerless maze. Most wagon trains had to move through the tallgrass country at a creep, inch by inch, with teams of men proceeding ahead of the line swiping at the grass with scythes, while the convoy's commander perched on the lead wagon peering down continually at a compass.

It was more prudent to try to outflank the tallgrass and travel inland as far as they could by river. The Missouri and its tributaries were the major routes over the north country; steamboats carried cargo to where the waterways dwindled down into muddy trickles. But eventually the travelers had to take their chances overland by wagon.

In the middle ranges the land was more arid than it was to the east, and big bluestem didn't flourish there. Instead, the tallgrass gave way to a proliferation of mixed grasses—short bluestem, wheatgrass, oat grass, switchgrass, needlegrass. These grasses tended to grow only three or four feet tall even in high summer, which meant that travelers at least got a look at the landscape they were moving through. Not that there was much to see: the land was a slow, regular, endless succession of immense swelling hills, like ripples in a gigantic pond. From the crest of each one, the view ahead was essentially the same: just the grasses and wildflowers evenly filling up the landscape out to the ring of the horizon. Sometimes the travelers would see meandering lines of darker green bulging up in the distance; those were scrub trees along the line of a riverbed. More rarely, there were faint white shapes on the horizon, remote broken hills and bluffs like motionless clouds, relics from some former age not quite worn away yet by the winds.

Guides warned travelers never to let their guard down while crossing the mixed-grass prairie. For all the openness of the terrain, it was still an extremely easy place to get lost in. Anyone who strayed from the wagons for more than a few minutes could become hopelessly confused among the maze of shallow valleys. Sounds barely carried in that region of the prairie; the grasses muffled them, and there were no solid prominences to send back echoes. The ground was so hard, and was so densely interwoven by the grass roots, that the heaviest wheels barely left an imprint. If the wagon train had begun moving in the meantime, there would be nothing to see from any ridgeline but the trackless uniformity of the unfurling land. Strayed travelers might spend days wandering hopelessly from one ridgeline to the next, looking for their missing companions. Their only chance was the hope that in the twilight they might spot the smoke trail of a distant campfire.

The landscape seemed to many travelers to be uncanny, as though they were moving through a waking dream. Strange signs and tokens were everywhere. Millions of years earlier the prairie had been submerged under a vast shallow salt sea, and its relics were still to be found underfoot. Along the hilltops and the slopes, wherever the grass roots were thinner, the earth was starred with countless fossil seashells—souvenirs of the Flood, obviously, and proof that this country was somehow more primordial than the rest of the earth. The land shifted in so many mysterious ways it sometimes seemed as though the floodwaters had never receded and the caravans were making their way across the bottom of the ocean. Not only were there no fixed landmarks, but the appearance of the grasses all around them changed day by day and sometimes hour by hour. The gorgeous tapestries of wildflowers were constantly shifting their colors, folding and unfolding with the sunlight. Each day at dusk the evening primroses would open, and hillsides that had looked brilliant green a few minutes before were suddenly as white as if they'd been buried by a blizzard.

The land was also a continuous seethe of winds. The winds were always blowing. There was an incessant succession of rushes and sighs and roars and rustles. The winds burned the skin as the sun did. They sent gusts of stinging sand hour after hour like plagues of flies. They kept people tossing and turning in their camps all night with tearing and flapping at the canvas of the wagons and sudden gusting stampedes through the campfires that sent up billows of choking, burning cinders everywhere. People believed that the winds were intolerable to live with for any longer time than it took to make the crossing; they said that people who tried to homestead in the isolation of the grasslands were invariably driven insane by the winds. They called it prairie madness.

But the greater danger were the storms. The storms were like nothing any of the travelers had ever seen before. They built up in gigantic, horizon-to-horizon tidal waves that swept over the prairie in crests of cataclysmic grandeur. Here is how the writer Fitz Hugh Ludlow described his first experience of a prairie thunderstorm:

> The lightning got broader, and its flashes quicker in succession; the thunder surpassed everything I have heard, or read, or dreamed of. Between explosions we were so stunned that we could scarcely speak to or hear each other, and the shocks themselves made us fear for the permanent loss of our hearing. One moment we were in utter darkness, our horses kept in the road only by the sense of feeling; the next, and the vast expanse of rain-trampled grass lay in one embrace of topaz fire, with the colossal piles of clefted cloud out of which the deluge was coming,—earth and heaven illumined with a brightness surpassing the most cloudless noon.

But there was something more. Concealed within the storm was some mysterious danger worse than the thunder and lightning, more devastating than the torrential downpours. Few of the travelers saw it. They would only come across its aftermath: they'd reach a settlement or a way station they were counting on for supplies, and they'd find it in ruins, its wooden or stone or turf buildings blown up as if by gunpowder kegs. The survivors would say that something had come out of the heart of the storm and vanished again and left nothing behind but a trail of wreckage and a mad spiraling scrawl in the earth.

One early traveler along the Platte River got a good clear look at the "sublime sight" and described it in his journal. He wrote that "a spiral abyss" seemed to form in midair. "It is very probable that if it had approached much nearer, the whole caravan would have made an ascension into the clouds." But instead, he wrote, "the spiral column moved majestically toward the North, and alighted on the surface of the Platte. Then, another scene was exhibited to our view. The waters, agitated by its powerful action, began to turn round with a frightful noise, and were suddenly drawn up to the clouds in a spiral form. The column appeared to measure a mile in height; and such was the violence of the winds which came down in a perpendicular direction, that in the twinkling of an eye the trees were torn and uprooted, and their boughs scattered in every direction." But it was over quickly. "What is violent does not last," the diarist noted. "After a few minutes, the frightful visitation ceased. The column, not being able to sustain the weight at its base, was dissolved almost as quickly as it had been formed. Soon after the sun re-appeared: all was calm and we pursued our journey."

In the 1840s only one or two wagon trains a month attempted the prairie crossing. For the most part, they were impoverished settler families who were making a last, desperate try for subsistence living on the West Coast. But that all changed at the end of the decade, when the news broke of the gold strike in California. Overnight tens of thousands of people were westward bound. All along the Mississippi River, where there were still no bridges across its miles-wide girth, so many people, animals, and wagons were piling up at the ferry points that the wait for a crossing often lasted for days. The cities along the river, and the scattering of settlement towns inland, were puffed up by a new growth industry: supplying wagon trains for the westward crossing. Upriver towns that only a year before had been nothing more than depots for the sparse steamboat traffic were transformed into crowded, brawling river ports, shantytown mazes of taverns and dry-goods stores, wagonmakers and gambling houses, milliners and brothels. They had large commercial districts that were wholly given over to stores and livery stables and smiths for the western journey. People were buying wagons, horses, oxen, and cattle; they were stocking up sacks of beans and flour and coffee and barrels of bacon and sugar and salt; they were buying maps and hiring guides; and the more devout families were arranging passage for their own preachers.

The wagon trains moved out from the settlement towns daily, sometimes hourly. Their lines gradually thinned out and scattered in the vast silence of the prairie. There could be anywhere between a few dozen to a couple hundred people in a typical caravan. As they traveled, they often turned into evanescent self-contained villages, with their own laws and customs, their own gossip, their own private histories. There were courtships and marriages along the trail, sometimes there were births, and often there were deaths. The great events punctuated the lulling sameness of the days. Weeks would pass with only the endless creak of the wagon wheels marking off the time. Sometimes the women would hang a bucket of cream from the frame of a wagon, and by the end of the day the rocking of the wheels had churned it into butter. Each evening as the camp was laid out on the trampled prairie grass and the fires were lit, the women would work in the cook wagons (most caravans had at least one, with its own stove and a flue poking up through the canvas roof), the men would be telling stories of the day, and the young lovers would be keeping their assignations in the distant low valleys beyond the firelight.

The caravans gradually wore down the prairie. The main trails west were so heavily trafficked that for the first time permanent ruts were dug into the soil. It was rarer now for wagon trains to get lost (though strays still often found themselves abandoned). But the crowding of the trails brought new dangers—particularly epidemic disease. Cholera was a continual threat. A stranger might stumble into the night camp with the first symptoms of infection, and by sundown on the following day everybody in the wagon train would be dead. At the same time, the prairie in those years accumulated a curious reputation as a healthy place, a place to recuperate, a place for miraculous cures. In the early 1850s, as the first torrent of immigration to California slackened, the caravans began carrying unexpected new passengers: wagonloads of invalids, the chronically ill, people with failing lungs or withered limbs, who only bought passage out to the heart of the prairie. They would set up camps and spend days or weeks in silent recuperation, idling in their wagons or on the trampled ground as the tallgrass seethed all around them, and then head back east.

The first permanent settlers began arriving in force before the Civil War. Most of them were there out of ideology and were only pretending to stay: driving up the voter rolls in Kansas and Missouri for the coming vote on statehood and slavery. Some were passionate abolitionists from the East who'd never imagined themselves west of the Mississippi, and they found themselves surprised and horrified by the life of the prairie. They particularly complained about the smell of the prairie grass, which got into their clothes and their drinking water and their bread dough. At night they found that the pillows in Kansas farms and rooming houses were all stuffed with dried prairie grass and they wouldn't escape the smell in their dreams.

After the Civil War, the drive to settle the prairies began in earnest. East of the Mississippi, in taverns and meeting houses and theaters and hotels, anywhere that advertisements were posted, there could be seen gorgeous topographical engravings of new prairie cities already being built. Most of the ads were placed by real estate speculators. They'd bought mile after mile of unoccupied land from the railroads (the government had handed it off to the railroads for free), and anyone foolish enough to purchase a plot from them would arrive to find nothing but deserted countryside scattered here and there with property stakes. The law was that ownership of a particular plot was established by the construction of a house, and a house was defined as a structure with a window, so some of the plots had lone stakes to which a little piece of glass had been glued. That was enough of a window to allow a deed to be upheld in court.

There were other ads, too—rather more modest and trustworthy ones, from organizations known as colony companies. These companies were determined to settle the prairie not through the random, slow accretion of farmers and tradesmen but in bold decisive strokes. So they were hiring the citizenry required for a complete town and sending them out en masse. A blacksmith, a milliner, a butcher, a wheelwright, a grocer—they'd interview for twenty-five or fifty jobs in all, and the hires and their families would travel together in a single wagon train. They would arrive to find the land already bought and cleared by the company, the plots already laid out and stocked with building supplies: within a few months, a windblown expanse of prairie was set with houses, smithies, stables, a hotel, a tavern, a church, and a crossroads general store.

The colony companies had all kinds of motives. Some of them were driven by religious passion, some by ideology; several colonies operated on principles laid down by the utopian theories of European intellectuals. There were one or two vegetarian colonies. Some were motivated by nationality or language: there were German and Swedish and Norwegian colonies where English was never heard. The first few colonies, before the Civil War, were fiercely abolitionist; the governor of Missouri, which was just as fiercely pro-slavery, not only refused them permission to settle but would not even allow them passage through his state to anywhere else.

Once the colonies were in place, though, they tended to lose their purity; within a decade, most of the ones that had survived were indistinguishable from the other new towns on the prairie. They shared the same remoteness, with only the outer tendrils of the railroads as lifelines. None of them had much in the way of official government. In many towns, the law enforcement, court, and jail were provided either by the colony companies or by private clubs of property owners. The federal government's presence was almost exclusively confined to cavalry garrisons, which had been dispatched into the prairie to reclaim it from the Native Americans.

But beginning in the 1870s, there was another odd manifestation of Federalism. A few days after any major disaster—a catastrophic flood or a prairie fire, and particularly a tornado—a stranger would appear. He was dressed in an army uniform, and he would introduce himself as an officer of the U.S. Signal Corps. Then he would politely ask the citizens to describe in detail what had just happened to their town.

10

The Night Watch

John Park Finley was born into a prosperous Michigan farming family in 1854. He was raised with the expectation that he would go into the family business and run a farm, but in that era few people thought that meant he was going to spend his life weeding cornfields. Agriculture was becoming a complicated and technical affair. When Finley was sixteen, he was sent to Michigan State Agricultural College, and after he graduated at nineteen, he spent a year at the University of Michigan Law School (law was an indispensable study for the modern farmer). All the while, though, he had been forming the conviction that he wanted nothing to do with the law, with business, or with farming. He wanted to be a meteorologist. In the 1870s, this meant only one clear first choice: a career in the U.S. Army Signal Corps.

The Signal Corps had essentially been the creation of one man, an army doctor named Albert J. Myer. Myer had spent several years before the Civil War working with soldiers who'd been deafened or rendered mute by battle wounds, and through this study he had devised many methods of nonverbal signing and signaling. During the war, he had used this knowledge to organize the Signal Corps: its brief was to provide the Union army with methods of communicating on the battlefield. By the time the war was over, Myer—who had turned himself into a skilled manipulator of the federal bureaucracy—had managed to extend the Signal Corps's duties to include building, maintaining, and operating the nation's large networks of military telegraph systems.

With peacetime, Congress and the military establishment considered the Signal Corps's usefulness to be at an end. They intended to dissolve the corps and fold its functions back into the regular army and turn over its telegraph networks to private companies. Myer had no intention of allowing that to happen. He began casting about for a large peacetime project the corps could take on in order to justify its continued existence. Toward the end of the 1860s, he hit upon the idea of creating a national weather service.

Congress had already debated a similar idea several times. There was a lot of pressure then for a national weather bureau. Much of the pressure came from the railroad companies, which had become major players in the American economy in the years after the Civil War: by the 1870s they in effect had a controlling interest in the federal government. Weather was a continuing and major factor in the efficient operation of the railroad system, and the industry wanted reliable data for everywhere its trains ran.

Congress first asked the Smithsonian to resume its ambitious prewar program of weather projects. But Joseph Henry, who was still the Smithsonian's director, informed Congress that he would have to refuse. There were several reasons. The spotters recruited by James Espy had dropped out of sight during the war, and many of them—particularly in the South—never got back in touch. Then, too, the Smithsonian's own weather offices had been severely damaged. In January 1865, a spark in a defective chimney had started a fire in an upper floor that had consumed several galleries and archives, including much of the Smithsonian's weather records. And then there was another factor: the economy was wildly unstable in the boom years after the war, and the Smithsonian's endowment and portfolio had taken several major hits. With the repairs to the building expected to consume the Smithsonian's budget for the next few years, such an ambitious project as a national weather service was simply out of the question. Henry suggested Congress try the Department of War.

This was what gave Myer his opportunity. In 1870, after years of tireless lobbying, he succeeded in getting Congress to approve legislation mandating that the Signal Corps create and maintain a national weather bureau. It wasn't going to be a small-time operation. Myer got not only the authority to build and staff weather stations around the

country, and the Smithsonian's old priority access to the national telegraph system, but also a discretionary budget to approach colleges and
universities and hire consulting professors and other experts—anybody
in the country who'd made a specialty of meteorology.

By the early 1870s, the first national forecasts were streaming out
from the Signal Corps's Washington City office. They rapidly became
absorbed into the routine of American daily life. In Washington City
they were posted at the War Department, the Capitol, the National
Observatory, and the Smithsonian; the corps had runners going out
three times a day to keep them updated. (The old map at the Smithsonian had been taken down during the Civil War.) Forecasts for the
rest of the country were produced by the Washington City office—the
forecasters there were called computers—and were transmitted by telegraph to the regional weather offices, where they were distributed for
display at local post offices and railroad stations. The corps also sent
the forecasts to local chambers of commerce, agricultural associations,
merchants' exchanges, and boards of trade. In many towns they were
displayed in the windows of newspaper offices. In luxury hotels, they
would be posted on an announcement board in the lobby; commercial
travelers and tourists formed the casual habit of checking them on their
way into breakfast.

The forecasts were known then as probabilities. This was because
they invariably began with the phrase "It is probable that . . ." Around
Washington City, Myer himself became known as Old Probabilities.
The data for the probabilities derived partly from volunteer observers
but mostly from the new weather stations. There were more than a
hundred stations scattered around the country, each staffed with a Signal Corps officer—known as an observer—and one or more assistants.
They transmitted a stream of weather readings three times a day, as well
as any reports of special or extreme conditions. Some of those conditions could be dramatic, even catastrophic: the Chicago weather station
sent in reports during the 1871 fire, up to the moment when the flames
consumed the station itself.

Myer found another way to make the Signal Corps essential to the
government. The perpetual uproar of the economy in those years was

causing waves of booms and busts; the reckless overexpansion of the railroad networks led to collapses that almost took out the entire country. In 1877 there was a nationwide railroad strike. Myer ordered the weather stations to observe the strikers along with the weather and to send coded reports on local unrest to Washington City. He passed these reports on not to his superiors but to President Rutherford B. Hayes himself (Hayes and Myer, as it happened, were childhood friends). Throughout the crisis, Hayes was discreetly kept advised on what cities were in turmoil or had quieted down, what regions were calm despite hysterical press reports of chaos, and what was most useful to the president—which local militias were proving ineffective or were actively going over to the strikers. That summer, when Hayes broke the strike by sending waves of federal troops around the country, his actions were specifically directed by the reports he'd received from Myer and the weather stations. If nothing else, Myer had insured that the Signal Corps would go on getting appropriations for years.

By the late 1870s the corps was known as the army's elite force. It had only five hundred officers and enlisted men and a waiting list more than a thousand names long. Not very many applicants were actually interested in the weather; the corps had become a fast track to the highest echelons of the military establishment. When John Finley of Michigan enlisted in the army and applied for the Signal Corps, he knew it wouldn't be easy. But he also knew that connections trumped regulations every time. He'd gotten excellent grades at college and law school, and when he arrived in Washington City in March 1877, he brought along certificates from both, but he also came with a sheaf of letters of recommendation his family had obtained for him from prominent Michigan businessmen and politicians who had heavy dealings with the federal government. He was initially told that he would have to wait for two years for a spot in the corps. He responded by handing over the letters. Six weeks later, he was advised that his application had been accepted and he was to report to the Signal Corps's training school at Fort Whipple, Virginia.

Fort Whipple was a spartan installation on a lush country estate. The estate had once belonged to Robert E. Lee; part of the grounds had been turned into the Arlington National Cemetery. The fort was on a hilltop with a commanding view—perfect for the cadets to practice their craft. Along with the basics of military drill, the cadets had to master hand signaling and signaling with flags, and they also had several hours a day of instruction in telegraphy (it took years before a telegraph operator was considered fully proficient). They also had to learn how to build and maintain telegraph lines. At that time, the Signal Corps was responsible for several thousand miles of lines, mostly in parts of the country where the commercial telegraph companies wouldn't go—the battle zones of the Indian Wars in particular, but also regions that were still too sparsely settled to make commercial telegraphy profitable. The cadets learned to set up what the corps called "flying wires"—temporary lines used on battlefields. The residents of rural Virginia got to know the sight of the cadets crashing around the countryside with their poles and lines, sending test messages back and forth over several miles of woods and fields, then disassembling their work and hurrying on.

John Finley was big—six feet three and more than two hundred pounds. He would always have difficulty cramming himself into a uniform. (The problem grew worse as he got older and stouter.) But he was a bear of a man, extremely strong despite his corpulence; he passed the physical and made it through basic training. Still, it was only after months in the countryside, spent red-faced and huffing, loading and unloading wagons as fast as possible, that he was finally transferred to Washington City to begin his formal training as a weather observer of the lowest rung: "assistant to a noncommissioned officer in charge of a weather station."

The Signal Corps's Weather Bureau office was a garish anomaly in the midst of a respectable Washington City neighborhood. It was on G Street and at first glance looked like most of the houses on the block: a squat three-story hulk of drab whitewashed stucco. But its mansard roof was a bristle of eccentricity: it was jammed with windmills, rain gauges, anemometers, and weather vanes. Above it, day and night, there hung a flock of swooping, quivering kites. It looked, one observer said, "like a gigantic playhouse."

The first things the visitor saw in the entrance hall were three enormous maps of America. They were pinned with cards displaying the last three sets of readings from the weather stations across the country. Beyond was a warren of cluttered cubbyhole offices. There was a library with more than a thousand books on meteorology (mostly in European languages, very little from the American storm war), a telegraph office strung with chaotic wiring, a maze of workrooms, file rooms, fact rooms, a cramped dining room, and rooms jammed with experimental apparatuses and floridly unlikely prototype gadgets designed to measure everything from dew point at high altitudes to the rise and fall of flooding rivers.

When Finley began at the G Street office, his job was lowly: sorting, collating, and copying the ceaseless stream of data flowing in from the weather stations. On the big table in the middle of the main workroom—which Myer had named the Fact Room—were large paper maps of the United States arranged in stacks of twelve with sheets of carbon paper between; the corpsmen would rapidly transcribe the coded figures for current temperature, pressure, wind speed, and precipitation to the maps. Another group of corpsmen and civilian meteorologists—the "computers"—would be compiling the data into usable form. The senior meteorologists used this work to compose the forecasts. Around the time that Finley started, Chief Signal Officer Myer decided to change what the forecasts were called—he may have gotten tired of being called Old Probabilities. His new name for them was "indications." They now began with the phrase "The indications are that . . ." From then on the senior staffers were supposed to be called "indications officers."

Final responsibility for the indications fell to the corps's chief civilian expert. This was Cleveland Abbe, a meteorologist and astronomer who had years earlier gained attention for issuing pioneering daily weather forecasts in his hometown of Columbus, Ohio. Abbe had been one of Myer's first hires. When Finley met him, Abbe was forty, vigorous, good-humored, and extremely quick-witted. The indications officers

Storm Kings

were amazed at how rapidly Abbe could take in a confused weather map and turn it into a lucid prediction. Abbe's accuracy rate with the indications was, the corps estimated, around 80 percent, which they thought was astonishingly high. Abbe's personal goal was to reach 90 percent. He thought it would probably be impossible to do any better than that.

Around G Street, Abbe was known as Acting Probabilities. The nickname caught on after Myer started spending less time in the office; he was traveling in Europe in 1878, and he fell ill with nephritis on the trip. But Abbe spent so long with the Signal Corps that ultimately he became known as Old Probabilities himself.

Early in his time at the G Street office, Finley caught Abbe's notice. Finley was hard to miss: he was a huge, clumsy man, with a nervous, irritable manner and a boundless capacity for sustained work. Abbe questioned him closely on his studies and was impressed that he had already mastered the basic textbook used by the corps, Elias Loomis's recently published *Treatise on Meteorology*. (Loomis, who had been around since the old days of the storm war, was now a professor of natural philosophy at Yale; his book was a substantial, conservative summation of the current state of meteorological knowledge.) Abbe recommended more books, and the sessions he and Finley spent in the Fact Room turned into an ongoing tutorial on advanced meteorological theory.

Abbe particularly wanted Finley to read a new book called *Storms: Their Nature, Classification, and Laws,* by William Blasius. Blasius was a businessman and amateur meteorologist who had been touring on the lyceum circuit since the 1850s. (Thoreau had heard him lecture and recorded that the audience was enchanted by his stories of people carried off by tornadoes but bored stiff by his science.) Abbe was hoping Finley would appreciate the extraordinary care and thoroughness of Blasius's work, particularly on the analysis of tornado damage tracks. Finley did so; in fact he remained an admirer of Blasius for the rest of his life. "His analytical map of the storm track," Finley would write in the 1920s, "is one of the best ever prepared and published of this class of storms." At his first reading with Abbe in the Fact Room, he was immediately inspired to do work on that level himself.

Abbe and Finley talked endlessly about tornadoes. Neither man had ever seen one, but both were fascinated by them. Abbe was growing increasingly preoccupied with the subject; reports had gradually been filtering into the Washington City office of the exceptionally large and violent tornadoes prevalent in the prairie states and territories beyond the Mississippi. The tornadoes of the prairies were something that Blasius had considered at length in his book. He had even offered a possible reason that they might be larger and more powerful than the ones that had been documented in the East. He believed that there was compelling evidence that tornadoes were formed in the collision between large bodies of warm humid air and cold dry air. There was one place in North America where this clash was a frequent, almost daily occurrence, and that was the central prairies. The thousands of miles of flat empty land that made up the Great American Desert, where vast currents of air from Canada and the Gulf of Mexico were continuously flowing together and colliding and mingling, would be a perfect breeding ground for tornadoes.

Was Blasius right? Abbe admitted to Finley that he had no idea. For all the furies of the storm controversy, many of the basic questions about tornadoes still remained unanswered—even unasked. Abbe was doing what he could to gather the basic research. Whenever he received a report of an unusually violent tornado, he had Myer send out a corps officer to make a field report. But he was beginning to think that the corps needed a full-time tornado expert, and he was wondering if Finley might be the man.

Finley was eager for the job. So Abbe decided to arrange a tryout for him. In May 1879, news came in from Kansas of a deadly tornado outbreak. Abbe persuaded Myer to send Finley, even though he was only an army private, on his first field investigation.

The railways west of the Mississippi were still spotty, the trains were usually overpacked with travelers and cargo, and their schedules were erratic, but the journey from Washington City to the heart of the prairie was now a matter of days instead of months. Finley arrived in eastern Kansas on June 12, not two weeks after the first reports of the disaster had been sent east. He spent the rest of June and into July piecing together what had happened—riding by wagon and horseback, sometimes making his way on foot; spending nights in fleabag inns and farmers' barns, sometimes, on rare occasions when the weather was clear, sleeping in the open. He guessed that before he was done, he had traveled at least five hundred miles.

That was still a sparsely settled country. It was scattered with a loose network of colonies, market towns, and isolated farmhouses. Much of the old prairie had been cleared and planted, but there were still trails everywhere that led out into the oceans of prairie grass and meandered off into nothingness. Complicating Finley's mission was the weather, which had been miserably rainy all spring and continued without letup through his stay. Ceaseless downpours made the roads like quicksand, swelled the streams into impassable torrents, and washed away the few rickety bridges. "Hardly three days," he later wrote, "was the weather at all pleasant or conducive to good work."

Still, he worked to reconstruct the events that had summoned him. A succession of violent thunderstorms had passed over the region on May 29 and 30. Several of the storms had spawned tornadoes. By Finley's count, there had been thirteen distinct tornado events. The exact number, though, was a matter of interpretation, because it became clear to Finley that some of the events had involved multiple tornadoes descending from the same cloud. That, Finley knew, was already going to make his report big news to Cleveland Abbe and the other meteorologists back home. The general view at the Washington City office was that tornadoes were rare and freakish occurrences. It was an exceptional year that saw more than two or three confirmed sightings.

Finley mapped out the trail of damage that each tornado had left behind. He walked the paths himself and interviewed everybody he could find along the way who had been caught up in or had witnessed the tornado's passage. Almost all the tornadoes, he found, had touched down in open country, and most of them had done damage to only a few isolated farms. But there was one great exception: the events in the town of Irving, Kansas, on the late afternoon of May 30.

As Finley pieced it together, a very large tornado had touched down southwest of Irving and moved rapidly through the hilly terrain toward the town. "Persons who watched its progress along this portion of its track," Finley wrote in his report, "stated that the demoniac fury of the cloud was appalling; whirling with most frightful rapidity, the intense black column would at times seem to level the whole bluff as it disappeared from view within the huge rolling mass of darkness." The tornado swelled up as it progressed; Finley estimated that by the time it crossed into the town itself, it was at least a half mile wide. It was moving so quickly that few people even had time to react. The destruction took only a few seconds to be accomplished, and it was total. Nothing remained but wreckage.

The funnel cloud had then passed back into the country beyond the north side of town. That was where it crossed over the new railroad bridge. This was an imposing construction of stone piers and iron spans; the two spans were 125 feet each. It had all instantly exploded into debris. "So completely twisted into shapeless ruin was the huge mass of iron rods and stringers," Finley wrote, "that it entirely disappeared from view in a few feet of water, except several ends of some of the long rods that reached out upon the shore."

By then the survivors were emerging from wherever they had fled to for shelter and were confronted by the ruin of their town. Within the swath of the debris trail were bodies half buried in the mud. The cries of the wounded could be heard coming from the collapsed houses and leveled storefronts. Some of the faintest cries were coming from the open country a half mile away. Rescuers began to venture into the rubble to look for the injured. But then there was a new alarm: all over town, people were suddenly yelling and pointing toward the western sky.

The storm there had broken up, and the sunlight was fanning out across the open country. It lit up an enormous gliding shape in the distance. The shape didn't appear to be a tornado; nobody saw a funnel. None of the townspeople, in fact, had the slightest idea what it was. One witness said it was like "the broadside of an immense mountain." From their descriptions Finley reconstructed it this way: "a cloud of inky blackness and enormous dimensions, presenting a square front of apparently two miles in width and a perpendicular height from earth to sky. It moved along slowly, but with the most inconceivable majesty of force, apparently annihilating everything within its reach."

When it came through the town, it proved far more catastrophic than the first cloud. A newly completed stone church was "whirled into a cone-shaped mass." Houses were torn from their foundations and spun in midair until they disintegrated. Loaded freight cars were upended on the railroad tracks. A new grain elevator burst, fell in on itself, and shed its contents across a mile of the countryside. Many people felt as though supernatural forces were at play. In houses St. Elmo's fire danced across interior walls and over the furniture. On the streets there was a curious updraft, which, one witness said, "acted so powerfully as to apparently reduce a man's weight about two-thirds." Small objects floated up from the ground to hundreds of feet in the air and then were swallowed in the blackness of the cloud. The noise of the cloud was deafening, like a continuous thunder of bank after bank of artillery. As it moved through the town, some witnesses saw writhing white shapes like waterspouts perpetually dancing and dissolving before its black featureless face. It began to dissipate as it crossed out of the wreck of the town and revealed in its last seconds two vast funnel clouds swirling side by side in its interior.

What was this storm? Finley was baffled by it. He didn't think it could be a conventional tornado. He wrote in his report that it must have been something unprecedented, some kind of freak combination of a tornado and a hurricane. Nobody he talked to had ever seen anything like it. They all pestered him with questions. This strange moving mountain: Was it something he had seen before? Was it something the federal government had studied? He wished he had an answer for them; all he could do was promise that he'd look into it.

They had other questions. Most of the townspeople were recent arrivals in Kansas. They'd never heard of tornadoes and wanted to know why they hadn't been told about them. They asked, Finley wrote, "whether or not this region was particularly subject to this class of storms, and the frequency with which they might and would occur." Farmers, tradesmen, and the most prosperous businessmen all wanted to know about how much danger they were in. He wrote that they all asked him, "Could the question be settled? Would it be settled by the Signal Service

Bureau? Does the Signal Service Bureau pay particular attention to this class of storms, so intimately affecting our welfare? Will the bureau be able to forewarn us next spring and summer?"

But something else came to trouble him even more: the behavior of the townspeople in the aftermath. They were putting on a great show of being practical, of bustling about the streets with urgent purpose, of cleaning away the debris, repairing the wrecked buildings, and rebuilding from scratch those that had been leveled, but they still had an unmistakably haunted air, an unshakable sense of dread. Finley saw that everything seemed to freeze whenever the sky clouded over. He wrote, "The terror depicted upon the countenances of the bravest men, at the sight of a dark cloud above the horizon, was something beyond description or realization."

For many people the aftermath was even more painful than that. The town was now filled with people who couldn't sleep at night. They had a kind of ritual they'd perform instead. Long after sunset they'd rise up and steal out of their houses. Carrying lanterns, they'd make their way to the damage track. And there they would stand or sit until dawn on the trampled, debris-strewn ground, keeping watch, looking to the western sky, waiting for the tornado to return.

II

Premonitory Symptoms

In the early 1880s, curious flags began appearing in prominent places all over America. They were seen flying above post offices and railroad depots and weather stations—enormous expanses of canvas, bearing bright and stark symbols that could be seen for miles away. They were the Signal Corps's new forecast flags. A flag of solid white meant fair weather, while one of solid blue meant rain; red with a large black disk at the center meant a storm; white with a black disk was a cold wave. They showed up first in the rural West, where they could be spotted at enormous distances by anyone with field glasses, but they were such an immediate success with the public that they quickly began flying from flagpoles in major cities. The flag for the cold wave was especially valuable in farm country, where advance word of a frost could mean the survival of a harvest. Railroads sometimes flew the cold-front flag from baggage cars so that every passing train could warn farmers in their fields if they needed to take action to save their crops. The flags were a familiar sight in America for decades; they lasted until the advent of radio forecasts in the 1920s.

They were the idea of General William Hazen, who took over as chief signal officer of the corps in 1880, after the death of the corps's first chief, Albert Myer. Hazen was a hero of the Civil War and more recently a decorated veteran of the Indian Wars. He was a successful and influential man from an exceptionally well-connected Ohio political family. His wife was the daughter of the owner of *The Washington Post*. But he had a better patron than that. Right around the time that he received his appointment to the Signal Corps, his childhood friend James Garfield was elected president of the United States.

Hazen was known as a fiercely contentious man who wasted no

energy in getting along with his superiors. During the Civil War, he had infuriated his old boss General Sherman by claiming credit for several of Sherman's triumphs during the March to the Sea. He had become a celebrity during the administration of President Grant, because of his exposure of the systematic corruption of the War Department's procurement system. His whistle-blowing testimony before Congress had led to the resignation of William Belknap, Grant's secretary of war. In 1876, during the Indian Wars, he had feuded so ferociously and so publicly with his commanding officer that he had to be reassigned. The officer was George Armstrong Custer, and that was the only reason Hazen missed the Battle of the Little Bighorn.

Hazen had no native ability as an administrator. But when he took over the Weather Bureau office on G Street, he was well liked—at first, anyway—for his determination to push the Signal Corps forward into new terrain. Unlike Myer, he was fascinated by basic scientific research. Myer had always looked for immediate results; Hazen was willing to back projects that might not bear fruit for years, if ever. He established a new work group at the Signal Corps headquarters called the Study Room, a companion to the Fact Room at the G Street offices. (There was no space left at G Street, though, so Hazen moved the Study Room out to the Signal Corps's base in Virginia; Hazen had just had its name changed from Fort Whipple to Fort Myer.) He sought out civilian experts in meteorology from university faculties and brought them in as consultants with the widest possible brief. Some he hired outright as full-time researchers, including William Ferrel, the man who had solved the feud between Espy and Redfield. Hazen paid him to keep abreast of all the current thinking about meteorology, with the goal of someday writing an advanced textbook.

Hazen backed another small idea that soon became one of the unquestioned givens of American life: standard time. At that point, timekeeping in America was a strictly local affair; each town set its own clock according to its best guess about when twelve noon was. This was gradually becoming a nightmare for the railroads, because as they grew across the country in those years, their schedules were turning into a hopeless maze of incomplete overlaps and partial synchronizations.

(One estimate around 1880 was that American railroads were using fifty different clock times.) With the enthusiastic public support of Hazen and the Signal Corps, a set of four standardized clock times, staggered across the country, was adopted by the railroads and the telegraph companies in 1883. Within a few years most of the country was using it, and by 1918 it had become a federal law.

Finley's field report on his Kansas expedition took him months to finish. The basic template for a corps field report was simple: go to the disaster site, interview witnesses and survivors, and reconstruct as closely as possible a chronology of the event. The officer was expected to stick to the facts and hold off on any theories or speculations. Finley did his best to follow the rules. But his report was unusual. The level of detail was unprecedented, even obsessive. He wasn't content to record the facts of the tornado damage; he cataloged them through a microscope. Where a typical officer might write that he had seen "debris" at one site, Finley wrote: "The creek to the SE of the house was choked up with a mixture of straw, rags, feathers, kitchen utensils, rails, boards, and pieces of farming implements." At another site he noted: "Lightning rods and wire fencing were wound into balls or twisted into ropes; tinware, cutlery, stove-pipes, harnesses, and furniture were broken and twisted in every conceivable manner."

As a result, Finley's report ran a hundred pages when the average report rarely went more than twenty. Finley also made room to talk about his own difficulties and shortcomings—something he would routinely do in his writings from then on. His report, he wrote, should have been much longer, but the horrendous working conditions, the impossibility of doing a thorough investigation of every tornado site, and the limited amount of time he'd been given to write up his findings had all forced him to cut his work short.

Nor could he forgo the opportunity to make recommendations. This was a brash, even arrogant move for a junior staffer who had no business expressing any opinion on Signal Corps policy. But Finley couldn't help offering a number of general observations about tornadoes and meteorological theory and suggesting several ways in which the Signal Corps could improve its methods of research. He urged most particularly that each spring the Signal Corps assign a special observer to the frontier; he even recommended where the observer should be based: Kansas City. The observer's goal should be to travel to tornado sites as quickly as possible so that the evidence would still be fresh. The goal should be to amass enough data to make tornado forecasts. The necessity for the forecasts, Finley observed, should be self-evident: after all, the Kansas tornado outbreak took place in one of the most sparsely settled areas of the country, and yet his estimate was that forty-two people had been killed and several hundred injured.

Finley ought to have expected a reprimand from his commanding officer, Hazen, for exceeding his brief. But he had a patron in the G Street office: Cleveland Abbe. Abbe was tremendously impressed by Finley's report, including the recommendations, and he talked it up to Hazen. Hazen agreed to let Abbe give Finley a new assignment. Search through the old archives, Abbe told Finley, and see how many accounts of tornadoes you can find. See if anything can be made out of them. At the least, get a sense for how often tornadoes really occur.

Finley was still expected to keep up with his regular duties for Abbe in the Fact Room. He spent much of his days preparing data for inclusion in the Signal Corps's regular publications, the *Weekly Weather Chronicle* and the *Monthly Weather Review*. But the rest of the time he was relentlessly burrowing through the archives. He read through the old weather logs kept by medical officers. He looked at the handfuls of surviving spotters' reports from Espy's day that had been salvaged from the disastrous 1865 fire at the Smithsonian. He went to the Library of Congress and read back issues of newspapers. Anytime he found a description of a tornado, he broke it down into quantifiable data—date, time of day, direction, speed, duration, fatalities.

He had a starting point for his own work, supplied to him by Abbe. This was a tentative list of American tornadoes that had been prepared years earlier by the Yale professor Elias Loomis, author of *A Treatise on Meteorology*. Loomis had recorded all the data he could scavenge for every tornado he'd heard about in the early years of the Republic. There were sixteen tornadoes in all.

Finley's list took him almost two years to put together. Its chronology began in 1794 and ended in 1881. Finley had cataloged every substantial account of tornadoes he could find and made a first assessment of their typical behavior. The title of the report was "Characteristics of Six Hundred Tornadoes."

Abbe realized that he had found his tornado expert. He wanted the report published immediately, but there were problems. Finley had poured so much exhausting labor into the research, had put in so much overtime, and had been so insistent on doing all the transcribing and copyediting himself that the final result was swarmed by countless tiny errors. Publication in its present form was impossible. What made the situation more difficult was that Finley grew overbearing and defensive whenever he was criticized. Abbe decided to delay publication until somebody could discreetly complete a corrected text. The job ended up taking another two years.

In the meantime, Abbe passed the draft on to General Hazen. Hazen was even more impressed by it than Abbe was—so impressed that he immediately promoted Finley to sergeant. He also found the report rather alarming; he'd had no idea that tornadoes occurred so frequently in the Great American Desert, even though he'd been stationed there himself during the Indian Wars. He decided at once that the corps should take a more active role in the investigation of tornadoes. He went back to Finley's recommendations in his field report from Irving, Kansas, and talked them over with Abbe. He agreed to have a man on extended assignment in the prairies during the spring and early summer; Finley's report had established that this was when tornadoes were most frequent. The only possible choice for the job was Finley.

Finley spent the spring of 1882 based in Kansas City. It was an active season: in early April, a large and powerful storm system crossed through the plains, with heavy winds and rain, severe hailstorms (the hail, which broke windows throughout central Kansas, was reported to be the size of hen's eggs), and multiple tornado touchdowns. One tornado destroyed all but two buildings out of eighty in the small town of Stafford, Kansas. Later that spring a tornado hit Phillipsburg, Kansas: the streets were said to be bathed in a ruby-red glow as the funnel moved into the heart of town. In June a storm spawned a tornado that cut through the outskirts of Kansas City itself; only one person was dead, but houses were described in newspaper accounts as being "crushed like eggshells." The same storm system the next day spawned a tornado that wrecked Grinnell, Iowa; it was so powerful that it blew trains off railroad tracks. A hundred people in Grinnell were killed.

Finley was kept on the move, visiting tornado scenes and interviewing survivors. But he also went on lengthy tours of his own. He traveled up and down the Missouri and the Mississippi; he toured around the Great Lakes to Michigan; he returned to Missouri and went on out to western Kansas. He visited the local weather stations wherever he went and collected copies of all their reports on tornadoes. He gave talks about tornadoes and the work of the Signal Corps at lodges and at businessmen's associations and at universities, where he enlisted volunteers to act as "tornado reporters."

Everywhere he went, he asked people to tell him their tornado stories. He was rarely disappointed. It seemed as though every city and small town in the plains and the Mississippi valley had been struck by a tornado. They called it a Texas twister or a Kansas cyclone. It might have happened the previous spring; it might have been forty years earlier. But everybody could still summon up every detail of that day, and they all wanted to tell it again to Finley. He heard the same thing in Kansas and Missouri and Oklahoma and Iowa and Illinois—the story of the Great Tornado. As often as not it was a tornado he'd never heard of before, but to the people of the town it was invariably the defining event of their lives. They dated everything about their local history by it. Somebody was born, some prominent family arrived or moved away, their beautiful church was built, the local college was opened, "a couple of years before (or after) the Great Tornado."

Finley meticulously collected their descriptions. It seemed as though no two tornadoes were alike. There were tornadoes like elephant trunks and tornadoes like snakes; there were gigantic tornadoes that calved off and reabsorbed smaller tornadoes, and twin tornadoes that collided and merged into one monstrous funnel, and multiple tornadoes that hung down from their parent clouds like crowds of icicles. Everybody remembered strange lights and glows. Usually, it was a deep ruby-red glow at the heart of the funnel like a demon's eye; that was the Red Wind of Indian folklore. Other times it was a diffuse, dark, sickly green aura that pervaded the surrounding clouds just before the tornado touched down; "tornado green," it was called. But other people had seen seethes of yellow and red around the base of the funnel like flames, and blue-white bands of lightning, and still others had seen that from close up the tornado funnel was continually sparkling and flashing up and down its length as though it were made out of diamonds. And then there were the noises the tornadoes had made, bellows and hisses, wails and moans and trumpet calls; it was as though the Indians were right: the tornado was sentient and was trying to get across an incommunicable message.

But there was something else, too: what the tornado had left behind. It was the same wherever Finley went. No matter that the tornado had been decades before, the townspeople could always point to someone who had never gotten over it. Finley recognized that haunted look, that air of perpetual anxiety, that he had seen after the strange twin tornado in Irving, Kansas. It might be a clerk in the law office, or a bustling housewife at the counter of the dry-goods store, or a sunken-cheeked wastrel in a corner of the saloon: they got the same look of blind panic whenever the southwestern sky clouded over.

Finley returned to Washington City at the end of the summer. He immediately threw himself into a round of feverish activity—as though to get everything settled all at once. In September he was furiously writing a copiously detailed new analysis of his tornado researches. In October he was enrolling in intensive seminars at the Johns Hopkins University, one of the first major universities to offer graduate studies in meteorology. In November he got married; his bride was a Washington City society girl named Julia Larkin (Signal Corps officers were considered highly desirable catches).

By December he was in an army mental hospital.

His diagnosis was "premonitory symptoms of neurasthenia." Neurasthenia was something of a vogue disease in that era. Its symptoms were exhaustion, anxiety, neuralgia, headache, and severe depression. Its cause was prolonged overwork. It was considered an affliction peculiar to the jittery energies of the Gilded Age; the famous psychologist William James suggested renaming it "Americanitis." Finley's doctor wrote less grandly that his patient was simply "doing too much brain work." His prognosis was: "He very decidedly needs rest. Should he continue to do as much as at present the consequences will be of very grave character."

Finley's recuperation was slow. Over the winter he was released from the hospital. He went back to his family home in Michigan and spent the spring of 1883 there. But he didn't find the stay restful. In fact, the longer it lasted, the more anxious he became. His illness, he wrote to a friend then, had caused him "a world of regret." Not because he had overworked himself to the point where he'd ended up in a mental hospital, but because he was tortured by the thought of all the new developments in his field he was missing out on while he was malingering here in the boondocks. He "trembled," he wrote, at the thought of how far he was falling behind.

Finley resumed his duties at Fort Myer, in its serene isolation outside Washington City. He instructed the cadets not only in the basics of service in the corps—signaling, telegraphy, and meteorology—but the essentials of fieldwork: the inspection of weather stations, the organization of river stations to report flooding, the strict technical requirements of making daily weather records. The cadets also became practiced at the physical labors required of corpsmen in the field: laying telegraph lines, digging postholes, repairing corroded cables. Sometimes they got such tasks as punishment for curfew violations or drunkenness or other derelictions of duty. This was actually against army regulations; legitimate duties weren't supposed to be imposed as punishments. But Finley, after serving at Fort Myer as a cadet and as an instructor, thoroughly approved. "An occasional dose of the laborer's job," he later wrote, "was good medicine for the recalcitrant Observer."

Fort Myer was also where General Hazen had placed his Study Room, and it was ideal for its staffers, too. Their job was to think—to think uninterruptedly. They were spared the grind of devising daily forecast maps; that was done in town at the Fact Room. They were free to spend their hours in the Study Room in extended researches without results. The placid setting—the base was on a hilltop, surrounded by great vistas of rolling forested countryside—was an encouragement to contemplation. It was meant to be a soothing alternative to the crammed and squalid streets of Washington City. Nor did it hurt that it seemed worlds away from the tangled, corrupt, patronage-driven labyrinths of the federal government.

When John Finley returned from his medical leave over the summer of 1883, General Hazen greeted him with the news of a promotion. Finley was now second lieutenant. He was also relieved of his scut-work duties in the Fact Room and was now officially in charge of the corps's tornado research project. That meant a transfer out of G Street to Fort Myer, where he was assigned a desk in the Study Room. He was also given two assistants. The assistants were to read and digest for Finley's benefit all the reports coming in from his national spotters network. Finley's job was to devise a formal method of predicting tornadoes.

He fell to the job with a burst of renewed enthusiasm. He reviewed his own fieldwork, he unearthed from the archives all the reports on tornadoes done by Signal Corps officers, and he had endless technical discussions with Abbe and with the other meteorologists in the Study Room. He was soon putting in more time on tornadoes than he had in the months leading up to his breakdown. (He was also spending several hours a day instructing cadets.) He found the subject maddeningly diffuse, but after several months he thought he had the basics within his grasp.

His core assumption was one he and Cleveland Abbe had made years earlier, which they had derived from their reading of William Blasius's book *Storms*: tornadoes formed at the meeting between a domain of hot humid air and one of cold dry air. But Finley had gone on to elaborate several further principles from this: for instance, that tornadoes tended to form in the southeast quadrant of low-pressure systems, at places of high contrasts in temperature and dew point. He had also massed enough evidence to confirm many rules of thumb that people had about tornadoes—that they rotated counterclockwise, that they generally appeared in late afternoon, and that they almost always moved from southwest to northeast.

But about other issues he wasn't so sure. What were conditions like inside the tornado? An idea was going around then, debated in the Study Room and in university science departments, that there had to be an area of near vacuum within the tornado funnel to account for the ferocious rush of inflowing winds. This was not a new idea; Franklin had suspected it, and Sir John Herschel had said as much during the debate over James Espy's steam-power theory. But it was realized now that the vacuum could account for the tornado's extraordinary destructiveness: if a funnel passed over a house, then the air pressure trapped inside would push outward into the vacuum, causing the house to explode.

Finley always regarded this idea with skepticism. But it proved to have a powerful hold on the imagination of other meteorologists: starting within the next few years, and persisting for more than a century, Weather Bureau officials and other experts would advise people to open their windows when a tornado was approaching in order to equalize the air pressure.

Meanwhile, did Finley have enough data to begin predicting tornadoes? General Hazen tried never to pressure the Study Room into delivering quick results. But the problem of tornadoes became more urgent early in 1884. In the third week of February, the forecasters in the Washington City Fact Room were tracking a large winter storm that was moving across the country. There were blizzards across the Great Lakes and violent thunderstorms in the lower Mississippi valley. On the nineteenth and twentieth, the office began receiving frantic wire messages from weather stations throughout the South. Tornadoes were touching down in waves, in families; at least fifty tornadoes within two days, leaving more than a hundred people dead. Nobody knew where the tornadoes had come from or how there could be so many of them. It became known as the Enigma Outbreak.

At the Signal Corps headquarters the news of the outbreak made

Hazen bump Finley's tornado project up to the highest possible priority. The time had come, Hazen decided, for an immediate full-scale test of tornado prediction. Finley was ordered to begin a three-month trial. He divided the country up into eighteen districts and subdivided each district into four forecast areas. Twice a day, he would make a prediction for each of these seventy-two zones. But these predictions were kept strictly within the Study Room. Even if they warned of an imminent tornado, Hazen declared that they would be kept entirely secret until the full test was complete.

Finley began the test in March and continued it till May. He was working at it at such a furious clip that Hazen midway through ordered him to slow down; one forecast a day, he decided, was sufficient. When Finley showed him his tabulation of the results, Hazen was amazed—and also suspicious. Finley was claiming a success rate of 96.6 percent. Hazen ordered him to begin another three-month trial. The results were the same.

But Hazen made no move yet to begin public tornado forecasts. In fact his ardor for tornado forecasting seemed to have cooled dramatically in the months since the Enigma Outbreak. When Finley presented the results of the second pilot study, he found that Hazen was barely interested. Instead, he was preoccupied with an issue that had nothing to do with tornadoes.

From the beginning of his tenure, General Hazen had been fighting countless bureaucratic battles with his superiors in the War Department and with Congress. He had assumed command in the middle of an ongoing scandal, a Signal Corps officer who had been embezzling funds. Soon after that, he had fought the War Department to keep them from admitting Negro soldiers to the corps. Now a new crisis was proving to be the bureaucratic war of his life.

Soon after he had taken over the corps, he had agreed to back a three-year expedition to the Arctic to establish a weather station. The expedition had gotten under way in 1881. It was led by Captain Adolphus Greely, a longtime Hazen protégé. Everyone considered it to be extraordinarily hazardous, but as it proved, they were still grossly under-estimating its dangers. Captain Greely himself had been fooled by the relatively mild Arctic summer of 1881 into thinking that relief missions would be able to reach his position above the Arctic Circle. But the first relief mission, in the summer of 1882, had only partially succeeded (it had left the supplies in an unmanned depot hundreds of miles south of the weather station), and the second relief mission the following year had been a calamity: one of the ships had gone down in an ice field, and the second had turned back. Greely and his team of twenty-four men had been left alone, with no supplies, their circumstances and condition a mystery.

The news of the second relief mission's failure put Hazen into a frenzy. He wanted its commander court-martialed and a new mission mounted immediately. He was overruled by his superior, Secretary of War Robert Lincoln, the son of Abraham Lincoln. The Arctic summer was ending; the ice was closing in; a second expedition, Lincoln believed, would doubtless meet a worse fate than the first. He decided not to risk any more men.

Hazen was outraged. He immediately had his staff at G Street compile at top speed two special reports: one excoriating the failure of the second relief mission, the other blasting Secretary Lincoln's refusal to send a third. The reports contained minute analyses of nautical charts and weather records, together with interviews with ships' captains familiar with the polar seas, all to demonstrate that the second mission had been incompetently commanded and that the third would surely have succeeded. Hazen included both reports in his annual message to Congress.

It was not a wise move. General Hazen was one of the best-connected men in Washington; Secretary Lincoln was one of the few who trumped him. Robert Lincoln was true American royalty—a homegrown Prince of Wales, a shoo-in for the presidency whenever he wanted it. In fact, since his father had been called "the Rail-Splitter," he was generally known around town as the Prince of Rails. It was not a joke he found funny.

General Hazen wasn't intimidated by Lincoln. In fact he openly despised him; in Hazen's eyes the secretary was a weakling, a coward, a civilian who knew nothing about the military and had no business commanding soldiers. But the secretary did have something Hazen didn't: the confidence of the president. That was no longer James Garfield, Hazen's childhood friend, who had been assassinated soon after taking office; it was Garfield's successor, Chester Alan Arthur—an old-school party hack from the New York Tammany Hall political machine.

President Arthur was a man who loved his pleasures, which among other things included gourmet dining, fine clothes, and luxurious accommodations. One of his first moves as president had been to have the antique furniture of the White House carted away and replaced by the latest from Tiffany. His intellectual curiosity was low, and his enthusiasm for science nonexistent. He took Secretary Lincoln's word on anything technical and was never going to overrule him in a matter like the polar expedition. "It is well known," one of Hazen's colleagues wrote later, "that the President felt no interest in Arctic matters, and that he would not have crumpled a single rose-leaf upon his couch, if by turning his body he could have discovered the North Pole."

But General Hazen was not the man to back away from a fight. His conflict with Secretary Lincoln came to a head in the summer of 1884, just as Finley was conducting his tornado forecasts. That was when the news came from the north that survivors of the polar expedition had been found.

Twenty-five men had set out for the Arctic; six had returned alive, including Captain Greely. The story of their rescue drew reporters from all over the world. Secretary Lincoln and his deputies in the War Department acted immediately to close off the survivors to any public scrutiny. The press was also denied any glimpse of the recovered dead bodies. The rumor spread that the bodies all too obviously displayed the marks of cannibalism.

Over the next several months, Secretary Lincoln systematically shut down any public discussion about what had happened to the expedition. Several review boards were held, each closely managed by Lincoln and each coming to the same conclusion: Nobody was at fault. The failure of the 1883 relief mission was unavoidable. The lack of a follow-up expedition was justified given the circumstances. Most important, the conduct of the Greely party during their long years in the Arctic was above reproach. General Hazen watched all this happen with mounting disgust. He told a reporter that the rumor of cannibalism was not a serious matter: What else were men trapped in the Arctic supposed to do? As far as Hazen was concerned, the real reason Lincoln was drawing a veil of circumspection over the whole matter was that he didn't want his own decision making questioned. If only Lincoln had sent that second expedition, Hazen insinuated, Captain Greely's whole team could have been saved.

What Hazen hinted at in public he declared explicitly in private. He sent the secretary a long confidential letter dismissing the review boards as a sham and accusing Lincoln of direct responsibility for the nineteen deaths among Greely's team. The letter ended:

> While the action of the Secretary of War was dictated by his sincere convictions of public duty, I believe it can be established beyond question that such action made certain that final disaster to Lieutenant Greely's Arctic party which the violation of their orders by Lieutenant Garlington and Commander Wildes [the officers commanding the failed relief mission] had rendered highly probable.
>
> I am, very respectfully, your obedient servant . . .

Secretary Lincoln was livid. But he was not one to strike back wildly. His bureaucratic counterblow against Hazen was slow, cunningly devised, and inexorable. It began when Congress came back in session in the autumn of 1884. A select commission opened hearings in Washington City. There were a lot of governmental commissions holding hearings in those days; nothing about this one seemed unusual. In fact its full name was a clear promise of tedium: the Joint Commission to Consider the Present Organizations of the Signal Service, Geological Survey, Coast and Geodetic Survey, and the Hydrographic Office of the Navy Department, with a View to Secure Greater Efficiency and Economy of Administration of the Public Service in Said Bureaus. The commission consisted of three senators and three representatives;

its chairman was Senator William Boyd Allison of Iowa, and so it was called, by the few observers who took note of its existence, the Allison Commission.

Its first several days of hearings were routine. Witnesses offered a careful bureaucratic review of several government agencies tasked with scientific projects. The first witness was John Powell, the director of the U.S. Geological Survey. Powell spoke ably, at length, and in copious detail about the survey's work—in particular, the creation of a set of topographical maps that would cover the entire nation. This was an enormous venture; years had been put into it already, and decades more might pass before it was complete. Powell went out on a limb and estimated that within three years they might be done with Massachusetts. The commission's questioning was cautious and sympathetic. The project, they all agreed, was of enormous value to the nation and needed the full backing of Congress.

The next witness was J. E. Hilgard, the supervisor of the Coast Survey. He also spoke at length about the difficulties and challenges of his task. Mapping the coastline was an extraordinarily complex, torturous process; the work was so open-ended that Hilgard couldn't even begin to guess when it might be completed. The senators and representatives were quick to congratulate Hilgard and his team on their work and to assure him of their ongoing support.

The following week, Secretary Lincoln arrived at the Senate conference room and took the witness chair. He apologized for not speaking first; that would only have been proper, since, as he made plain, the commission had largely been his doing. But the press of business had prevented him. The recent presidential election meant a change of administration, and he had many duties that needed to be finished before he could turn over his office to his successor.

Then he turned to his purpose. He barely acknowledged the Geological Survey, the Coast Survey, and the Hydrographic Office. His only concern was with the Signal Corps. In his years as secretary, he told the commission, he had become increasingly convinced that the Signal Corps was suffering from what he called "radical defects." It was poorly run, and its fundamental mission had become hopelessly confused. He believed that it had been a grave mistake for the corps to take on the job of weather prediction at all; it had proved to be wholly unsuited for the job. The Weather Bureau needed to be transferred at once to a new civilian agency, preferably one somewhere other than in the Department of War, and the corps needed to be reintegrated into the regular army.

Lincoln's speech might have been seen for what it was, a broadside attack on Hazen, if anybody had been paying any attention. But nobody was. The opening hearings had barely been attended, and anyway reporters were not inclined to write up in detail the testimony of a cabinet officer about the fine points of departmental bureaucracy. After the holiday recess, when Cleveland Abbe, the corps's chief civilian forecaster and John Finley's mentor, appeared before the commission, he clearly had no idea what he was in for.

Abbe arrived at the hearing room prepared to give testimony similar to that of the earlier witnesses on the importance of the corps's work for the American people, with accounts of its ongoing research projects. The commission allowed him to do so, more or less—except that he was continually interrupted with questions about the military structure of the Weather Bureau and whether it would be possible to change it into a strictly civilian agency. Abbe was flummoxed. He replied in generalities about the heavy burden of work the corps had taken on and how that burden was only going to increase. He predicted that sooner or later every American would want a personalized weather forecast delivered each day by telegram. The commissioners pressed him again about the logistics of transferring weather service to civilian control. All he could say was, "You are asking me a question in military matters that I am hardly fit to answer."

If Hazen hadn't been aware before that the commission was specifically gunning for the Signal Corps, he knew it then. A few days later, Abbe requested an opportunity to provide additional testimony before the commission. He delivered a long, carefully prepared speech on the excellence of the Signal Corps, the absolute necessity of continuing it in its present form, the eminent practicality of employing both civilians and military officers, and the wholly admirable administration of

General Hazen. Hazen himself appeared the next day and gave a relaxed and amiable statement about how successful the Signal Corps was, how harmonious and pleasant the working conditions were, and how well he himself got along with his superiors in the War Department.

Hazen then arranged for several of the officers in the Washington City office to appear before the commission. All dutifully repeated the gist of Abbe's and Hazen's testimonies. The goal was obviously to wear the commission members down and get them to produce the sort of vague and noncommittal report that usually came out of federal hearings. The plan might even have succeeded, too, if it hadn't been for John Finley.

By the time the commission got to Finley, it was growing increasingly somnolent. Representative Robert Lowry, taking Finley's testimony, was almost listless: "Lieutenant Finley, you are connected with the Signal Service, I believe?"

"I am," Finley answered.

"In what department?"

"In the Signal Corps proper. I am now stationed at Fort Myer, Virginia."

"You have some particular information upon the subject of tornadoes, their origin and characteristics?"

"Yes, sir; I have devoted some study to that subject."

"You may give the Commission, if you please, such information upon that subject as may be within your possession."

"That information is rather extended and diverse," Finley answered. "I could not give in brief, perhaps, a very comprehensive statement; but I will say that I have been studying the subject for about five years specially." He then summarized briefly his fieldwork and his study of the Enigma Outbreak.

The representative heard him out and rephrased his question, with the first hint of impatience: "It has been suggested to us by the Chief Signal Officer that you might give us the result of your investigations upon that class of storms."

"I can submit my papers upon the subject," Finley answered.

"You allude now to the full reports you have made?"

"The special papers," Finley fussily corrected. "There are three professional papers and one Signal Service note."

The representative held up the copies of the papers that Hazen had already forwarded to the commission. He plainly felt that this thick wad of technical analysis was too much to expect anyone in Congress to read. "What would be the practicability," he asked, "of your giving us an epitome of these documents in such form as to be incorporated in the testimony?"

Finley considered. "I dare say I might do that in a short note. I would prefer, however, to prepare anything of that nature at my desk rather than to attempt to present the matter without deliberation."

Lowry was probably surprised by Finley's reluctance to fulfill such a routine request. Witnesses were expected to arrive with these sorts of epitomes already prepared, and if not, to supply them soon afterward for incorporation into the record (which, it was understood, nobody was going to read anyway). Lowry said, "I will suggest to the Commission the propriety of having that epitome rather than these documents embodied in the record."

Senator Eugene Hale then spoke up. He clearly wanted to avoid any imputation that the commission was criticizing Finley in any way. "I think if Lieutenant Finley could prepare a paper of that kind," he said, "showing the method of his investigation, and showing also the results and the application of them which could be made throughout the country by our different industries generally, that it would be very valuable."

Lowry was ready to wrap up and move on. He asked Finley, "How soon could you prepare such a summary?"

Finley had been chafing under this apparently innocuous line of questioning, and he burst out: "I can hardly say. My duties are such that I have not a moment of spare time. For the past three months I have been working about seventeen hours a day, and I do not see how I can prepare such a paper as Senator Hale suggests without being relieved from some of my present duties."

That woke the whole panel up. Senator George Pendleton asked, with a certain cautious alertness, "Will you describe, if you please, the occupation or occupations that keep you engaged for seventeen hours a day, as I think you said?"

Finley was only too happy to oblige. "About that many hours. The whole time here indicated is devoted to the course of instruction at Fort

Myer, the performance of my duties at the office of the Chief Signal Officer, and the pursuit of special studies in connection with tornado work. The course of instruction at Fort Myer embraces the performance of military duties, instruction in tactics, electricity, military signaling, international signals, military surveying, the construction and practical operation of telegraph lines, telegraph practice with the key in sending and receiving messages, and practical work in topographical sketching. If you desire such a statement I could give you one to cover minutely every moment of time devoted to the performance of my duties."

Pendleton mildly observed, "Seventeen hours a day is a very heavy strain."

"I know it is," Finley replied, "but I think that I can give you a statement to cover every moment of that time."

"That is not necessary," Pendleton murmured. "You have answered sufficiently."

Lowry then asked, with great sympathy, "Are your duties likely to continue so arduous as to require that expenditure of time?"

"I can hardly say," Finley answered.

Lowry then wound up: "How soon can you prepare the statement we have spoken of?"

Finley, apparently soothed by the kindness of the commission, answered airily: "I dare say, as I understand the desire of the Commission is a brief note, I can prepare it in a couple of days."

He was then excused.

Finley plainly didn't realize what he had done. But Hazen understood the situation all too well: if the commission was looking for proof that the corps was badly managed, Finley's testimony that he was forced to work seventeen hours a day was exactly what was required. It would be useless for Hazen to claim that this overload was the result of Finley's personal obsessiveness on the subject of tornadoes. He wouldn't have been believed, and in any case it should never have been permitted to happen no matter what the reasons were.

Hazen knew he had to act quickly to limit the damage. At all costs, Finley must be kept from giving further testimony to the commission.

There was no telling what he might say if he was encouraged to talk at length. So Hazen immediately relieved Finley of all his current duties and gave him a new job. He was made inspector of the corps's weather stations, and a few days after his testimony he departed Washington City on an extended tour of the stations west of the Mississippi.

General Hazen probably felt then that he'd dodged a bullet and that now he only had to wait Secretary Lincoln out. The 1884 election was bringing in a new administration: Chester A. Arthur and the Republicans were leaving; Grover Cleveland and the Democrats were coming in. Lincoln was finishing up his duties in the War Department that winter before retiring from government service. (While routinely mentioned as a possible presidential candidate, he never ran; he spent the remaining decades of his life occupying highly lucrative positions in the private sector.) But, as it proved, Lincoln wasn't yet done with General Hazen.

That winter, Hazen's angry private letter to the secretary about the Greely expedition had been leaked to the press. When and how exactly this happened, nobody knew, but it first saw print in the *Chicago Tribune* in February 1885, a few weeks before the inauguration of the new president. Everybody assumed Hazen had been the leaker, and they all took it to be a particularly cheap shot at the departing secretary. A reporter for the Washington *Evening Star* happened to catch up with Hazen at one of the city's most fashionable meeting places, the lobby of a downtown hotel called the Ebbitt House. He asked Hazen about the story, and Hazen off the cuff admitted that the letter was genuine but denied that he had leaked it. The reporter immediately published Hazen's remark. That proved to be provocation enough for Secretary Lincoln. In one of his last official acts before he left Washington City, he had Hazen court-martialed.

General Hazen's trial took place in the middle of March, almost immediately after Grover Cleveland's inauguration. It was a grand affair. It was held not in some cloistered War Department meeting room but in a public room of the Ebbitt House. The hotel was then jammed with guests in town for the inaugural celebrations—reporters, politicians, lobbyists, power brokers, and visiting dignitaries. Every seat was taken when the court-martial began.

The judge advocate prosecuting the case made it sound perfectly straightforward: General Hazen's letter to Lincoln was grossly insubordinate, and Hazen had compounded the insubordination by making the letter public. Hazen's attorney (he'd been permitted to bring in a civilian lawyer) replied for the defense: the letter may have been vigorously worded, but it wasn't technically insubordinate. In fact Secretary Lincoln had always encouraged forthright debate and disagreement. Hazen had simply been expressing his honest opinion. As to the second charge: Hazen denied that he'd leaked the letter, and he had no idea who did; his lawyer broadly hinted that it could perfectly well have been Secretary Lincoln himself, just to make the general look bad.

From such a clear-cut beginning, the trial rapidly devolved into a legalistic shambles. On the face of it, General Hazen's defense was untenable. The letter was plainly insubordinate to the point of insolence. The problem for the prosecutor was to find a way of saying so without raising the question of whether Hazen's charges had any merit. He wanted all discussion of Secretary Lincoln's decision making, and in fact all discussion of the Greely expedition in general, excluded from the trial. In practice this meant he was obliged to raise a barrage of objections every time Hazen's attorney opened his mouth. Hazen's attorney, meanwhile, had a different tactic. He didn't exactly mount a defense; instead, inch by inch, hour by hour, in the face of a ceaseless string of sustained objections from the other side, he set out to confuse the issues so thoroughly that nobody listening would have a clear idea what exactly Hazen had done, if he had done anything at all.

By the second or third day of this ordeal, any practiced courtroom observer would have concluded that the entire business was a sham. The judges were probably sympathetic to Hazen, and they almost certainly had doubts about Secretary Lincoln's conduct—and besides, Hazen's attorney really had succeeded in muddying the waters about who might have leaked the letter. But a not-guilty verdict would have been tantamount to an indictment of Lincoln. The members of the panel there-fore came to an unorthodox—in fact flagrantly illegal—solution. They took it upon themselves to rewrite the charges against Hazen so that they were watered down almost to the point of nonexistence and then found him guilty of those.

The verdict was sent on to the new president, Grover Cleveland, for final disposition. Cleveland may have been a beginner at his job, but he seems to have understood the matter perfectly—and besides, he was determined to go lightly on Hazen anyway. It so happened that he and Hazen were longtime friends. Cleveland wrote Hazen a letter of censure so vague it was barely detectable as a rebuke. Then he officially declared the matter closed.

12

Violent Local Storms

From the veranda of the Antlers Hotel in Colorado Springs, when the weather was right, the Signal Corps's weather station on Pike's Peak could be seen gleaming on a high mountain ridge. In April 1885, the hotel guests often gathered with field glasses to observe it. They were looking for signs of life. No reports had come in from the station in months; the telegraph lines had been taken out by strong storms and avalanches early that winter, and the trails had all been obliterated by unusually heavy snow. The corps's chief observer at the Colorado Springs base had reported back to Washington City that the Pike's Peak station was hopelessly cut off and that not even the local mountaineers were willing to attempt a relief mission.

The Pike's Peak station was famous. Among the more than one hundred stations the corps had then established, it was the only one to have caught the public imagination. This was partly because of its remote and exotic location, and partly because its observers had their own (officially discouraged) tradition of tale-telling. They were notorious for making up grandly theatrical stories, which they solemnly passed off to the press as scientific truth. One time an observer had claimed that his wife and children had been trapped in a cave by a blizzard and had been eaten by gigantic rats. (The observer was unmarried and childless, and the rats remained unknown to science.) Another year an observer issued an urgent warning that Pike's Peak had erupted and that the lava flow would soon engulf Colorado Springs. But this year, without a word from the station, it seemed as though the worst had befallen it. Stories had been circulating in the local newspapers for months, and were now beginning to spread out to the national press, that the current crew of six men at the station must already be dead.

Among the guests at the hotel that April was John Finley. It was part of his tour as inspector. He had come to Colorado Springs to inventory the base weather station in town. This had proved to be quick work. "Unserviceable property," he remembered later, "had been accumulating at the Base for years." He began lugging the old gear and supplies out to a vacant lot. "As fast as it was inspected," he wrote, "I had it removed from storage and piled there." Then he soaked it all in kerosene and set it ablaze. He had the base station observer and his staff stand guard to protect the crowd that had gathered: the townspeople had been unaware that inventorying a military base could be so exciting.

His next job had been to see to the relief of the Pike's Peak station. He listened to the talk on the veranda each morning and consulted the base station observer and talked to local mountaineers. All of them told him that his assignment couldn't be completed because an ascent of the mountain was impossible. The weather was consistently foul: day after day, the summit was continuously shrouded and enfolded by snow clouds. Most of the guests were saying that the mountain station would remain inaccessible until high summer.

Finley was having none of it. "Notwithstanding all of the arguments presented by the mountaineers," he wrote, "I firmly informed them that, as an Army Officer I was under positive military orders to make an inspection of the station at the Peak and ascertain the condition of the Observer in Charge and his assistants. Also I was to take important meteorological observations at the Summit and test out the station instruments." He was particularly insistent on this point with the observer at the base station in town, who was profoundly unhappy to hear it; his orders were to accompany Finley up the mountain.

The local mountaineers did try one more time to get Finley to reconsider. They cataloged the dangers ahead: the trails invisible beneath the snow, the streams that couldn't be forded, the treacherous crevasses and fields where the snow might be a hundred feet deep; the whiteout storms at high altitudes, the dangers of oxygen deprivation above twelve thousand feet, the constant threat of mountain lions and other predators. All of this was capped by the impossibility of crossing a promontory called Windy Point—a place known for its catastrophic avalanches.

Finley was unmoved. The constant presence in his thoughts was the fate of the Greely polar expedition. He was determined that he wasn't going to fail the men of the station the way the relief missions had failed Greely. Nor was he going to let Hazen down. This was his chance to redeem himself after what had happened at the commission hearings.

When it became obvious that Finley was going to go in any case, the mountaineers came through for him with supplies and gear. They had alpine pikes, hunting knives, and revolvers. They also had fresh instruments for the weather station: Finley had a bulky mercurial barometer fastened to his back, while the observer carried an array of thermometers. As a final preparation against the intolerable cold, both men were sewn up into several layers of gunnysacks.

The two set off on muleback. Their mounts were white government mules that proved to be well trained and more competent at mountain climbing than the men. Finley, who had little practice with mules, was relieved to find he could give his mount free rein at any perilous or doubtful point, on the thinnest of ledges or the most fragile of iced-over streams. "I learned to deeply appreciate the wonderful knowledge of these faithful animals," he wrote. He was awestruck at the careful way they tested each path, one hoof at a time, whenever the passage was narrow or risky.

They spent their first night on the mountain at a halfway house with another mountaineer. The mountaineer made his living by supplying the station at the summit with firewood. That was a job that took him all summer: he could only bring the wood up the trail by burro, and each burro could only carry two four-foot sticks. The winter months he spent collecting wood for the next year when the trails were open again.

The halfway house was a squalid and rat-infested den; the rats threw everything off the shelves and ransacked the kitchen supplies and banged at the pots and kettles. They were so agile jumping from tables to shelves that Finley became convinced they could fly, and he spent the night cowering in bed under a pile of buffalo robes, with his head covered for protection. "Sleep was out of the question while these devils were performing," he wrote. But fortunately, "between 1 and 2 a.m. they left the shack, having ransacked every quarter in a vain search for more food, after having devoured the waste from the kitchen and table that was placed where they could easily obtain it."

The next morning they set out for Windy Point. They were obliged to leave the mules behind with the mountaineer and trudge up on foot. The snow grew so deep they were often wading up to their armpits. The weather became increasingly foul. Storms were cresting the mountaintop and spilling down along the slopes; there was thick fog in the ravines and a continuous pelting of rain, sleet, and snow. There were terrifying lightning displays and gigantic echoing booms and crashes of thunder. At one point they were caught in a mysteriously charged snowstorm, where every flake left a trail of cold fire through the air, and their hair and beards and fingertips were emitting endless showers of sparks; a wave of his arms, Finley wrote, "was like the sweep of flaming sword-blades." Meanwhile, as they crept onward, they were constantly listening for avalanches, and they kept their bodies pressed flat against the rock face in hope that they would feel the warning vibration from up the slope.

They were wholly worn out by the time they approached Windy Point. When they stopped to rest, they remained standing and leaning on their pikes, for fear that if they sank to the ground, they wouldn't have the strength to get up again. The wind was growing stronger, and it was thickening with stinging pellets of ice; the two men were cut by the flying ice, and their cheeks and foreheads began bleeding; the blood kept freezing on their eyelids and blinding them. The observer led the way up the last stretch, desperately warning Finley not to lose his balance.

A few yards short of the crest, Finley slipped and crashed to the ground. He didn't have the strength to rise. The observer tried vainly to get him to his feet; that would have been tough under the best of circumstances, given Finley's size, but in the midst of the storm, with both men exhausted, and Finley weighed down even more by the gear he was carrying, the observer found it impossible. He had to stagger on alone; he made it over the crest and down to the station, where he collapsed against the door.

The station crew were astonished to hear the noise; they flung the door open and dragged the observer in. He was able to get out that a second man was still out there at the crest. The crew immediately went out after Finley. They barely found him in time; the furious snow had almost entirely covered him over where he lay, and wrapped in his burlap sacks, he was almost impossible to tell apart from the other boulders heaped along the mountain slope. Only his pike, which he was still clutching upright, let his rescuers spot his position. He was unconscious and half frozen; he came to himself lying on a big office table while the crew frantically rubbed his hands and feet to restore his circulation.

Finley and the observer stayed at the station until the warm weather came in. Finley assiduously collected data from the instruments he'd lugged up the mountain, which he later proudly wrote were found to be hugely useful to Professor Ferrel, back at the Washington City office. The whole rescue mission itself, though, turned out to have been superfluous. "The station force," he wrote, "was found in good health with plenty of food and sufficient firewood to carry them through the winter season. They were greatly surprised to hear of the big excitement of the country as to their alleged desperate situation, and wondered most of all at the successful venture we had made to reach them. The trip was looked upon as quite impossible at that season of the year."

Finley returned to Washington City that summer hoping—maybe even assuming—that he could get back to his tornado work and begin issuing public forecasts. But he found that General Hazen was still worried about the Allison Commission. The commission had adjourned in the spring, while Finley had been in the Far West; its members had taken no actions and had issued no report. But Hazen knew that didn't mean anything. Government commissions ground on, according to their own logic, long after their occasions had been forgotten; Secretary Lincoln was gone from Washington City, but the Allison Commission would go on pursuing his revenge.

There was another problem for the tornado project. Finley had prepared a technical report summarizing his forecasting methods and results, and this had been circulated among the civilian scientific community. The response had been uniformly hostile. Finley's claim of a near-perfect success rate was met with derision. He had arrived at it honestly: he hadn't fudged his numbers; he had taken his forecast maps and added up his daily successes and failures. But it was his method of defining "success" that other meteorologists found preposterous.

Finley's mistake was sheer naïveté: he had given his positive and negative predictions equal weight. This meant that if one of his forecast zones had never seen a tornado in its recorded history, and Finley had predicted that it would not see a tornado on that day, then when there was no tornado, he counted that as a success. He justified himself this way: "It requires as much, and often more, study to say that no tornadoes will occur as to make the prediction that conditions are favorable for their development."

This was doubtless true, but to his critics it was comparable to predicting that the Gulf of Mexico would not dry up overnight and then taking credit for a successful forecast when the next morning it proved to still be wet. His method, according to his critics, needed to be judged primarily on his positive predictions. A reanalysis of Finley's numbers showed that in the test period he had made one hundred positive predictions of tornadoes, and there had been only twenty-eight confirmed touchdowns—a success rate considerably worse than if he had just tossed a coin.

Given all this, General Hazen might have been tempted to cancel Finley's project entirely. But he had one great strength as an administrator: he was loyal to his staff. He believed that Finley was onto something. So he offered a compromise: if Finley was certain that one of his forecast zones was going to see a tornado, then the corps would issue a public warning. But Finley was not to use the word "tornado," for fear it would cause a panic. Instead, Hazen suggested that he call it a "violent local storm."

Finley accepted the deal, and it became the official (though never publicly declared) corps policy from then on. Warnings of "violent local storms" began to be issued, and the observers around the country got to know what that meant—even if the public didn't. How useful they were, though, remained unclear. Finley's positive success rate that summer remained steady at around 25 percent, but his warning areas were so broad that there was no way of knowing the risk for any specific location.

In any case, the arrangement in its original form only lasted a few months. By the end of the summer of 1885, Hazen had been obliged to send Finley on another and longer round of inspection tours. The commission was about to reconvene after the summer recess, and Hazen had learned that now it was going to focus specifically on working conditions at the Signal Corps, based on Finley's revelations in his testimony.

At the commission's public hearings that autumn, several ex-cadets and one current officer came forward to provide critical testimony concerning General Hazen and the corps. The officer, Lieutenant W. A. Glassford, gave a thorough analysis of the military organization of the corps and pointed out numerous technical and practical problems. He was particularly harsh about Fort Myer, which he described as "unmilitary and weakly controlled, perhaps corruptly."

The cadets also talked about Fort Myer. They went into great detail on the miserable conditions there, and they described at length how they had been systematically overworked and mistreated. The drills were interminable; their duties, especially those of policing the fort grounds, were demeaning; the food was unwholesome; and they had to endure constant verbal and physical abuse from their instructors—particularly Lieutenant John Finley.

Some of the complaints would have sounded frivolous to older veterans, particularly those who'd served in the Civil War, but they were heard out by the commission in shocked solemnity. In part it was a reflection of the military culture of the Signal Corps. The corps was drawing its cadets from well-connected families and from elite colleges; these were young men of privilege who had rarely been treated harshly or critically by anyone in their lives. It was not surprising that Finley, a man who appeared to take seriously the traditional ideals of military conduct, would be portrayed in the commission testimony as a short-tempered tyrant, a martinet who had brutalized the cadets by shouting at them when they laughed or reprimanding them for getting distracted while at attention.

Other charges at the hearings were more substantial. The universal complaint was that the food at the camp was poor—not just unappetizing, but sometimes actively rotten. General Hazen was so concerned by this charge that he sent the camp medical officer before the commission to refute it. The officer testified that he had regularly inspected the food and found it wholesome. Unfortunately, he wasn't prepared for the tough cross-examination he got from the commissioners. Under close questioning he admitted that there had been occasions when the meat served to the cadets was spoiled and even maggoty. He was asked if he had rejected it. He had to confess that he hadn't. Why not? He stammered out an unfortunate defense: the cadets hadn't been given a direct order to eat it, so if they found it not to their liking, they could have refused it.

General Hazen himself showed up to testify again soon after that. This time he was angry, and he was defiant, and compared with his affable demeanor the previous winter, he was plainly desperate. The criticisms made by Lieutenant Glassford had enraged him. "Mr. Glassford had never been fully in sympathy with our work," he told the commissioners. "He has never yielded willing and able assistance to the methods of the office, but had always tended, in some degree, to insubordination. He has always been serious and fault-finding . . . He has never been fully efficient as an officer. He has been wilfully neglectful on many occasions."

As for the complaints of the cadets that they'd had to police the camp: "Every soldier in the world has to do policing. I did it when I was at West Point . . . every man at West Point had to do it. Everybody in the whole Army has to do it. It is the same way in every camp." About the food: "Now, with regards to the complaints of those men at Fort Myer respecting their rations, I want to say this. There never was a recruit in the world who did not complain about his rations. It is a sort of acknowledged privilege."

About the cadets' complaints of mistreatment by their instructors he was more conciliatory. It probably was true, he conceded, that the cadets could have been treated better, but that was because of a systemic flaw in the structure of the corps: it wasn't military enough. Men were being promoted because of their scientific or technical abilities rather than their fitness for command. A man like Lieutenant John Finley, he said, might have been excellent at his meteorological duties but had no skill whatever at leading men in the field, and his unacceptable behavior at Fort Myer clearly showed it. Hazen admitted: "I have not had officers of proper experience and tact to put in charge of these men."

All that said, however, there was no reason for the commission to contemplate taking away weather duties from the Signal Corps. "I here state, and I am ready to maintain it, that the work of the Signal Service is not only highly efficient and satisfactory everywhere with people and communities having interests in it, but that not a word has come from them to this Commission, so far as I have ever known, favoring this transfer." The only people who wanted weather forecasting to be under civilian control, he said, were the scientific community, as represented by the recently founded National Academy of Sciences, "who appear to have always wanted to control it." And, of course, there was one other faction: "my personal enemies, who wish to strike at me."

The commission concluded its hearings soon afterward and issued its report with unusual speed. But its conclusions were no surprise. Short-term, the commissioners recommended the immediate closing of Fort Myer. They also recommended the immediate elimination of the Study Room as an unnecessary and impractical expense—as ever with the federal government, the need to appear hardheaded and realistic trumped the necessity of funding basic scientific research. Long-term, they recommended that the Weather Bureau be removed from the corps and transferred to a new civilian agency that should be created in some part of the government other than the War Department.

Lieutenant Finley had remained out of town as the commission finished its hearings and never testified again. He knew he was being kept out of trouble, but he found to his surprise that he liked the job he'd been given. He took well to his duties as an inspector of the weather stations. He was thorough and conscientious. He learned to act quickly to restore military discipline when he found the observers slacking off; in fact, even though he'd entered the corps strictly to do meteorology, he was increasingly finding everything about military life congenial. He also enjoyed the sheer oddity of what he found traveling around America. He arrived in one town to find the weather station empty of its gear: the observer, an inveterate gambler, had had to hock it all to pay his debts. The G Street office hadn't suspected a thing, though, because the pawnbroker kept the gear in his storeroom and allowed the observer to take his readings and file his reports from there.

Finley also liked being an ambassador for the corps. He was a good public speaker, and he was always comfortable giving his standard talk about tornado preparedness. He told his audience about the latest ideas about tornado warnings: someone had proposed stringing telegraph wires around the outskirts of towns, for instance; when a tornado approached, it would break the wires, and a special signal would ring in the telegraph office. He also stressed the importance of digging storm shelters, which were generally known then as tornado caves. The most basic dirt cave, excavated in a yard or a field, deep and wide enough to hold several people, was the safest place to ride out a tornado or other violent weather. And he continued to enlist volunteer tornado spotters; when he returned to Washington City in the summer of 1886, he had accumulated almost two thousand spotters in his network.

But on his arrival he found himself without a job. The first part of the commission's recommendations had already been implemented: Fort Myer had been shut down, and the Study Room, without a home, had been dispersed. There was no question of Finley resuming his work on tornadoes and no indication of when, if ever, that would change.

General Hazen had not been defeated by the commission report. He had reconciled himself to the loss of Fort Myer and the Study Room and was already planning his counteroffensive. He knew he still had two powerful weapons on his side: his friendship with President Cleveland, and the inertia of the federal government. It could be years before any further action was taken on the commission's recommendations. There was plenty of time for Hazen to work out a deal that would keep his corps in the weather-forecasting business, retain its elite status within the War Department, and prevent it from being merged back into the regular army.

His big goal in the autumn of 1886 was to obtain larger housing for the Signal Corps offices. This was a practical necessity, even without the closing of Fort Myer. The corps had expanded during his years as chief signal officer; the Weather Bureau in particular had long since overgrown the office on G Street. The corps had been refused space in the War Department's own new office building and was instead occupying a series of makeshift rented and commandeered buildings scattered around the city. Hazen wasn't the only one who found this situation intolerable. The archive of meteorological records was kept in a warehouse building notorious for its stench: the joke in the corps was that the prehistoric Washington City swamp was seeping up through the basement. Hazen wanted a large new headquarters built for the corps with fireproof rooms for its archival storage. Failing that, he wanted the War Department to rent or buy him an existing building that he could remodel for his long-term needs.

He spent that autumn charging around the city inspecting real estate. He assigned Finley to be his combined chauffeur, bodyguard, personal assistant, and caretaker. This was not a job Finley accepted with any enthusiasm. He knew by then how Hazen had thrown him to the wolves at the commission hearings. But this was another part of military discipline he had absorbed: neither then nor later would he ever publicly speak a word of criticism of his commanding officer. Besides, he didn't have to spend much time in the general's company to see why his help was urgently required. Hazen was dying.

Hazen was suffering from chronic nephritis, which was then usually called Bright's disease. This was a progressive and untreatable form of kidney failure that caused severe back pains, testicular pains, and difficulty breathing. Hazen, it was more and more clear to Finley, was in daily agony and was finding it almost impossible to perform the simplest tasks, but he was refusing to reduce his workload. He wouldn't even admit that he was sick.

In the meantime, he had found the perfect place for his new head-quarters. It was a sprawling house at the corner of Twenty-Fourth and M Streets. In fact it was a mansion, one of the city's showpieces—a mock-Spanish hacienda built around an open court and surrounded by forested grounds. It belonged to a prominent family who'd made a fortune mining in Mexico and who were now going back south to manage their investments. Hazen kept returning to the hacienda day after day and talking excitedly about how he'd remake the interiors and assign all the offices.

He and Finley paid their last visit to the mansion in late December. It was a bitterly cold and stormy day, and the empty building was unheated. Finley later wrote: "I protested with the General that our visit was a very dangerous exposure for him, in fact for both of us, but nevertheless we finished the inspection, in a very thorough manner, including the basement of the structure, as was customary with the General in the performance of all of his duties."

The next day, Finley came down with a severe cold. When he next saw Hazen, he discovered him to be so sick he couldn't get out of bed. He was alone, except for a body servant. His family happened to be spending the season in Europe; he had closed up his lavish mansion (actually his wife's mansion—it was a gift to her from her father) and had taken rooms for himself near the G Street offices. Finley visited him there every day.

At New Year's, Hazen roused himself to attend a formal reception at the White House. The weather was still wretched; that evening the city was hit by a major snowstorm. But Hazen still showed up at the reception in a resplendent full-dress uniform, which he had covered only with a fashionable cape. He was miserably sick. Finley kept worrying at him to take things easy and make an early evening of it. But Hazen, surrounded by the glittering pomp of Washington City society, felt wholly in his element and insisted on staying long past midnight. Finley offered to go back to Hazen's rooms and at least fetch him a warm coat. Hazen told him to stop being so foolish.

At last the reception began to break up. Hazen gallantly insisted on helping several of the most glamorous women into their carriages. The storm was then at its height, and Finley was horrified to see Hazen standing in the midst of the fierce gusts of snow in nothing more than his uniform. He hadn't even bothered to put on his cape. Finley immediately fetched it and tried to wrap it around him, but the winds were so strong that they kept the cape fluttering behind him like a pennant.

The next day, Hazen couldn't bring himself to leave the apartment. The day after, he couldn't get out of bed. The final decline took two weeks. Finley stayed with him, along with Hazen's body servant. When Hazen's death finally came, Finley wrote, it was "agonizing in the extreme." There were times when Hazen was writhing around so violently that it took both Finley and the servant to hold him down.

13

How to Escape

General Hazen's death was the beginning of the end for the Signal Corps's Weather Bureau. Everybody knew that without him as the corps's champion, the recommendations of the Allison Commission could not be staved off for much longer. There was nobody left who could maneuver within the federal bureaucracy as he could, nobody who was as well connected in Washington City society, nobody who was as certain of his own rectitude, and nobody who was as ruthless.

In the meantime, though, the daily work at the grand new Washington City office and the weather stations had to continue. Hazen's successor as chief signal officer was Adolphus Greely—the commander of the doomed polar expedition. Greely had always been Hazen's man and tried to rule the corps with Hazen's style. (One of his first acts as chief was to take on the federal bureaucracy in order to ensure that the survivors and the relatives of the deceased from the Arctic expedition received full military benefits.) But nobody thought Greely was half the commander Hazen had been. Not only did he lack the connections and the fearsome reputation; he just didn't have the heart for it. He was a man perpetually haunted by the sense that everyone was judging him unfairly. He was certain that he would never be free from what had happened on the Arctic expedition. Nobody ever asked him about it directly, but (as he revealed in his letters) he was certain that the dread word "cannibalism" was never far from their thoughts.

But then, Greely had been put in an impossible situation anyway. The Allison Commission had undermined in advance any standing he might have with Congress or the War Department. Sooner or later Congress would act on the commission's central recommendation and remove the Weather Service to civilian control. In the meantime, the

service was being whittled away. Year after year, Greely was faced with
new rounds of budget cuts and demands that he do more with fewer
resources.

But he continued to support his old mentor's pet projects. That
meant he did what he could for Lieutenant Finley. In the spring of 1887,
he put Finley in charge of the new Meteorological Records Division.
This essentially meant that Finley was spending most of his time checking incoming field reports for obvious errors, a job for which he was
profoundly unsuited, but Greely also took the trouble to specify that
the study of tornadoes was still included in his duties.

The problem was that the study had turned into a charade. There
was no budget for Finley to do any field researches, and Greely wasn't
particularly interested in the results anyway. In his first progress report
for the new division, Finley complained that he was simply compiling
the reports from his own spotters network. The reports were coming in
from all over the central prairies and throughout the South, but he was
doing nothing with the data.

At bottom, despite his gesture of support, Greely clearly considered
tornado prediction to be a dead issue. In his report to Congress in the
summer of 1887, he essentially dismissed Finley's forecasting project as
a failed experiment. The problem with forecasting tornadoes, he wrote,
was that any prediction would surely result in a panic, and no prediction could be specific enough about the tornado's likely path to serve as
an effective warning. "It is believed," Greely concluded, "that the harm
done by such a prediction would eventually be greater than that which
results from the tornado itself."

Greely's view was shared by the civilian scientific community. In May
1887, the meteorologist William Blasius gave a speech to the American
Philosophical Society in which he savaged Finley's work on tornado
forecasting and mocked his warnings for "severe local storms." Blasius
asked, "Has the Signal Service saved a single life or any property by
its tornado predictions?" To Blasius the answer was clearly no—and
would remain so, probably forever. Tornado prediction, Blasius said,
"can never be done with any certainty, except in so general a way as to
be valueless." In fact he considered the corps's whole approach to the

study of weather to be a waste of time: "What additions to meteorological science has it ever made? Is there even one valuable result in all its voluminous literature that cannot be found in the prior works of others? If so, where and what is it?"

Finley's only response was to continue making public speeches about tornadoes and their dangers. He assembled a little book out of his talks and his papers and had it published in 1888. The title was *Tornadoes: What They Are and How to Escape Them.* It was a simple and straightforward guide to what was then known about tornadoes. There were nontechnical explanations of the various theories of tornado formation, descriptions of the local weather conditions favorable to tornadoes, and warning signs that a tornado was approaching. The longest and most fervently written section was a detailed plan for constructing a tornado cave, which Finley claimed would offer "*absolute* security to life and limb and *nothing* can *replace* it for that purpose."

The book was published not by the Signal Corps but by a commercial publisher, and the corps took no public stand on the book one way or the other. But the next year, Greely published a book of his own, titled *American Weather,* designed to puff the work of the Signal Corps and its continuing importance to American life. He went out of his way to praise Finley's tornado work. "No other person," he wrote, "can be accorded greater credit for collecting and arranging data respecting these storms."

But this was just another empty gesture. As it happened, Finley was just then engaged in the most impassioned fight about tornadoes he'd ever had, and Greely was about to side with his opponent—somebody Finley worked with every day in the corps's headquarters.

The late general Hazen had been a man passionately devoted to his family—not just his immediate family, but a whole tangled tree of first cousins, second cousins, great-aunts, and great-uncles by marriage. This is how it happened that he had brought into the Washington City office a distant cousin of his named Henry A. Hazen.

Henry Hazen had been born in India, the son of Congregationalist missionaries, but educated in America and sent by his relatives to Dartmouth College. After graduation, he had been appointed assistant professor of meteorology at Yale, under Elias Loomis. He had come to the attention of his august cousin the general early in the 1880s, just as the Study Room was first being set up. The general had sent his chief civilian forecaster, Cleveland Abbe, on a scouting expedition for meteorological talent. Abbe had thought of approaching the famous and well-regarded Loomis, but he then heard through the academic grapevine that Loomis's work was really being done by his assistant Hazen. Abbe interviewed Hazen and quickly concluded he would be the better hire. The general was only too happy to accept Abbe's recommendation and put his young relative on the Signal Corps payroll.

Professor Hazen proved to have a vigorous and original mind. At the Signal Corps he did work on the design of thermometers; he studied the microclimates of urban environments like Chicago; he researched ways of using railroad lines to deduce altitude above sea level. He often gave volunteer lectures on meteorology at local colleges. He took on the editorship of the corps's *Monthly Weather Review*. He published papers on sunspots, on the possibility of lunar influences on the weather, on methods of calculating flood stages of rivers, on the calibration of anemometers, and on the reason for the spectacular sunsets seen all over the world after the eruption of Krakatoa. He was also a passionate advocate for meteorological exploration of the upper air and several times made balloon ascensions to take readings—this was when ballooning was still considered a fairground stunt.

Among the duties that Professor Hazen ultimately took on was assisting John Finley in tornado research. But this proved to be a disaster. The two men were a poor match from the start. Finley was bluff, clumsy, dogged, and overbearing; Professor Hazen was brilliant, cultured, aristocratic, and haughty. Finley's main, if not his only, interest was meteorology; Hazen had many wide-ranging interests, but his deepest enthusiasm was for the genealogy of the Hazen family, which he discussed continually and at length. Hazen did not trouble himself to be anything other than contemptuous toward Finley, and soon they found themselves at war.

Their first skirmish was over a narrowly technical issue about tornadoes. Professor Hazen published a letter in *The American Meteorological Journal* claiming priority for a key principle of tornado formation.
Lieutenant Finley, Hazen noted, had written in one of his papers that
tornadoes formed in the southwest quadrant of a large region of low
pressure. Professor Hazen himself, shortly beforehand, had been quoted
in an article in *The Washington Post* identifying the quadrant as the
southeast. He therefore deserved credit for being the first to identify the
correct quadrant.

Finley found this claim petty and infuriating—and factually incorrect. "Southwest" had plainly been a transcription error, one of many
that dogged that particular paper. He could prove it: several of his earlier publications had specifically stated that tornadoes formed in the
southeast quadrant. He demanded that Hazen withdraw his claim.
Hazen backtracked, but only partway. He published a follow-up letter
in which he asserted a new claim. It was true, he conceded, that Finley
might be technically correct, but Hazen himself still deserved priority,
because of his own "definite mention and emphatic calling attention"
to the southeast quadrant. "Of all the ways of retreating from an inde-
fensible position," Finley countered in his own follow-up, "the method
adopted by Professor Hazen is both unique and original."

Their argument soon broadened out to take in the nature of tornadoes in general. In fact it became a kind of claustrophobic replay of the
great storm war of the previous generation—except that it was conducted over the distance of an office desk, close enough for the combatants to feel each other's breath when their voices were raised.

The grounds of this quarrel were both personal and scientific. Finley
took for granted that he was the corps's tornado expert and that his
views should naturally be taken as settled. Professor Hazen considered
himself the only true authority on the subject—even though, or particularly because, his views were sharply divergent from Finley's, and in
fact from every other meteorologist's.

Hazen was a figure recognizable in almost every bureaucracy: the in-
house skeptic. No matter what the prevailing view was on any issue, he
was certain to take the opposite position and argue it with cool conde-

scension and implacable tenacity. With the subject of tornadoes, Hazen considered his role to be the necessary corrective to Finley's air of certainty. As far as he was concerned, Finley and every other expert had gone off the rails about tornadoes, and it was his job to bring to the subject some long-overdue common sense.

Hazen's working premise was that tornadoes were an exceptionally rare phenomenon about which there was almost no reliable information. He didn't believe that any of the basic facts about them had been established. He had reviewed the history of tornado studies, going all the way back to the works of the principals in the storm war James Espy and William Redfield and had concluded that they had all been thoroughly wrongheaded. There was no evidence of an upward movement of air in funnel clouds, as Espy had claimed; nor was there any evidence that the funnel rotated, as Redfield had believed. So what did the wind do in a tornado, if it neither rotated nor ascended? Hazen thought the question was still entirely open.

He did concede one possibility. He thought there might be something worthwhile in the long-neglected views of the third combatant in the war, Robert Hare. It could be that tornadoes were primarily electrical. One strong piece of evidence, according to Hazen, was the roaring noise so often heard around tornadoes. Hazen didn't think this had anything to do with the inrush of wind; it was more likely to be the sound of an electrical discharge like that of a gigantic generator. He also thought electrical discharges accounted for the mysterious flashes and glows of colored light seen within the funnel. But most important, electricity explained the extraordinary destructiveness of the tornado: as the funnel passed over buildings, it was blasting them apart with lightning bolts.

Hazen refused to accept that there was an area of low pressure at the center of the funnel. He thought it was more likely to be an area of high pressure, and the tornado's winds were in fact flowing outward. (He did not accept that a rapidly falling barometer was a sign of violent weather, either.) He was equally certain that reports of tornadoes half a mile wide or more were nonsense. He suggested that all such reports be "thrown out" from the study of tornadoes. He was aware that there were reliable reports of such storms, the most famous being the mile-wide funnel that had destroyed Natchez, Mississippi, in 1840. He didn't deny that it had happened, but he didn't think it was possible that it was a tornado. It was some other type of storm, possibly a hurricane. His own studies of the subject had proven to his satisfaction that a true tornado was almost never more than a hundred yards wide and that an observer should be able to get within ten yards of it in perfect safety.

Ordinarily, Hazen's views might not have gotten much of a hearing. But they happened to coincide with a backlash against Finley's ceaseless talk of the dangers of tornadoes. Over the previous few years, a number of people in and out of the Signal Corps had been growing increasingly unhappy with the way Finley had been traveling around the Midwest as an authoritative spokesman about tornadoes and other forms of violent American weather. Local government officials in the states and territories beyond the Mississippi, real estate speculators, business associations, and all those involved in the clearing and settlement of the prairies had begun to speak out against the pernicious idea that tornadoes were common in their part of the country and that they posed any significant risk to the population. The head of the Iowa Weather Service, Gustavus Hinrichs, published an article in *The American Meteorological Journal* (which Professor Hazen was then editing) dismissing Finley's tornado researches as fantasies. Most of the tornadoes Finley had recorded in Iowa, Hinrichs wrote, had never happened; "they have never existed outside the archives and publications of the Signal Service." Hinrichs's own researches plainly demonstrated that Iowa rarely saw more than "one real tornado a year." This, he wrote, "is bad enough, and needs no amplification by professional tornado manufacturers."

The corps's own section chief in Oklahoma published a letter in the *Monthly Weather Review* (also edited by Hazen) attacking Finley. "Long-range forecasters, through their ignorant predictions of tornadoes, are causing much unnecessary alarm to the inhabitants of Oklahoma," he wrote. "The constant fear and excitement have certainly a tendency to cause nervous troubles." He was quick to be reassuring to those sufferers: "Not a single tornado has occurred this year, very few in other years, and the Weather Bureau has not as yet issued a single forecast of

'Conditions favorable for severe local storms.'" And yet, because of Finley, "every time a thunderstorm occurs, or a rain cloud appears in any part of the sky, accompanied by even moderate winds, every cave and cellar is filled with frightened men, women, and children." He didn't approve of the use of tornado caves anyway: "This undoubtedly causes more deaths as a result of exposure in these damp places than have been caused by all the tornadoes that ever occurred."

Professor Hazen himself magisterially summarized the situation in an editorial for the *Monthly Weather Review*. "When the Bureau began to collect and publish fairly correct statistics relative to these storms," he wrote, "the sum total of their number and the attendant destruction was so large as to be very impressive." But the calm analysis of these numbers had shown that the dangers had been vastly overstated—twisted by "sensational writers" to give "a most alarming picture of the condition of the atmosphere in this country." It was important, he wrote, that meteorologists "did not join in the popular cry 'beware of the western tornado.'"

On the evening of March 27, 1890, an unusually violent line of thunderstorms came across Louisville, Kentucky. The barometric pressure fell so quickly that the gas streetlamps all over town were snuffed out. Then a rapidly moving gust front knocked down the telegraph wires. A torrential downpour began falling. In the midst of the fury a tornado roared through the heart of town. One witness said it was like a turnip. Another compared it to a balloon lit up from within by orange fire. It was exceptionally powerful and so tightly organized that even though it passed a few hundred yards from the Signal Corps's weather station, the anemometer there barely registered a flicker of rising wind. Because the telegraph lines were down, the observers couldn't send on a warning.

The tornado was only around seventy-five yards across when it was first seen. By the time it had cut through the residential neighborhood in the southwest side of Louisville and crossed into the downtown commercial district, it had swelled to more than half a mile wide. It wrecked warehouses, office buildings, churches, factories, and meeting halls.

Most of the commercial and industrial buildings were empty at that hour, but the meeting halls were packed. The people of Louisville, as was common in the Midwest then, frequently passed their evenings by attending lodges, membership associations, and quasi-mystical orders. Downtown Louisville on that night saw gatherings of the local branches of the Independent Order of Odd Fellows (the lodges of both the white and the black members), the Roman Knights, the Knights and Ladies of Honor, the Daughters of Samaria, and the Sisters of the Mysterious Ten (these two last were lodges of African American women). At every one of these lodges there were injuries and deaths. In one hall fifty-five people were killed. By the time the tornado crossed out onto the surface of the Ohio River, more than a hundred people were dead.

Even though the Signal Corps still didn't make tornado predictions as a matter of policy, it was widely blamed for not giving any advance warning. What made this criticism most painful to Greely and his forecasters in the Washington City headquarters was that they actually had decided to break their own rule and issue a warning. They had been monitoring the progress of the storm system as it crossed Kansas and Missouri, and they had recognized the strong probability that it would spawn tornadoes. At some point during the late afternoon of the twenty-seventh, the situation looked so dangerous that somebody— possibly John Finley himself—had persuaded Greely to issue the old public warning for "severe local storms." But it arrived in Louisville too late to make the evening newspapers. The earlier forecast was still posted around town, as a kind of inadvertent monument to Weather Bureau ineptitude: "The indications for today in Kentucky are fair weather, followed in the western portion by rain, easterly winds, and stationary temperature."

But the corps's reputation took a much worse hit the day after the Louisville tornado. That was when the chief observer for New York City, Sergeant Elias Dunn, took upon himself to warn the people of the lower Mississippi valley of imminent disaster. Dunn happened to be a well-known figure in New York; he was called Farmer Dunn, because New Yorkers thought that only a farmer could care as much as he did about the weather. On March 28, Dunn gave interviews to several newspapers about what had happened in Louisville and what was likely to come. When the tornado had crossed the Ohio River, he said, it had stirred up a gigantic tidal wave that was even now rushing downstream. His best guess was that on April 1 it would reach Cairo, Illinois, at the confluence of the Ohio and Mississippi Rivers, and over the next several days travel down the Mississippi to the delta. He estimated that it would reach New Orleans around April 15. The wave then, he said, would be fifty feet high.

This prediction appalled and outraged the citizens of New Orleans and the lower Mississippi River valley. The corps was obliged to issue a public disavowal of Dunn's views. No such tidal wave had been observed, the corps declared, and none was expected. Dunn had been speaking only for himself and had no business associating such a pronouncement with the corps.

There was one practical result of Dunn's warning and the storm of criticism that followed. Chief Signal Officer Greely was forced to revisit the whole issue of tornadoes and attempt to settle the conflict about them within the corps once and for all. He believed that the most urgent practical necessity was ending the war between Finley and Professor Hazen. He did so by following the example set by his predecessor, General Hazen, whenever Finley got into trouble: he sent Finley away.

Finley was reassigned from the Washington City office to the most remote point Greely could find: San Francisco. There Finley was put in charge of forecasting for the entire Pacific region. Finley proved to be a reliable and popular forecaster who immediately won the trust of San Francisco's newspapers and the public; one of his first public pronouncements was to correctly forecast the end of a severe drought that had been ravaging Northern California. But he said nothing at all about tornadoes: there had, after all, not yet been a single confirmed report of a tornado west of the Rockies.

Back in Washington City, meanwhile, Greely made several public statements about tornadoes. All of them echoed, or even parroted, Professor Hazen's views. Their gist was that tornadoes were not as dangerous as Finley had claimed and as was popularly believed. The official view of the Signal Corps, as articulated by Greely, was that tornadoes were a minor and rare phenomenon that was not worth the resources for extensive study.

It was a bad position to argue. Given the destruction the tornado had left behind in Louisville, Greely's remarks came in for open ridicule and contempt in the press. He was frequently reminded that he had earlier praised Finley's tornado work. So why had he changed his mind? Greely had no answer. But it didn't matter anyway; he was soon forced to backtrack.

The weather that spring and summer proved to be unusually bad across America. In the months after Louisville, several other very destructive tornadoes were reported from the Midwest and the South. There was widespread speculation in the nation's press about why. The general consensus was that the American climate was growing dramatically worse; the most widespread popular theory was that it was caused by the deforestation of the eastern half of the continent. At the end of the year, Greely responded to the public concern by announcing in his report to Congress that he was reopening Finley's tornado research project. But this time he was determined to make sure it would have responsible leadership. Greely wrote: "Impressed with the number and violence of destructive tornadoes during the past year, it is believed that an investigation of phenomena of this kind on their numbers, area devastated, lives lost, and other such information might be of current interest. This work was intrusted to Professor H. A. Hazen, who has given much time and attention to these phenomena."

The morale within the corps grew steadily worse. The staff at the Washington City office was grossly overworked and undertrained. Observers were being sent out into the field knowing only the barest basics of meteorology. Instead of the relentless schooling earlier cadets had undergone at Fort Myer, new graduates were simply handed a copy of Loomis's old introductory textbook on meteorology (now rapidly growing out of date) and told to pick up the subject on the job.

The regional forecasts came out twice rather than three times daily. They covered larger areas and were noticeably vaguer. And, what was more to the point, they were more often wrong. Several newspaper editorials reported a new trend: farmers were giving up on the corps's predictions and returning to the traditional almanacs to get their weather news.

Public criticism of the bureau was becoming routine. "There is of late," William Blasius wrote in the *Proceedings of the American Philosophical Society*, "a growing impression in the public mind that the Signal Service Bureau is degenerating, and is less effective than during its earlier days." Blasius, as it happened, didn't agree—but only because he had never believed the corps's weather predictions were worth anything anyway. An editorialist for Philadelphia's *Public Ledger* was more concerned. Not only was the corps doing nothing to alert people to dangerous tornadoes, but it had recently failed to predict a major Atlantic storm, which the editorialist said was the kind of mistake it would never have made in the old days. (Not true; the corps had never had much luck forecasting Atlantic weather.) The bureau, the editorialist wrote, might be made a useful service again if only it could be "restored to its former 'probability.'" But nothing would improve unless attention was first given "to failures of somebody at the Washington office to do as good work there as the service is capable of doing, or has heretofore been done."

It was in the midst of this public unhappiness that Congress at last took up the recommendations of the Allison Commission. Four years had passed since the report had been issued. The current president, Benjamin Harrison, had already called repeatedly for its recommendations to be adopted and for the bureau to be transferred out of the military altogether. In the 1890 session, the legislation was finally approved. At the end of the following year, the Weather Bureau would be removed from the Signal Corps and placed with the Department of Agriculture, which had recently been elevated to cabinet level.

Where did that leave the military meteorologists of the corps? In limbo. They essentially had two choices. They could remain in the U.S. Signal Service, which was now resuming its original specialties of tactical telegraphy and battlefield communications, or they could go with the new Weather Bureau, which would require them to resign their commissions and become civilian meteorologists.

Lieutenant Finley wanted to remain a meteorologist and had no desire to leave the army. But there was a third option: according to the final congressional legislation, the bureau could retain on its staff four officers as meteorologists with their traditional military rank preserved. Finley was determined to be one of those four officers. He applied to the War Department—only to be torpedoed by his superior officer Greely.

Greely's required annual evaluation of Finley for that year was highly critical. Greely wrote that Finley only had "moderate ability in discussing weather data and to somewhat less degree in weather forecasting." This was manifestly absurd and suggests that Greely was still taking cues from Professor Hazen. Another criticism was more just: Finley, Greely wrote, "is unsuited for any duty involving the control or handling of any large number of men, as he is lacking in administrative work which demands clear, unbiased judgment and breadth of thought." His final judgment was in fact a fairly shrewd assessment of Finley's strengths and weaknesses: "Cannot organize, but is himself one of the most indefatigable workers the Chief Signal Officer has ever known. Fair education; indomitable energy; excellent habits; and will always be a most valuable subordinate officer. Is not successful with his subordinates, as he is apt to be unreasonable in his demands upon their time, expecting from all the same intense application he himself displays."

Finley considered this evaluation to be a personal affront. He was immediately determined to get it overturned. Not only did he have "indomitable energy" on his side; he also had his wife, Julia, who had her own connections in high Washington City circles. On his return from San Francisco, with Julia doing the introductions, Finley privately met with a number of the most influential people in town in order to press his case. His gist was that Greely didn't really know him and in his negative assessments was simply parroting the foolish and unfair things that General Hazen had said in the commission hearing.

This backdoor campaign worked. Over the next year, Finley was granted several new opportunities by the War Department for reviews and appeals of his case. In the end Greely's evaluation of him was tossed. Finley was promoted to first lieutenant over Greely's objections, and the new civilian Weather Bureau formally accepted him as one of their four assigned military officers.

At the end of 1891, the Signal Corps officially went out of the weather-forecasting business. It returned to its original mandate as the army's communication service. Greely stayed on as its commanding officer. It did well under his guidance. During the Spanish-American War, the corps constructed and operated thousands of miles of telegraph wire in Puerto Rico, Cuba, and the Philippines. Later Greely was highly praised for setting up and running an emergency military command in San Francisco after the 1906 earthquake. Greely was perennially successful, but he never lost the sense that his career should have gone better. He was still convinced that everyone he met regarded him with suspicion and distaste. After his retirement, he turned to writing and became a popular author of light history specializing in books about Arctic exploration—without any awkward autobiographical admissions. Shortly before his death in 1935, he was not particularly assuaged by receiving the Medal of Honor.

It did not take long for Lieutenant Finley to realize that his decision to stay on with the civilian weather service was a terrible mistake. The new culture of the place made him instantly uncomfortable. The problems came in with the first civilian chief, Mark Harrington, who had been a professor at the University of Michigan. Harrington had taught astronomy and mathematics, but he also knew meteorology well: he'd founded *The American Meteorological Journal* and was a close friend of Cleveland Abbe's. But he was not an ideal administrator. He was hot-tempered and paranoid, quick to antagonize both his superiors and his staff. He was also intensely suspicious of the military holdovers from the Signal Corps. His particular nemesis was his nominal assistant, Major H. H. C. Dunwoody, one of the oldest survivors of the Signal Corps era (he had been with the corps even before Finley). Harrington was convinced that Dunwoody wanted to depose him and return the bureau to the corps. Soon Harrington was writing a stream of letters to his superiors in the Department of Agriculture like the following: "Dunwoody is a selfish intriguer and a source of discord in the Weather Bureau. I request that the President recall him. We do not need military control of the Weather Bureau."

Harrington didn't like Lieutenant Finley, either. In this case, though, his objections took a more theoretical form. While Harrington himself was a solid and expert meteorologist, he disapproved of the kind of meteorology that Finley had been practicing. He had no interest in tornadoes or other forms of violent weather. In fact, he thought the whole focus of the Signal Corps on short-term forecasting had been a mistake. After all, who really benefited from the prediction of the weather? As far as Harrington was concerned, it was the farmer, and only the farmer. But to the farmer, Harrington wrote, "the problems of the climate have a permanent, while those of the weather predictions have only a passing, interest . . . It is the average weather or climate which determines the agricultural capacity of a region." In other words, it hardly mattered to the farmer whether on one particular day it was going to rain or be sunny; what did matter were the long-term climate trends. As long as Harrington was in charge, that was going to be the principal focus of the new Weather Bureau.

Finley lasted with Harrington's bureau for less than a year. Then he put in for a transfer. But he didn't ask to be sent back to Greely and the Signal Corps—what was the point, after he'd fallen out with Greely so spectacularly? Instead, he requested duties in the regular army. He received the transfer in October 1892, and his career as a government meteorologist was at an end.

14

The Desert Is No More

The great Trans-Mississippi Exposition of 1898 was built at the outskirts of Omaha, Nebraska, between a decaying industrial district and the open prairie. The entrance was a triumphal arch sixty feet high, topped by a group of warriors and goddesses holding aloft the American shield. Beyond was an enormous white promenade. Down its center ran a glittering canal two thousand feet long, spanned halfway down by an ornate bridge and dominated at its far end by an intricate Renaissance fountain. On either side were gigantic exhibit halls, mock-Ionic and Romanesque and Palladian, ornamented everywhere by pseudo-classical statuary and elaborate friezes. There were swans clustering and squawking on the waters of the canal and a fleet of Venetian gondolas, each with a gondolier who spoke with an ostentatious Italian accent and sang Mediterranean folk songs. At night the canal, the fountain, and the pavilions were illuminated by thousands of brilliantly colored incandescent bulbs, as though the exposition grounds were sketched in lines of light.

The exposition was always crowded. There were more than two million visitors over the course of that summer. The visitors swarmed the colonnades and the Midway Plaisance, stood in long lines at the restaurants, exclaimed at the fireworks shows, roared their approval of the frequent patriotic parades. That was during the crisis of the Spanish-American War, and its great provocation—the destruction of the American frigate *Maine* in the harbor of Havana—was recalled by a regular small-scale re-creation of the disaster on the canal near the fountain. At the conclusion of every speech, as the crowd furiously waved small American flags on sticks (for sale throughout the exposition grounds), the thunderous cry would go up: "Remember the *Maine*." On the

Fourth of July, when the speeches and parades went on from dawn to midnight, breathless messengers would run up to the podium and interrupt the speakers with an urgent dispatch: news of a great victory in Cuba. The roar of the crowd could be heard throughout the whole city.

But the great message of the exposition was development, trade, and peace. Exhibit hall after exhibit hall—the Mines and Mining Building, the Fine Arts Building, the Liberal Arts Building, more than a hundred of them in all—told the same story: the heartland now meant spectacular economic growth, inexhaustible natural resources, and a burgeoning civilization. The Machinery and Electricity Building was a continuous roar of motors and turbines, of flashing lightbulbs and popping circuits. There were six hundred exhibits of cultivated fruits, flowers, and grains in the Horticulture Building; the Nebraska exhibit alone took up two thousand square feet. Railroad cars of fresh melons were shipped in by the Texas exhibit and given away to visitors. The Manufacturers Building had seventy thousand square feet of exhibit space and included working factories that made hats, saddles, and bridles; there were bakeries selling their goods out of the oven and a chocolate maker giving away free samples fresh from its vats. At the center of the hall was an electric refrigerator, thirty feet high with double-paned glass sides, displaying dozens of kinds of dressed meats. The Agriculture Building was a labyrinth of garish color; every pillar and arch was hung with riotously colored wreaths and scrolls and festoons and banners made out of grasses and grains. Spears of wheat, oats, corn, barley, and rye were woven into liberty bells, candelabra, cornucopias, hourglasses, and spinning tops. There was an enormous American flag woven of cornstalks. The Great Seal of Nebraska was worked out in thousands of seeds.

On a separate stretch of the exposition grounds was the Indian Congress. "This unique exhibit," the fair's official historian later wrote, "enabled thousands of visitors to see what the government had done for the benefit and welfare of the aborigines." The encampment was around four acres, and over the course of the summer several hundred Native Americans stayed there. They were employed to stage mock battles and hold imaginary tribal councils. On special occasions they re-created the Ghost Dances—the religious rite that had swept through the plains earlier in the 1890s, by which the surviving nations had sought to summon the ancestral spirits of their greatest warriors and drive the whites back to wherever they'd come from. The crowds gathered around the barricades to watch the Native Americans solemnly admit defeat.

As the exposition's president, Gurdon Wattles, proclaimed during his speech of welcome on opening day: "The Great American Desert is no more."

Among the side events held on the exposition grounds, and spilling out through the hotels and meeting halls of Omaha, were conventions. The Retail Grocers Association and the Association of Theatrical Stage Employees, the Association of Railway Telegraph Superintendents and the National Convocation of Bohemian Turners, the Beekeepers and the Scottish Rite Masons, the Pure Food Congress and the National Road Parliament—there were around a hundred conventions, a new crowd of delegates arriving almost every day through the late spring and summer, to talk business and to see the fair. The last convention, as the great events were over and the exposition itself was beginning to break up, was the first annual meeting of Weather Bureau officials.

As everyone at the convention knew, the early years of the civilian bureau had been tumultuous. The first chief, Mark Harrington, had always been difficult, and he had eventually become impossible. He had recently been fired by the secretary of agriculture, and in his place had come Willis Moore, a career meteorologist who had been an observer in the Midwest since the early Signal Corps days—well liked, a competent meteorologist, and a good bureaucrat. He opened the Omaha convention with welcome words: "There are no dissensions at the Central Office of the Weather Bureau. There is harmony there, and that means much to the rest of you." The applause was deafening.

Moore was followed on the speaker's podium by Cleveland Abbe. Abbe seconded everything the chief said about the new harmony in the central office, and he added that the bureau's relations with the Agriculture Department were excellent. He attributed this (with much applause) to Moore himself. He then asked for a cheer to be given for Major Dunwoody, Chief Harrington's old nemesis, who after so many years of service in the central office had returned to the Signal Corps and was now serving in the Philippines. (Harrington himself, showing signs of severe mental instability, had abandoned his family and disappeared soon after he was fired; years later he would be found working at a lumber camp in the Pacific Northwest. He spent his last years in a mental asylum.)

Then the business of the convention began. For the next three days the officials heard and debated papers on improving relations between the Weather Bureau and the public; on issuing weather warnings for the benefit of transportation companies; on the effects of forest clearing on the climate; on whether the bureau's signal flags were the optimal shape; on issuing warnings for lake storms, flash floods, and cold snaps; and on the question "Are changes in the present forms (1053 and 1054) for reporting weekly climate and crop conditions advisable?"

So they went on, as the Trans-Mississippi Exposition closed and the workmen began disassembling the great ephemeral city of plaster all around them and as, day and night, the shoreless sky of Nebraska endlessly filled and emptied with clouds—and not once, in any prepared paper, or in any of the question-and-answer sessions, or in any of the open discussions, did anyone mention tornadoes.

After John Finley's departure to the regular army, the only person left at the Weather Bureau who had gone on taking an active interest in tornadoes was Professor Hazen. Hazen was still, despite the transfer of power and the restructuring of the bureau, the designated tornado expert. He took the job seriously. In the early 1890s he began traveling around the country as Finley had, lecturing business groups and town meetings on the practicalities of tornado preparedness. While his boss, Chief Harrington, had already made plain his lack of interest in tornado research and would have preferred that Hazen do something else (he particularly wanted Hazen to work on technical problems of instrumentation and measurement), the tours were officially tolerated, because Hazen's attitude toward tornadoes proved to be an excellent fit with the new bureau policy. Hazen wasn't an alarmist, the way Finley had been. He reassured his audiences that tornadoes were not a serious problem in the Midwest.

He was especially disdainful of Finley's endless propagandizing for tornado caves. Hazen thought this was nonsensical at best and corrupt at worst; he insinuated, and sometimes said outright, that Finley had been seduced by the insurance industry, which was deliberately cultivating public anxiety about tornadoes in order to drum up business.

Hazen meanwhile had inherited Finley's enormous tornado archive. In his idle moments at the Washington City offices he was working his way through it. He didn't think much of it. He was particularly contemptuous of the reports from the spotters network (which were still coming in, even after Finley's departure)—hundreds upon hundreds of tornado sightings and, as far as Hazen was concerned, all useless, because neither Finley nor his informants had made the slightest effort to distinguish major tornadoes, minor tornadoes, and harmless funnel clouds that hadn't reached the ground. Hazen thought that some kind of classification system was the essential first step to the serious study of tornadoes. Since tornadoes were so elusive, he concluded that the only sensible criterion should be the amount of destruction they left behind. It was an idea several decades ahead of its time, but when Hazen proposed it to his superiors, they dismissed it with barely a shrug and told him that if he had a problem with the spotters network, he should simply discontinue it.

As for the raison d'être of Finley's whole tornado project, the issuing of tornado warnings, Hazen had been and remained thoroughly skeptical. He thought Finley had in fact done about as well at it as could be expected, given the current state of knowledge about tornadoes. The problem was that there were simply too many fundamental questions about tornadoes that were still wholly unknown. Specifically, Hazen wondered about the conditions within the upper altitudes of severe storms. He thought that the only way tornado prediction would ever become a reality was by penetrating the hidden reaches of thunderstorms. He pressed his superiors at the bureau for permission to make high-altitude balloon ascensions in order to take readings. They did agree to that, and in the first years of the civilian bureau he arranged for a few flights, one of them above ten thousand feet. But his initial results were inconclusive, and the flights were soon discontinued. (Their only

lasting effect was to confirm Hazen's own lifelong enthusiasm for ballooning; he began working on a grand scheme for mounting the first
transatlantic balloon flight.)

Despite there being so many unknowns, Hazen did have several
practical proposals to make about tornado safety. He described them in
detail in his lectures, articles, and press interviews. He urged that communities in the Midwest adopt them, because "as the so-called cyclone
belt becomes more thickly populated, disasters from this cause will grow
more frequent." His solutions, he said, were simple, cheap, and sensible.

The first was to plant trees. Hazen shared the general belief that the
rise in the number of tornadoes was due to deforestation. Logically,
therefore, tornadoes must be unable to cut through forests. So if cities
and towns would only cultivate dense thickets of trees on their southwestern perimeter, the majority of tornadoes would be stopped in their
tracks. Alternatively, since, as Hazen believed, tornadoes were primarily
an electrical phenomenon, it should be possible to disrupt approaching tornadoes by means of barrier walls of electrified wiring. But he
believed his best and most practical method of tornado defense was
what he called a tornado trap. He proposed building a line of lookout
stations along a town's western boundary, each connected by wire with
caches of dynamite. "On seeing a funnel cloud approaching," Hazen
explained, "the operator would simply wait until it got near enough
and then touch off the cartridge which would blow it to smithereens."
In fifty years, he predicted, "not a big town in the southwest will be
without a tornado trap."

Professor Hazen's public career as a tornado expert did not last long.
The end came at roughly five o'clock in the afternoon on May 27, 1896,
when a large thunderstorm crossed over St. Louis, Missouri. The storm
was a spectacular apparition. The banks and towers of black and green
clouds were so vast that many witnesses described them as the most
impressive thing they'd ever seen. It spawned a gigantic tornado funnel
that touched down on the hilltop grounds of a hospital complex near
the southwestern city limits. In the twenty minutes that followed, the

funnel blasted through several of the most densely occupied neighborhoods in the city, skimmed across the Mississippi River, and wrecked the
industrial and freight railroad districts of East St. Louis on the Illinois
shore. At least 250 people were killed, probably more; the exact number
was impossible to estimate because of the number of unrecorded boats
sunk when the tornado raked across the riverfront.

In the days after the disaster, Hazen gave several interviews in which
he expressed his sorrow over the deaths and his regret that his plans for
tornado traps had not been adopted. He said that every one of the casu-
alties could have been prevented if only he'd been listened to.

Shortly afterward, the Weather Bureau issued a public statement:
"Certain interviews with Prof. H. A. Hazen, U.S. Weather Bureau,
have recently appeared in the public press, in which the planting of
forests on the southwestern edge of cities and the discharge of dynamite bombs have been advocated as a protection against tornadoes.
It should be clearly understood that the Weather Bureau—using that
term as expressing the collective thought of its Chief and members of
the scientific staff, Professor Hazen alone excepted—does not endorse
the theories set forth in the interviews above referred to. The opinions
expressed and the methods of executing them are Professor Hazen's, and
he alone is responsible for them."

Chief Willis Moore, who had just been put in charge of the bureau
after Harrington's departure, worried that this press release didn't go
far enough. He was in fact immediately determined to put an end to
Professor Hazen's public career. He followed up the press release with a
letter to every newspaper that had published interviews with Hazen or
had even quoted his remarks. It read: "I have to inform you that these
statements were not authorized by the Weather Bureau, and that the
theories advanced are not held by scientific men generally. The interview came from Professor Hazen as a private individual, and not in
his capacity as an official of this Bureau. From personal observation of
the havoc wrought by several tornadoes, I am fully convinced that any
attempt to destroy them by the means suggested will be a failure."

After that, Professor Hazen gave no more interviews on tornadoes.
Moore made plain to him that he was no longer the bureau's tornado

expert. Hazen was to stick to his principal job: forecaster. While the bureau had been de-emphasizing the importance of the forecasts, it still issued them daily. There were now four forecasters at the Washington City office preparing the forecasts for the whole country. Hazen was reassigned to the night shift.

He didn't seem to mind all that much. He took to his nightly duties with amiable good humor. He became an avid bicyclist—there was a great vogue for bicycles in the late 1890s, shortly before the advent of the automobile—and he grew to be a familiar figure around his neighborhood in Washington City, barreling to and from the bureau offices sometime after sunset and just before dawn. He maintained his air of diffidence with the bureau staff. At the Trans-Mississippi convention, his only contribution was a lighthearted paper making fun of the idea that meteorologists would ever be able to make long-term forecasts.

15

The Book of Failure

In the summer of 1899, a man named Lyman Baum sat in the basement den of his house in Chicago, writing the book that he thought would make his fortune. Baum was in his forties then, and he'd already chased after several fortunes. He'd managed theater companies back east, where he was originally from. He'd taken his family into the West, to the town of Aberdeen, South Dakota, where he'd opened up a store called Baum's Bazaar that sold Native American glassware, assorted lamps, wicker baskets, children's toys, novelties from Japan, and "Gunther's Celebrated Chicago Candies." He'd run a newspaper in Aberdeen for a couple of years. He'd moved to Chicago, where he worked as a commercial traveler in fine china and glassware. He also did freelance reporting for several local newspapers. He kept a private notebook of ideas for stories that had been rejected, which he labeled "The Book of Failure."

For a while he ran a trade magazine called *The Store Window,* which was a practical business guide to the latest ideas in retail displays. This was in fact the subject of the book he was writing that summer: its working title was "The Art of Decorating Dry Goods Windows and Interiors." But Baum had never been able to make a go of anything without also jumping at five other ideas at the same time. So as he accumulated the pages of his business guide, he was also trying his hand at a children's book.

This was not on the face of it a promising venture. He had no special knack for writing for children. He wasn't even especially imaginative. But children's books had recently become an extremely popular genre, after the worldwide success of Lewis Carroll's Wonderland books. Baum thought he could cash in. He had published two children's books already, under the name L. Frank Baum (Lyman, a name he'd never liked, seemed all wrong for a children's author)—one called *Father Goose* and another called *A New Wonderland*. Neither one was successful, and the titles are a fair indication of the originality of the contents.

Nor was this new one intended to break fresh ground. Its first pages sketched in the scene as quickly as possible: a young girl on a Kansas farm is carried off to wonderland by a tornado. For the name of the young girl, Baum recalled a grotesque detail from newspaper reports of the famous double tornado that had destroyed the town of Irving, Kansas, in 1879 (the town that had been the subject of John Finley's first field report): the name of one of the victims, who had been found buried head down in a mud puddle, was Dorothy Gale. And as for the name of the wonderland, he got that by looking around his basement den. His gaze fell on his filing cabinet, where there were two drawers. One was labeled A–N, and the other, O–Z.

Baum was not a strong prose writer, and his book can be a tough slog for readers now. The best, and virtually the only, stretch of vivid writing occurs right up front, in his description of the harshness and dreariness of the Kansas prairies. This was something that Baum had known well in his years in the Dakotas:

> Not a tree nor a house broke the broad sweep of flat country that reached to the edge of the sky in all directions. The sun had baked the plowed land into a gray mass, with little cracks running through it. Even the grass was not green, for the sun had burned the tops of the long blades until they were the same gray color to be seen everywhere. Once the house had been painted, but the sun blistered the paint and the rains washed it away, and now the house was as dull and gray as everything else.

(This description may have led the makers of the movie, forty years later, to shoot the Kansas scenes in black and white.)

As for the rest of the scene? It's a blur of generic prose. The worst is the tornado itself. Baum mentions that "it was very dark, and the wind howled horribly." Then the tornado appears: "The north and south winds met where the house stood, and made it the exact center of the cyclone. In the middle of a cyclone the air is generally still, but the great pressure of the wind on every side of the house raised it up higher and higher, until it was at the very top of the cyclone; and there it remained and was carried miles and miles away as easily as you could carry a feather."

This passage suggests that Baum may have been following the ongoing controversies about the nature of tornadoes, particularly the competing theories of Lieutenant Finley and Professor Hazen, without really understanding much of the science. What it does not suggest is that Baum had any idea what a tornado looked like or how it behaved. If he wrote about the prairie from firsthand experience, he wrote about the "cyclone" without ever having seen one.

But that was typical for writers then. Tornadoes were growing in the public consciousness—partly because of great disasters like Louisville and St. Louis, and partly because of widespread newspaper coverage of the appearances of Finley and Professor Hazen. Tornadoes were becoming part of the humorous folklore of the plains states; residents talked with a certain whimsical pride about Texas twisters and Kansas cyclones as though they were personal property. The hero of a comic novel from 1895, *The Adventures of Jones* by Hayden Carruth, travels around the Midwest in a "globular cyclone-house"—a large metal sphere that is bounced from place to place by tornadoes like a soccer ball. Another novel, *A Ride on a Cyclone* by William Ballou, is about an Idaho tycoon who is mysteriously carried by a tornado across the whole country in the course of a single night and is deposited in Manhattan at dawn. The tornado is nowhere described, nobody witnesses it, it leaves no damage behind, but nobody regards its astonishing continental passage with the slightest surprise or interest. It's just the sort of thing that happens out there in the plains.

Today there would no doubt be spokesmen available from the National Weather Service to explain exactly what these authors got wrong about tornadoes; no one bothered then. That was not exactly because the Weather Bureau experts were inclined to be indulgent; it's because the bureau no longer had any tornado experts.

A few days after the start of the new century, a small item appeared in *The New York Times*. Its headline read: "Weather Forecaster Succumbs to Injuries Received in Bicycle Collision with a Negro." Professor Henry Hazen had been careening through the streets on his bicycle as usual, on his way to work, when he'd hit a pedestrian (*The New York Times* apparently thought Negro pedestrians were a menace) and been flipped to the pavement. He died the next day without recovering consciousness.

The obituary notice by Cleveland Abbe of the bureau appeared shortly afterward in the *Monthly Weather Review*. Abbe recalled Hazen's pride in his family—"which includes very many distinguished names in theology, literature, commerce, and military matters"—and identified the Hazen family traits as "great tenacity of purpose, independence of character, boldness in the defence of personal convictions and energy of execution." He also praised Hazen's original contributions to the design of meteorological instrumentation. And he thought Hazen was quite forward-looking in his attitude toward ballooning and upper-altitude exploration, which Abbe thought would be major factors in the future development of weather forecasting.

About other questions, particularly—though Abbe didn't say so—tornadoes, it was harder to be just. "It must be confessed," Abbe wrote, "that a peculiar temperament sometimes led him to beliefs and statements in scientific matters entirely untenable at the present day, but to which he adhered with such pertinacity that to some he occasionally appeared obstinate and headstrong. This was simply a result of the intense earnestness of his own convictions which so completely absorbed his mind that there was no place for further considerations."

After Hazen's death the bureau essentially closed out its interest in severe weather altogether.

The bureau in those years was intent on fulfilling what it saw as its main mission: providing weather information to the nation's farmers. The regional weather stations kept lists of local farmers and mailed them overnight forecasts. In areas wired for telephone service, the switchboard operators would call subscribers with the forecasts each morning. By the second decade of the twentieth century, a few hundred newspapers around the country had begun running daily weather maps. By modern standards the forecasts were only the vaguest of generalities: "warmer," "colder," "stationary temperatures," "dry," "rain," "snow"— that was about as far as they went. They didn't bother to specify highs and lows in Fahrenheit degrees. There was only one type of emergency warning the bureau ever issued: for a cold snap that might seriously endanger a crop.

As for tornadoes—into the new century, no records of tornadoes, not even raw counts of tornado occurrences, were kept by the bureau. No attempts were made to predict tornadoes; the old ban against using the word in forecasts remained the fixed policy. No research of any kind was financed or conducted on tornadoes. A standard reference book on the Weather Bureau published in 1922 (*The Weather Bureau: Its History, Activities, and Organization*) did not mention the existence of tornadoes. A textbook on meteorology published at around the same time, written by one of the bureau's own meteorologists (*Physics of the Air*, by W. J. Humphreys), devoted three sketchy pages to tornadoes in its general chapter on atmospheric circulation. There was only one suggestion for further reading: John Finley's book on tornadoes, which had been published almost forty years earlier.

In 1892, when John Finley departed the bureau, he joined the Ninth Brigade of the regular army. The brigade was shipped to the Philippines early in the Spanish-American War, and Finley served there as a regimental officer until he was invalided home with severe dysentery. (This was a common fate for American soldiers in that war.) When he had recovered sufficiently stateside, he was reassigned to the army recruitment office. He spent the next several years traveling around America making speeches about the success of the Philippine campaign. He returned to the Philippines in 1903, as part of the ongoing American occupation, and there he was appointed military governor of the island of Mindanao.

Mindanao was a large, complex, crowded place. The landscape was a tangle of green mountain ranges, lush plateaus, and dense lowland swamps. The population was a jumble of antagonistic cultures and languages—Christian, Muslim, and pagan, with a heavy Spanish Catholic influence. There was also a new revolutionary insurgency spawned by the American invasion. Finley was stationed in Zamboanga, the largest city on the island. He made frequent travels inland to try to broker peace treaties among the various tribes, who were continually skirmishing with the Americans and with each other. He became a familiar and grudgingly respected figure in the villages of the deep jungle. He was notorious not only because of his peculiar appearance—the fat pale old white man wearing his full uniform in the hottest weather—but also for his fervent sincerity and his casual willingness to trust his life to people who plainly meant him no good. He often traveled alone and unarmed in the jungle, and he would stay overnight in any village that would give him welcome.

Finley approached colonial administration almost exactly as he had his tornado research. He didn't want small incremental successes; he hungered after the big all-encompassing solution. After he'd been there a year, he thought he'd found it. He called a meeting to lay out his proposal. He invited the religious and political authorities from all the settled towns on the island, along with all the tribal chiefs he could reach inland. Their delegations arrived in Zamboanga in a gorgeous parade—thousands of people in armadas of native boats, all draped and festooned in flowers and fabric streamers. They were greeted by crowds blasting away at the *agongs* and *kulintangans* and *lantakas*—the clangorous native drums and weird bell-like trumpets and rocketing cannons. The scene, Finley later wrote, was an "indescribable din" that had a "matchless barbaric splendor."

For the next few days, Finley talked. His scheme was for an enormous central market that would be open to everyone and where all the island's goods could be bought and sold. He wanted it to be held in a new building, not in some arbitrary open space—a substantial building that would draw sightseers from all over Mindanao and the surrounding islands. He cajoled, persuaded, and threatened; gradually, he won some sort of grudging acquiescence from the assembled delegates.

Finley's market took a year to build. It was a vast open-air hall of bamboo pillars and arches and woven fronds. The opening day was a triumph. Finley watched in deep satisfaction. He described the scene later: "Slaves jostled masters, hill people traded with coast people, sworn and bitter enemies forgot their feuds, timid women and children joined heartily in the excitement, new acquaintances were made, new agreements were entered into, new and strange things were purchased for loved ones, and the slave and the peon experienced the first thrills of freedom, and the quickening impulse of self-conscious control, in the possession of that which was lawfully and rightfully theirs, as the product of their own ingenuity and labor."

Finley immediately began traveling around the islands urging everyone to adopt his market scheme. He pitched it as a solution to the old, corrupt colonial system so despised by the people of the Philippines, and, he said, it would also reduce the tensions created by the new American occupation. Several colonial administrators were interested. The American government was impressed. Finley, in recognition of his initiative, was promoted to major.

After a few years, Finley arranged what he hoped would become another Philippine tradition: a great countrywide fair, modeled on the American expositions of the 1890s. It was put on in Zamboanga in 1907. It ran five days, and it featured crafts shows, games, feats of strength, and an assortment of prizes. For years afterward, Finley was delighted to find prize certificates proudly displayed in native houses. The fair ended in a grand dance of previously warring tribes; there were, as Finley was pleased to note, no arrests.

In 1909, supreme military authority of the Philippines was assumed by the famous general John "Black Jack" Pershing. Pershing was a colonial administrator of a different type from Finley. He was contemptuous of the native populations and always on the lookout for the quickest military solution to any political problem. Pershing had once been an instructor at West Point, where he had been loathed by the cadets for his toughness and unyielding military rigidity. Behind his back they called him "Nigger Jack," because he had once commanded a regiment of African American soldiers (the famous buffalo soldiers of the Indian

Wars); the nickname had dwindled to "Black Jack," and it stuck with him for the rest of his life.

Just as soon as Pershing assumed his post in the Philippines, he collided with Finley. He despised Finley's market plan at first sight. Nor did he have any use for Finley himself; he considered him "an old pessimistic windbag of the most inflated variety." Finley was, Pershing wrote, "an impossible person in every way: he is brusque, gruff, overbearing and exclusive." Worse still, Finley, as was his habit, had taken to grossly overestimating his success. He claimed that his markets were taking in millions of pesos a year—a figure Pershing considered absurd.

They were soon at war. But Finley had gotten much better at bureaucratic politics since his old days with the Signal Corps. Pershing soon came to suspect that he was being deliberately undermined; everybody somehow had gotten the idea that Finley was solely responsible for the peace that prevailed on Mindanao. Pershing also suspected that Finley's well-connected society wife, Julia, was bad-mouthing him in Washington's elite circles and was also spreading rumors about him to the press.

Pershing got his chance to strike back in 1913, when Finley went to Washington. Finley was there on a curious diplomatic mission. He was acting as a representative for the Muslim community of Mindanao, and he wanted official sanction from the Islamic authorities of the West for Mindanao's Muslims to cooperate openly with the American occupation. The mission turned out well; in fact some historians rated it as one of the few diplomatic triumphs of the Spanish-American War. But it proved to be Finley's undoing. Pershing used Finley's prolonged absence as an excuse to appoint a new administrator for Mindanao, and he persuaded the War Department to reassign Finley permanently to stateside duty.

Finley accepted defeat. He took the transfer. As a consolation prize he was promoted to lieutenant colonel. He worked at the War Department's shabby warren of offices in Washington, D.C. (the construction of the Pentagon was still a couple of decades in the future). He had a hard time getting used to the city; even after a few years away, it was a Rip van Winkle experience. Its paved and cobblestoned streets were now jammed with hooting automobiles, and there were fantastic tangles of power lines and phone lines and trolley wires looming down over every intersection. Still, he resumed his old round of speech making on the virtues of the American occupation of the Philippines, and he wrote articles for American periodicals about his Mindanao market scheme. His major effort in those years was a scholarly work of ethnography on the Muslim population of Mindanao—a pioneering study that is still cited by anthropologists and historians today.

Finley was promoted to full colonel in 1916. He went on making speeches, but other than that he took no direct part in the run-up to the American intervention in the great European war. He retired from the military in April 1919 after forty years of service.

He was sixty-five then, still hale, and in need of a new career. He naturally thought of returning to meteorology, his first passion. He had never given it up entirely; during his years in the Philippines he had published an article in the *Monthly Weather Review* on the different Asian words for "typhoon." But the Weather Bureau of the twentieth century was no place for him. It had lost all its old schoolboy exuberance. None of the garish characters Finley had known in his youth were still around. The last holdout had been Cleveland Abbe, who had continued with the bureau all through its civilian years (he'd long since stopped doing research on storms; instead, he had worked on improved devices for collecting weather data). Ill health had forced Abbe to take a leave of absence from the bureau in 1915, when he was seventy-seven years old, and he had died the following year.

The new bureau was a somnolent place. Its staffers were timid and colorless drones. They had not the slightest interest in new ideas. Finley had been keeping up avidly with meteorological research, and he was aware of all the exciting new developments then taking place in Europe. A group of Scandinavian scientists had come up with a dazzlingly original method of analyzing weather systems in terms of the clashing edges of air masses, which they called "warm fronts" and "cold fronts" (they'd gotten the idea during the Great War, from newspaper maps of the western front). But the U.S. Weather Bureau would have none of it: it rejected the idea of frontal analysis out of hand and would go on rejecting it for decades.

Finley decided to ignore the government bureau. Instead he tried his luck as a private meteorologist. He reconnected with some of the survivors of his old network of storm spotters, and he made new friends among amateur weather enthusiasts. Through them he got access to a wealth of meteorological records. He was able to build up an impressive private library of statistical data. With that he moved to New York City in 1920, took offices there, and opened up a company he called the National Storm Insurance Bureau.

The bureau was a great success from the start. His first clients were the big insurance companies and underwriters; later he was hired by real estate men, agricultural speculators, and maritime investors. He provided them with risk assessments for tornadoes, windstorms, and other forms of violent weather. He also became a frequent speaker at trade conventions and businessmen's lunches, where he talked about the deficiencies of the government's Weather Bureau and the peril of ignoring the possibility of catastrophic weather events. His message was dramatic and ominous: If nobody was studying, predicting, or issuing warnings, then what was going to happen when the next great tornado came?

16

An Awful Commotion

The Weather Bureau's national maps for the third week of March 1925 showed a large and powerful storm system forming in the Pacific Northwest and dropping down out of Canada. On March 17 the system was rolling through the Great Plains. It reached Kansas by sundown, and sometime toward morning on the eighteenth it was approaching the Oklahoma border.

That was desolate country even in the green season—flat land, a scattering of scrub trees, and nothing at the horizon but the bristling towers of the oil fields. The storms that came down from the north country had nothing to impede their cresting grandeur for hundreds of empty miles. Normally, the storms came through the plains in late spring or summer. But now and then one would arrive earlier, at the beginning of spring, when the wild blackberry bushes were just starting to flower. Such a storm was sometimes called a blackberry storm. The storm of March 1925 was the greatest blackberry storm in generations.

Back in the old days of the Signal Corps, the situation on the weather maps would have immediately led someone like Finley to raise the alarm. The atmosphere in the southern valley was unusually sultry for March; a large body of colder and drier air was moving in swiftly from Canada behind the storm; there had already been very large areas of violent thunderstorms in the northern plains. It was virtually a guarantee of dangerously severe weather around the central Mississippi valley. But the Weather Bureau's forecast for that region on March 18 was typically cautious and tepid: mild weather in the morning, colder by evening.

Just before dawn on the eighteenth, the storm line intensified as it approached the Oklahoma border and a tornado touched down. It was a small tornado and didn't last; it held together just long enough to destroy a gas station on a remote country road outside the small town of Dearing, Kansas. After sunrise the storm crossed through the northeast corner of Oklahoma into the Mississippi Ozarks. This was a wild and inaccessible country. If the storm left any severe damage behind that morning, it went unrecorded—hidden behind high limestone ridges, unseen within remote wooded valleys, the way storms had passed for thousands of years.

By around noon the storm had crossed most of Missouri and had reached Reynolds County, in the southeast. There it was seen by a mail carrier making rural deliveries in the hill country. The carrier was on the road leading north out of the town of Ellington when he glimpsed a strange cloud gliding swiftly through a gap between two hills. The cloud had no distinct shape and was surrounded by a shroud of fog. The mail carrier couldn't imagine what kind of storm it was. But he did later report that he'd heard somewhere in its depths "an awful commotion."

Across the eastern county line from Ellington in Iron County was the village of Annapolis. It was a sleepy place. Most of the townsmen worked at the lead mine and were gone all day; housewives did their shopping early; the children were in school. A stranger walking the silent streets on any ordinary afternoon would think that the place had been abandoned. Along the one commercial strip, the hours after lunch were when the clerks in the law offices and the general store could doze without fear of discovery. A customer who arrived then could count on the uninterrupted attention of any proprietor; a traveler was sure to have the corner restaurant to himself.

At around 1:15 p.m., the streets of Annapolis were enveloped in a thick, smoky fog. Several people emerged from their seclusion to find out why the day had grown so dark. They heard a mysterious sound, a gathering roar, that seemed to be coming from all directions at once.

Then every building in the center of town simultaneously exploded.

Seconds later the fog bank was gone, and a torrential rain was falling. From the wreckage of the houses and office buildings and warehouses, people were staggering out into the streets, screaming for help, collapsing helplessly, wonderingly touching the shards of wood or metal that had impaled them. Others, apparently uninjured, were standing in the midst of the soaking rubble and staring obliviously into the distance. Debris was raining down everywhere: roofs that had been torn off from houses, bricks from disintegrated walls, beams that were like tumble-weeds of splintered lumber. There were nearly a hundred houses in Annapolis, and only seven of them were still intact.

As the survivors shook free from their daze, they found themselves spellbound by an apparition: the biggest house in town, an old-style gabled mansion, was still upright and untouched in the middle of the ruin. But as they watched, they could see smoke and flames begin to flower from the roof. A party of rescuers crashed through the front door and began searching the ornate interior rooms. They found the mansion's inhabitants on an upper floor, gathered around the sickbed of the family matriarch, all unaware of what had happened outside. The rescuers herded the family downstairs and carried the old woman out to the sodden, debris-choked street just in time.

Meanwhile, the strange fog bank was sweeping onward. It skimmed the small mining town of Leadanna and destroyed a third of the houses there. Then over the next hour it traversed the wilderness country west of the Mississippi River. The land was still largely unknown, and the storm went unobserved. But when investigators later traced out the damage track in the deep forest, they saw unmistakable signs that at the interior of the fog bank had been two gigantic funnel clouds moving side by side.

At around 2:30 in the afternoon, the storm emerged from the Missouri hill country and rapidly churned across the Mississippi to Illinois. Seventy-five minutes had passed since the storm had crossed over Annapolis, which meant that the cloud was moving at more than sixty miles an hour.

The area of Illinois on the far bank was known as Egypt. No one knew where that name had come from. One story was that a traveling preacher in the early nineteenth century had compared the lush, rolling landscape to the Land of Goshen, the paradisial region of Egypt that the Pharaoh had given as a reward to Joseph. Many people evidently agreed with him; the maps of the region were speckled by names out of Egyptian history: Thebes, Dongola, New Memphis, Karnak, Cairo.

But Egypt was a place with its own culture—generally isolated from both north and south, with its own preoccupations, customs, and slang. Drugstores were called jelly joints, and after school the kids would say they were going to go jelly. In the evenings the kids played Go, Sheepy, Go and Annie Over. They had their own ball game, where the teams would stand on either side of a barn and use brooms to knock a ball up across the roof; this was called Over the Rainbow. There were the Catholic kids and the Public kids (called that because the Protestant kids went to public school); they would stand on opposite sides of the street that divided their neighborhoods and yell insults at each other: Catlickers and Puplickers.

In early 1925, the outside world seemed particularly remote. All the talk in Egypt was of a local gang war that involved bands of bootleggers, the police, and the Ku Klux Klan. The shifting allegiances among the players were as complex and fractured as the medieval wars of the Guelphs and Ghibellines. In some towns the Klan had taken upon itself the job of enforcing Prohibition (many Klansmen regarded alcohol as a European and Catholic vice); they had their own jails and detention camps where they were holding bootleggers they'd arrested in house-to-house searches. The gangsters, meanwhile, controlled several Illinois counties outright and guarded them like fortresses. Everyone in the region had become used to the dread noise of gunfire in the distance. When the strange cloud came through Egypt, many people took the commotion for the sound of yet another gun battle.

The cloud reached Murphysboro, Illinois, shortly after 2:30 in the afternoon. Murphysboro was a town of around twelve thousand people. At the local school, the kids were woolgathering toward the end of a hot day of classes, just before the final bell, when the streets outside darkened with fog. Many of the kids suddenly began complaining of intense earaches. Then the kids near the windows cried out: all the buildings along the block were disintegrating, and the clouds of debris were streaming straight up like chimney smoke. Violent gusts of wind came shrieking down the school hallways. The principal was running from room to room pounding on doors, yelling for the building to be evacuated. Some of the teachers found that their classroom doors couldn't be budged: the air pressure in the hallways had fallen away almost to nothing. The principal and the teachers who could began herding the kids outside—directly into the heart of the storm. That was when the building caved in on itself.

The fog engulfed the town. Block after block of houses and factories and storefront buildings erupted. Water mains burst; gas lines detonated; the streets were bombarded by burning debris. In the space of a few minutes, more than 150 square blocks and ten thousand buildings were destroyed.

The cloud crossed out of Murphysboro and moved northeast through open country. The landscape was hilly and broken there. But a few people managed to get a good look—travelers on the remote roads, passengers on distant trains. They were all stunned by the sight. No one reported a funnel cloud or anything they could recognize as a tornado. The cloud was a dense black billowing ball rolling over and over on the ground, with bands of sickly yellow lightning sizzling around its circumference and vast blurred shrouds of fog spreading all around it.

Town after town, all the way across Illinois, the same events repeated. The fog appeared in the streets; the roaring rose from all directions; and the buildings were gone. In the mining town of West Frankfort, the heart of the storm passed directly over the mine entrance, and the conglomeration of buildings around the shaft—the hoist and the tipple and the feeder and the towers—all vanished in an instant. This was in the middle of the afternoon shift, and the miners deep underground had no idea what was happening. They heard a weird wind spring up within the inner chambers of the mine, and then all of a sudden every loose stave and pick and lantern and brace and ax and coal wagon rose up into the air and went hurling in a flying tumult toward the main shafts. The lights all went out, the elevators and the conveyor belts stopped, and the power lines went dead. The miners had to ascend by foot through the darkness, up a rough-hewn emergency passage, all the way back to the surface.

When they emerged into the late-afternoon sunlight, they found their town was gone. Hundreds of houses had been destroyed, the land scoured down to the foundations, and the families that survived were wandering helplessly through the traces of where the streets had been. Even the heaps of debris seen in other towns were missing; almost all of it had been carried off by the cloud and was raining down on the earth miles away.

There had been a storm like this once before: the great mysterious tornado of 1805 that had cut its way through the forests of southern Illinois and had left the endless windroad behind. The 1925 storm followed almost the same track and lasted just as long. It crossed from Missouri through Illinois into Indiana, hour after hour, through the course of the afternoon. It didn't come to an end until some time after four o'clock, somewhere in the Indiana farmland. There witnesses reported that it destroyed itself in the open country in a vast collision of dissipating and undulating funnel clouds.

It was called the Tri-state Tornado, and its damage track of 219 miles is still the longest on record. The Tri-state Tornado is also the deadliest tornado in American history. The 1805 tornado had been as powerful a storm, but its path had taken it through the uninhabited wilderness country; by 1925 the landscape of southern Illinois had been cleared and occupied. The fantastically lush world of southern Illinois that had once been called the American Bottom had been supplanted by an endless clutter of mines and factories and farms. The Tri-state Tornado crossed small mining towns and new industrial towns and old agricultural market towns strung out in skeins along the tangles of the rail lines. In its wake nine hundred people were dead.

By late afternoon the news of what had happened was spreading out from eastern Missouri and through Egypt and out into Indiana. The storm had been so peculiar, so tightly organized, and so swiftly moving that in many towns its passage had almost gone unnoticed outside the areas of immediate destruction. In Murphysboro and West Frankfort, people on the opposite side of town had heard and seen nothing at all; they weren't even aware anything had happened until they saw the smoke rising from the dozens of raging fires.

The rescuers converged erratically, without plan, with no idea what had happened or what kind of help was needed. Their ignorance was compounded by the destruction of the phone lines and the telegraph lines. Special trains bringing medical personnel and supplies began arriving along the tornado damage track after dark; the engineers were uncertain what towns to make for, and they often found the rails destroyed or buried in debris. The rescue work was also hampered by the weather, which was turning bitterly cold. Snow was falling along parts of the damage track by midnight.

Over the next few days and weeks, the Red Cross arrived with food and other supplies; tent hospitals were set up in public squares; the Illinois Public Health Department was vaccinating people for typhoid. People all over Egypt were already calling the tornado God's judgment on the gang warfare. Even those less sure of God's role were concerned that the gangs and other undesirables would somehow find a way to take advantage of the chaos. There was a public announcement in Murphysboro two months after the tornado: "Women and girls are asked to stay off the streets by city and county officials due to men of all character swarming into the city since the tornado. These are men of character such that they have no respect for women."

Egypt today has no direct traces of the Tri-state Tornado. But it remains a pervasive presence in the region's history—particularly the long, unrelieved decades of economic depression and physical decrepitude that followed. An oral history of Murphysboro published in the 1990s was called *When the Whole World Changed*—changed for the worse, and changed because of the tornado. The tornado was blamed for everything from the decline of local industry to a widespread rabies epidemic that followed in the summer of 1925. Nobody knew what a tornado had to do with rabies. It was really just a way of expressing the belief that the tornado had opened up a wound that could never be healed.

PART IV

THE MYSTERY OF SEVERE STORMS

17

Canvas and Cellophane

The USS *Shenandoah* was the first large rigid airship built in America. It was a monstrous construction: almost seven hundred feet long, and filled with more than two million cubic feet of helium. It was an immense undertaking even to inflate—particularly then, since in the 1920s, helium was extremely scarce and expensive. (It was extracted in small quantities from the natural gas fields of Texas and the Oklahoma Panhandle.) The helium was contained within twenty enormous fabric bags that were suspended from the frame within a spiderweb of wire braces. Beneath the bags, running the length of the airship, was a keel corridor that held the crew's quarters, galley, food lockers, and oil tanks for the propellers. The propellers and the control car (for the captain, navigator, pilots, and engineers on duty) were lower still, attached by metal struts to the underbelly of the ship. The entire ship was encased in a cotton sheath coated with a brilliant aluminum adhesive paint that could be seen from miles away.

By 1925 the *Shenandoah* had already made one transcontinental voyage. This was a grand soaring tour through the South and the Southwest, up the West Coast, back south again, then a swing around the Rockies, and then northeast across the plains and through the Ohio valley. The crew of forty-three, together with a reporter and an artist from *National Geographic* magazine, watched with dreamy euphoria as the great vistas unfolded below them: the endlessly meandering track of the Rio Grande, the shifting tans and grays of the scrublands, the oceans of the prairie pieced out into farmland and crisscrossed by new networks of dirt roads—and everywhere, in cultivated fields and at rural gas stations, in the parking lots of roadside diners and the public squares of market towns, people staring upward in astonishment as the vast silver airship glided puttering over their heads. The trip was such a success that the army immediately proposed an even grander voyage: due north across Canada, to take part in the latest Arctic expedition. But there were too many worries about its stamina in polar conditions. Instead, it was sent out on a more colorful and amiable expedition: a tour of state fairs in the heartland.

The airship departed from its base in New Jersey on September 2, 1925. Its top speed was seventy miles an hour; the weather was good, and it was able to keep up a decent clip all day and into the evening. By midnight it had crossed Pennsylvania and was passing into Ohio. The air was growing still and sultry. The crew found the conditions ominous, but the forecast from the Weather Bureau was reassuring: continued clear and calm through the night. The ship's commander, Captain Zachary Lansdowne, made the decision to trust the bureau forecast and continue on. He retired for the night to his quarters.

Around 3:00 a.m., the crew in the control car spotted lightning on the northwestern horizon. Then the airship began to be buffeted by strong winds out of the northwest. Lansdowne was summoned to the control car. He took one look at the sky and immediately ordered a change of course.

The airship took a wide turn toward the south. It moved away from the storm through clear air, with the Ohio countryside spread out below. It was a placid scene—the headlights of a few cars and pickup trucks moving along the winding roads, the lights of a town (it was Cambridge, Ohio) in the middle distance. But the air around the ship grew turbulent again. The skies ahead and behind were muddy with clouds, and the winds were growing stronger. The airship's forward progress came grinding to a halt in a flood of contrary winds. The storm was closing in. The airship had no escape route open; it was simply going to have to ride out the storm.

Around 5:00 a.m., the airship was engulfed by the forward edge of a gigantic, horizon-to-horizon squall line. Immediately within the billowing wall of clouds the airship encountered a swiftly ascending convection column. The ship was caught and was buoyed upward at high speed. The crew members began a frantic release of helium. They managed to level off at above a mile up. But too much helium had been released, and the ship had lost its buoyancy; the moment the ship drifted out of the convection column, it began a rapid dive. Now the crewmen had to release ballast (several thousand pounds of water) as the ship took its sickening slide. They were able to pull out of the dive and bob up into a zone of calmer air at around three thousand feet. But there was still nowhere for them to go. They were surrounded by the steeps and cloud canyons of a raging thunderstorm. They drifted helplessly into another big convective column, this one with strong rotating winds. The airship was sucked into an ascending current so powerful its nose was pulled almost vertical.

The crew knew that this ascent was one the ship couldn't survive. As it shrieked up the column, it began to twist. The rotating winds were inexorably pulling its midsection apart. The crewmen could only grab hold of whatever fixed objects were in reach and hang on. They watched in horror as the vast latticework of steel struts and cables that held the rows of helium gasbags in place began to disintegrate. The silvery exterior sheath bent, bulged, and finally ruptured: great gaps in the skin opened up to the storm. The bow and the stern pulled away from each other, and the ship tore in half. Two crewmen lost their grip and fell out through the widening gap into the titanic, lightning-lit abyss. As the heavier stern section began to descend, its still-attached cables yanked the control car out of the struts that kept it bolted to the bow section. The control car swung loose; its weight pulled all the cables out with it, and they tore away from the engines at the stern. Then the whole tangle went tumbling to the earth. All the trapped men in the control car—the captain and eleven crewmen—were killed in the crash.

The two halves of the airship sailed free from each other. The stern section floated out of the convection column and began a slow meandering descent through the lower depths of the storm. Twenty-two crewmen were still aboard that section. Within a few minutes of rain-lashed, wind-buffeted chaos, they were jarred by a shattering impact: the stern had come down in the open countryside. Then it began skimming and bouncing along the ground, pushed by the fierce rainy gusts at the surface. There was a tearing collision with a stand of trees; the branches ripped another gaping hole in the skin, and four of the crewmen were hurled out to the ground. They were badly bruised in the fall, but they all survived. The stern bounced several hundred yards forward into a shallow valley. Once it was out of the winds, it sank in a heap into the muddy ground. The eighteen crewmen still aboard were all alive. They emerged cautiously into the rainy predawn air, where they were met by a party of local farmers awakened by the fearsome commotion.

Meanwhile, the bow section, once it was freed from the control car, was carried upward by the convection column into the higher reaches of the storm. There it drifted in wide slow circles at the top of the column, among billowing cloud tops and above long crackling and booming trails of lightning. Seven crewmen still clung helplessly to their perches in the wrecked latticework. The storm continued to rage below them, while the sky above was lit up by the gathering dawn. After almost an hour of circling, the crewmen were able to reach the release valves of the surviving gasbags. They began a cautious descent.

The wrecked bow coming down out of the clouds was a spectacular vision: a gigantic ragged tube trailing silvery shreds of its skin. The crew began shouting and waving to the farmers who were emerging into the dawn to marvel at the sight. One farmer caught a rope that was dangling down from the ship and tied it off around a tree trunk; the bow bobbed and tugged, but the line held, and the crewmen began hopping down to the earth. They seized more ropes and got the bow lashed. Then they and the farmer took turns shooting at the exposed gasbags with pistols and rifles until the wreck finally deflated.

The blame for the *Shenandoah* disaster was universally laid on the Weather Bureau for failing to predict the thunderstorm; some smaller measure of blame went to the ship's captain for believing the bureau. In all the critical editorials, the ruling assumption was that the bureau's forecasts had never been particularly useful or trustworthy. What was new was the belief that accurate forecasts mattered.

American society was becoming more mobile. That was the time when the first commercial aviation companies were carrying passengers and cargo around the country. The army was expanding its Air Corps and establishing new air bases. And there were flocks and schools of private planes popping up everywhere; some manufacturers of private planes were encouraging their use for suburban businessmen to commute into the city. All these aviators required for their own safety specific, localized, and detailed weather forecasts. All of them were consistently appalled at the vagueness and uselessness of the bureau's product.

The army's pilots were so frustrated by the bureau forecasts that they began lobbying the army command for a forecasting system of their own. They were successful: the Signal Corps was tasked with providing detailed weather forecasts for military aviation. Not forty years after the Allison Commission and the power struggle over military versus civilian control of the National Weather Service, the corps was back in the weather business. By the end of the 1920s, it had weather stations at most of the major air bases on the East Coast and through the heartland.

Civilian aviation companies had to be more ingenious. They developed their own networks of weather spotters. The system was simple: a pilot flying a long route would periodically land in a convenient town, find the nearest telephone, and place calls down the line to his list of spotters to ask them what the weather was like where they were. It was far more useful than listening to bureau forecasts. The most celebrated aviator of the age, Charles Lindbergh, was one of those most openly contemptuous of the bureau. In a quickie memoir published immediately after his first transatlantic flight, he made a particular point of saying that he always flew "paying almost no attention to weather forecasts." They were so unreliable, he said, that "I do not want to condition my mind with them."

Bureau officials could hardly be oblivious to these sorts of insults, and in the wake of the *Shenandoah* they did make some efforts at modernizing their approach and engaging with cutting-edge research. Their most daring move was to bring in a young and brilliant meteorologist from Sweden named Carl-Gustaf Arvid Rossby; he was hired to set up a meteorological service for civilian aviation and to train the staff meteorologists in the latest European ideas. Rossby's specialty was the study of air masses and weather fronts, concepts that the old-school staffers at the bureau had been resisting for more than a decade. They complained that his methods of frontal analysis would require hundreds of new weather stations just to obtain enough data; Rossby told them that they hadn't needed data before because they were obviously just making their forecasts up.

Rossby lasted at the bureau barely eighteen months. He went off to a professorship at the Massachusetts Institute of Technology. There he would become famous among meteorologists for his studies of global atmospheric circulation and the jet stream—the meander waves he discovered in the jet stream are now called Rossby waves—and for his reanalysis of the role the Coriolis force plays in violent weather. Rossby would also offer a conclusive refutation of an idea that had been around since William Ferrel: that tornadoes were affected by the Coriolis force. The violent rotation of the tornado, Rossby's work showed, is not related to the rotation of the earth; it's caused by the interplay between the tornado vortex and the angular momentum of the inflowing winds, a phenomenon now known as cyclostrophic balance. (Technically speaking, the ratio between inertia and the Coriolis effect is now quantified by "Rossby numbers": the high inertia of a tornado gives it a high Rossby number; hurricanes are Coriolis-driven and have a low number.)

The bureau missed out on all of this. But then, it had no use for Rossby's ideas generally. The staff meteorologists continued their old methods of forecasting as though Rossby's time with the bureau had never happened. It would require another ten years, a new chief, a new head of research, and a new generation of university-trained staff meteorologists before the bureau was finally brought to acknowledge the existence of warm fronts and cold fronts. But this was about par. One estimate made in the 1920s was that the minimum length of time it took the bureau to approve and implement any change in policy, no matter how minor—even upgrading to a better brand of thermometer—was seven years.

An automobile left behind
by a tornado in Omaha,
Nebraska, circa 1913.
(Library of Congress)

The great tornado at St. Louis, Missouri, and East St. Louis, Illinois.
Newspaper panorama of the catastrophic 1896 tornado. (Library of Congress)

John Park Finley in later life.
(Library of Congress)

William Hazen, chief signal officer
of the U.S. Army. (NOAA, Wikimedia Commons)

Adolphus Greely, survivor of the
polar expedition and successor
to Hazen in the Signal Corps.
(Library of Congress)

Fig. 135. — Two Views of the same Tornado at Goddard, Kansas, May 26, 1903, about
4 P.M. (No barograph disturbance was noticed at Wichita about 18 miles distant.)

A pair of early tornado photographs, untypical because
they haven't been heavily retouched. (NOAA)

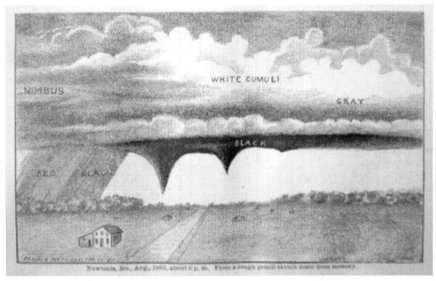

A sketch of tornado development, from John Park Finley's 1887 book, *Tornadoes*.
(Finley's *Tornadoes: What They Are and How to Observe Them, with Practical Suggestions
for the Protection of Life and Property* [1887], p. 23)

"After the Blow." In a cartoon by Udo J. Keppler,
men emerge from a shelter after weathering the tornado
of "November Elections." (Library of Congress)

Wreckage of the USS *Shenandoah*. (U.S. Naval Historical Center)
(Historical Marker Database, Jessica Tiderman/J. J. Prats)

A Kansas tornado, from a stereoscopic print.
(Kansas Historical Society/Foundation: Kansas Memory)

An exceptionally good early-twentieth-century tornado photograph from Kansas.
(Kansas Historical Society/Foundation: Kansas Memory)

E. J. Fawbush and Robert Miller in the Severe Weather
Warning Center at Tinker Air Force Base, early 1950s.
(American Meteorological Society, NOAA)

The bureau might have done as well to look at older ideas. If it wasn't comfortable with young hotshots like Rossby, it could have taken some inspiration from the earlier generation of meteorologists like John Finley. He was still around and still dispensing advice to anyone who'd listen. He had made a go of his National Storm Insurance Bureau for years; by the late 1920s, he'd expanded its scope and was dealing more and more with aviation companies and underwriters who wanted data on the weather-related risks of air flight. Finley himself, though he was in his late seventies, was spending almost all his time on the road, traveling around the country to do field reports on the causes of airplane crashes.

The Weather Bureau did ultimately get in touch with him—but only out of nostalgia. It was compiling a historical archive and soliciting memoirs from all the old survivors of the Signal Corps days. Most responded with a few brief and jovial paragraphs about the wild old days in the frontier weather stations, the camaraderie in the Fact Room, the dangers of signal work during the Indian Wars. Finley wrote page after page. His old obsessiveness about detail hadn't slackened; three times he withdrew his submission, saying he wasn't satisfied with it, and he rewrote it to make it longer.

Finley remained vigorous well into his eighties. During the Great Depression he moved full-time into aviation work: he closed up the National Storm Insurance Bureau, moved back to his hometown in Michigan, and opened a new business, which he called the National Weather and Aviation School. He was the principal instructor. He gave lectures on applied meteorology, theoretical meteorology, climatology, and his new specialty—practical weather forecasting for civil aviation. He was as strong and lively as ever. When his beloved wife, Julia, died in 1934, he remarried a few months later. He didn't retire from teaching at his school until 1939. He died on November 24, 1943, at the age of eighty-nine.

Finley's chief legacy could be seen throughout the Midwest and the plains states: the tornado caves. They were known more elegantly as cyclone cellars; sometimes they were called storm cellars, by those who didn't want to be reminded that tornadoes existed. They had become common sights in rural Oklahoma and Nebraska and northern Texas. They could be glimpsed in a farmhouse backyard, a few dozen feet from the kitchen—a plain wooden door set at an angle in a low mound of grassy earth. Below was a simple but sturdy excavation, large enough to hold a table and chairs and a couple of cots; there'd be a shelf with a lantern and a supply of matches, and from the late 1920s on there'd usually be a radio. Families would sit and tell stories through the roar of the night, parents forcing joviality, children fearfully cradling a pet or a doll, waiting to see if their house had been blown to flinders and everything they owned scattered a mile downwind.

But cyclone cellars were rare sights in cities, even at the heart of the tornado zone. People believed they were safer from tornadoes in a city than they were in the open country (a belief that persists today). They also believed that tornadoes didn't cross rivers and couldn't go into valleys—ideas that were left over from the previous century and wouldn't be refuted by the Weather Bureau for decades more. The bureau in those years was still silent about tornadoes. People in general knew less about tornadoes than they had in Finley's time. Nothing about tornado safety was taught in public schools; a common theme in stories from tornado survivors was that they had no clear idea what a tornado was and didn't understand what was happening to them.

In the popular imagination, tornadoes remained an unseen, vague, surreal, almost comical menace. In a Mickey Mouse cartoon from the mid-1930s (*The Band Concert*), Mickey is sucked up into a tornado and does a kind of slapstick ballet with the flying debris in the middle of a funnel cloud as an entire house is randomly assembled and disassembled all around him. A similar scene appeared a few years later in the movie version of *The Wizard of Oz*: as Dorothy Gale rides the tornado out of Kansas, she sees weird apparitions out the window—an old woman knitting in a rocking chair with a cat on her lap, two men in a rowboat, other Kansans swept up into the funnel cloud who are comically carrying on their ordinary lives as though nothing has happened.

But *The Wizard of Oz* was also the movie that put the most effort into creating a plausible image of what a tornado looked like. The tornado was an elaborate mechanical effect: a thirty-five-foot-tall canvas sock suspended from a moving gantry; it was partially filled with fuller's earth to create a realistic wreath of dust around its base, and there were big sheets of cellophane laboriously arranged to create believable shadows of clouds. The result was nothing like the feeble throwaway description in L. Frank Baum's original novel but a stunning vision of dread. Whole generations of Americans would remember it as the most vivid image of a tornado they'd ever seen.

On September 29, 1927, a tornado passed through St. Louis and killed 80 people. On March 21 and 22, 1932, there was an outbreak of tornadoes through the Deep South as a storm system passed from Texas through to South Carolina; more than 300 people were killed. On March 14, 1933, a tornado cut through the heart of Nashville, Tennessee, killing 11 people and shattering the windows in the state capitol. On the evening of April 5, 1936, a tornado destroyed the residential districts of Tupelo, Mississippi; houses on Gum Pond were carried into the water, and the pond was filled with bodies. Close to 250 people died, maybe more: no accurate count was made in the black neighborhoods. One of the survivors was a fifteen-month-old infant: Elvis Presley.

The Weather Bureau was keeping records of tornadoes again. It was also funding some research on upper-level conditions, using weather balloons. But mostly it was letting the tornado stories accumulate, just as it had in John Finley's time. In the bureau's *Monthly Weather Review* there were occasional reports of unusual and bizarre tornado events, presented without commentary. The May 1930 issue, for instance, contained an account sent in from the Dodge City, Kansas, office of a tornado witnessed by a local farmer named Will Keller. Keller said that on an afternoon in June 1928, he saw what he described as an "umbrella-shaped cloud" in the southwestern sky. As it approached, he could make out three tornadoes dangling from a greenish-black base. By the time he got his family into the cyclone cellar, one of the tornadoes was passing directly overhead. Keller looked up from the entrance to the storm cellar straight into the interior of the funnel cloud.

"Everything was as still as death," he said. "There was a strong, gassy odor, and it seemed as though I could not breathe." Then he heard "a screaming, hissing sound"; it was coming from around the base of the funnel, where smaller tornadoes were forming and breaking free. Above them was a great whirl of rotating cloud streams, crisscrossed by lightning bolts, that opened up into a vast cathedral of clear air. In its upper reaches was a small hovering cloud, rising and falling and pulsing like a heart.

18

The Unfriendly Sky

The Pantlind Hotel, in downtown Grand Rapids, Michigan, was a huge old Beaux Arts hulk of brown brick, with pale stone arches and an ornamental cornice. In 1943 the army commandeered it, moved out all the long-term guests, and shipped in several hundred army air-force cadets. The cadets slept there each night: the luxurious beds in each room were replaced by standard army cots. They had their meals in the lavish dining halls, which had been made over as much as possible into cafeterias. After breakfast each morning the cadets were marched in squads through the glamorous lobby, across the street, and into the city's Civic Auditorium, where they were trained to become meteorologists.

By the end of the 1930s, the U.S. Army Air Corps had almost two hundred men with at least some basic knowledge of aviation meteorology. But with the onset of the war, as the Air Corps rapidly swelled into the mammoth U.S. Army Air Forces, with tens of thousands of planes and hundreds of thousands of personnel, the need for trained meteorologists became urgent. American air bases were going up all over the world, and each required a fully staffed weather station. The Grand Rapids instructional school, together with several other ad hoc schools set up throughout America, would ultimately graduate more than twenty thousand weather officers.

The director of the Grand Rapids school was Colonel Don McNeal. He was not remembered fondly by the cadets. He made sure the school was punishingly difficult. The classes ran for seven hours a day, every day but Sunday. In the evenings, after an hour of physical training, there was a compulsory two-hour study period monitored by officers and senior cadets. McNeal was also known for his spectacular temper. He fought constantly with his superiors about academic standards and

the school curriculum: he was determined to turn out genuine meteorologists, while they were, he felt, satisfied with any warm body. But he
reserved his deepest rages for the civilian Weather Bureau. There was
supposed to be a general spirit of civilian-military cooperation then, as
everyone pulled together for the war effort, but McNeal despised the
Weather Bureau men who were being brought in by the Pentagon as
administrators, instructors, and advisers. He thought they were insuf-
ferably arrogant about their superior meteorological knowledge and
looked down on his cadets with contempt.

His cadets actually felt something similar about him. He was notorious for sneaking up behind them in the study period, peering over
their shoulders at their workbooks, and then berating them for their
mistakes. At graduation, as the cadets waited in line for their diplomas,
he would pace back and forth in ill-disguised fury until he couldn't
stand it any longer, and then he would yank out of the line the cadets he
thought didn't measure up and flunk them on the spot. Ultimately, he
only allowed slightly more than half of any class to graduate. The cadets
came to call him Sudden Death.

Among the first graduates at Grand Rapids was a cadet named Robert
C. Miller. He was from Southern California originally. His family had a
prosperous business selling sashes and doors, but his own ambitions ran
elsewhere. He'd attended Occidental College in Los Angeles; he'd gotten married there and was planning on becoming an algebra teacher. At
the time of Pearl Harbor he was taking classes in differential and inte-
gral calculus. The draft board rejected him because he was overweight
and out of shape and had unusually poor eyesight. He was determined
to serve anyway and tried four times to enlist; he said he only succeeded
the fourth time because the army physicians got tired of seeing him
waiting in line.

After Grand Rapids he was sent to the South Pacific. He was stationed on bases in Netherlands New Guinea and the Philippines. He
moved with the Air Corps as its bases went up on island after island. He
came in after the construction battalions had done their work—landing

in force, cutting metaled airstrips into the deepest jungle, erecting hangars and barracks and mess halls and officers' clubs where there had been impassable swamps. It was a matter of only weeks before planes were buzzing in and out like wasps.

Miller liked the camaraderie of the corps, but he remembered the islands as impossible challenges for a meteorologist. He had nothing to work with—no spotters network, no meteorological data, no model in general for the behavior of the vast weather systems of the Pacific. He had to find his own way to master his craft. He did it by learning from the enlisted men who'd already been serving in the South Pacific for years. They knew nothing about meteorological theory, but they had picked up countless rules of thumb and weather signs that let them read the sky and the ocean.

He also learned to trust his own intuition. He had a knack from early on of being able to visualize weather not as a flat map but as a three-dimensional process. This was a style of thinking that had been encouraged by one of his professors at Occidental who'd taught him to understand physical processes like ocean waves as evolving dynamic systems. The instructors in Grand Rapids had also helped him by teaching him the latest European theories of meteorology and forecasting (still regarded with some caution by the civilian Weather Bureau), which emphasized the complex and shifting patterns of upper-air flow. All this enabled him to make good guesses about the weather that was gliding over the archipelagoes and the open waters of the Pacific. He got into the habit of drawing his maps freehand, at the last possible minute, to make sure the pilots always had the latest data. This was a skill that would awe civilian meteorologists when they encountered Miller after the war.

Miller himself had no doubt about what would happen to him once the war was over. He was never going to go back home and take over the family's sash and door company. ("I couldn't see that business as a life-long proposition," he wrote in his memoirs, "and unfortunately it caused a great rift between my dad and me.") Many of his fellow meteorologists were going into the civilian world; some were even joining the Weather Bureau, which he found unimaginable. He had inherited from old McNeal at the Grand Rapids meteorological school a contempt for the bureau that he never lost. But then, he had acquired through his training and his service a certain contempt for civilians generally. He was determined to stay on in the military as a weather officer.

Tinker Air Force Base, on the outskirts of Oklahoma City, had been built as a depot and staging area during the war. It had grown into an enormous sprawling complex covering nine square miles. It was essentially an autonomous city with hundreds of buildings and thousands of personnel; by the early postwar years it had become the largest single employer in the state. In 1948, among its other functions, it had become a vast parking lot for surplus military aircraft. Hundreds of planes left over from the war were being stored there—kept in fenced airfields, wing to wing, like puzzle pieces on a limitless board.

The great meteorological challenge for the base weather station was in predicting severe storms. These were a major issue not only for pilots in flight but for all the matériel being stored out in the open; a brief hailstorm could do hundreds of thousands of dollars' worth of damage. There was also the threat of tornadoes; the base had never seen one, but that didn't mean there hadn't been close calls. The year before Miller arrived, a disastrous tornado had crossed through central Oklahoma. This tornado had been almost two miles wide, and its damage track was more than a hundred miles long. It had leveled the city of Woodward, Oklahoma, and killed more than 150 people; the funnel had blasted through an industrial complex and sent a storm of blood-red toxic mud falling for several miles downwind.

Miller, though, was not initially inclined to take the weather in Oklahoma particularly seriously. He later said that he'd assumed it was essentially no different from the weather in his home in California, where people made a great show of alarm over showers and fogs; certainly there would be nothing as dramatic as the typhoons he'd seen in the Pacific.

On the evening of March 20, 1948, Miller was on duty at the base weather station. The station was in the Operations Building, a low squat construction near the control tower. The twilight air was warm and placid. After dinner, Miller and his backup forecaster, a staff sergeant, did a routine analysis of the current weather maps. They had surface maps, which were built up from civilian and military weather stations around the Midwest, and they also had upper-air data supplied by the Weather Bureau in Washington. Miller concluded after a few minutes that there wasn't much happening. The prairie was quiet, except for some strong surface winds blowing across the empty country to the southwest. He wrote out his nightly forecast for the base: dry weather, with gusts up to thirty-five miles per hour.

Shortly after 9:00 p.m., as Miller and the sergeant kept an idle watch on the military Teletype, they saw reports from other Oklahoma weather stations of lightning strikes out in the remote prairie. Around 9:30 they did something that would become an automatic routine for any meteorologist but was then a novelty: they checked the radar.

Radar was one of the great meteorological legacies of the war, even though its connection to the weather had been wholly accidental. The British scientists who had done the first experiments with a prototype military radar system had been troubled by strange signals on their monitors: here and there, amid the blips of aircraft they were tracking out to sea, were faint, transitory blobs and glows of no known origin. These phantoms were dismissed as interference patterns or mechanical failures—except that they didn't have any detectable cause. Only gradually did the scientists realize that the radar was picking up the echoes of falling rain.

The Allied military didn't make that much use of the discovery during the war. But afterward, the weather stations at U.S. Air Force bases began salvaging the radar units from old aircraft. The radar at Tinker AFB was from a disused B-29. It was cranky and erratic, and the weather officers tended to leave it off as much as possible to coax more life out of it. But it was unusually powerful, with a range out to near a hundred miles. When the monitor lit up, Miller was dismayed to see bright blobs strung out along the southwestern limit of the screen. This was a line of fully mature thunderstorms crossing the empty Oklahoma prairie directly toward them.

By 10:00 p.m. the line had reached Oklahoma City's civilian airport, seven miles to the southwest. The weather station there transmitted its report—torrential rain and wind gusts up to ninety miles an hour. A few minutes later came an urgent bulletin: a tornado was on the ground south of the airport and moving rapidly to the northeast.

Miller was still new to the Midwest. and found the drama of a severe weather warning excessive. He did know, or at least had been told, that he should immediately take shelter when a tornado was approaching. But he didn't think of it; instead, he ran outside to watch.

By then the storm was lighting up half the sky, and its towering crest was directly overhead. In the glare and flash of the lightning he could see the awesome silhouette of the tornado funnel. Miller always remembered how large and monstrous it was: a titanic flickering shape looming over the base. As it swept past the control tower, all the windows simultaneously shattered. The staff, too astonished to move, were seriously cut by flying glass. All the windows of the Operations Building blew out, too, and Miller flattened himself against a blank wall as the clouds of glass rained down on the parking lot. The funnel roared on through the row of airplane hangars along the edge of the airfield. Then it crossed onto the field itself, where the planes were parked. The tornado destroyed more than thirty planes before melting away into the darkness near the fences at the far side of the base.

A plane landed at the base airstrip early the next morning. It was a priority flight from Washington, D.C., and it was bringing in an investigative board of five senior officers from the Pentagon. They spent an hour touring the damage track through the base, which was then being swarmed by repair crews and cleanup crews. Then they found an office for themselves and summoned Miller and his supervisor, Major E. J. Fawbush, to explain just how the air force could have lost more than ten million dollars' worth of aircraft in under a minute.

Miller sat miserably in the waiting room before the hearing began. It was hardly fair, he repeated to himself, that a California kid like him could have been expected to understand Oklahoma weather. He also had a more constructive excuse ready. He believed that he had been led to make the wrong call in his evening forecast because he hadn't realized how untrustworthy the upper-air data supplied by the civilian Weather Bureau was. His mistake, as he put it in his memoirs, was that he hadn't been "astute enough" to grasp that civilian meteorologists as a class were worthless. He grew so impassioned on this point as he waited to be summoned before the board that Major Fawbush had to tell him to lay off and let him do the talking.

But the hearing itself turned out to be a mild and perfunctory affair. Major Fawbush gave the board a summary of the night's events. He stressed how difficult it had always been to predict tornadoes, and he provided a brief history of, and rationale for, the civilian Weather Bureau's ban on tornado warnings. He did not mention Miller's complaint about the upper-air data, much to Miller's fury. He explained to Miller after the hearing that he wanted to avoid picking a fight with the bureau that would be of no use to either side. Miller grudgingly acquiesced.

The board members considered the matter over lunch. In the afternoon they came back with a report exonerating the weather officers. The tornado was an act of God, they ruled, and "due to the nature of the storm it was not forecastable given the present state of the art."

They did inevitably have recommendations. They wanted the air force's weather officers to collaborate with the civilian Weather Bureau in order to devise procedures for predicting tornadoes and issuing tornado warnings. This idea was, as the saying went in government circles, a nonstarter, and the board probably knew it. The Weather Bureau really did look down on the military's weather officers, just as Miller darkly suspected, and any spirit of cooperation they may have felt during the war had long since melted away.

More realistically, the board ordered Tinker, and all the other air force bases in the Midwest, to devise and implement emergency preparedness plans in the event of a tornado. Tinker's base commander, General Fred S. Borum, immediately seized on this last idea. That same afternoon, almost as soon as the board's plane was back in the air for Washington, he had operational teams at Tinker working out procedures for the rapid securing of aircraft and other base matériel. He also ordered Miller and Fawbush to come up with a practical method for making tornado forecasts.

Borum knew nothing about the sorry, centuries-long history of failed tornado prediction. He didn't think there was any reason Miller and Fawbush couldn't come up with a workable method in a matter of days. The two weather officers couldn't think of a good way of telling him he was wrong.

So, the next morning, they began an immediate ad hoc double-overtime seminar on the nature of tornadoes.

They didn't have much to go on. The only known authority on tornadoes, even then, was John Park Finley; his book from 1888 was still the standard reference. There were a handful of research papers in the scientific periodicals; the Weather Bureau had also been doing some statistical studies of tornado occurrences and severity. But not a single book had been published on tornadoes since the 1880s.

The most substantial work that Miller and Fawbush could draw upon had been done by the military. The Pentagon had commissioned a major study of midwestern weather during World War II. This had been a practical necessity: the vast industrial structure of the war had taken over much of the prairie. The military had deliberately scattered bases and factories and industrial sites throughout the midwestern states as a way of helping the regional economy recover from the Depression and the Dust Bowl years. But the appearance of so much military construction had led to a growing public anxiety: Was it dangerous? What would happen if a tornado struck a munitions plant? The workers in the plants themselves were particularly jumpy. The appearance of black clouds in the southwestern sky was sometimes enough to have a plant's warning sirens sounded and for everyone to run for the emergency shelters.

The Pentagon study concluded that the real danger of a tornado setting off a munitions explosion anywhere was vanishingly small (though it still recommended the organization of a tornado spotters network, just in case). But in order to reach this conclusion, the authors had to assemble a substantial body of research on what was and what was not known about tornadoes, and it was this that Fawbush and Miller devoured. Most of what they read was not essentially different from the ideas John Finley had worked with in the previous century, when he'd first set out to predict tornadoes. The stress was still on the clash between warm humid air at the surface and an overrunning domain of cooler air aloft. Tornadoes appeared when this atmospheric tension became catastrophically unstable. But what triggered the formation of the tornado's violently rotating funnel cloud? It was still a complete mystery.

One recent piece of research particularly fascinated Fawbush and Miller: there appeared to be a correlation between tornadoes and upper-air wind shear. This made sense to them. The old idea, dating back to William Ferrel in the nineteenth century, was that the rotation of tornadic storms was caused by the Coriolis force; this had been disproven by Rossby. But there was no doubt that the interior of a severe thunderstorm was a chaotic environment where winds were moving violently in contrary directions. If a rising convection column were continuously deformed by wind shear—no matter where or how the shear originated—it would begin to rotate, and this could be the genesis of the tornado funnel. Fawbush and Miller then set out to collect every surface and upper-air weather chart they could find that recorded the conditions when tornadoes had touched down to see if they could locate consistent evidence of wind shear.

By the end of their three-day immersion, they took stock of what they'd come up with. Fawbush didn't think much of it. They had some promising leads for research projects, particularly on conditions in the upper altitudes. They had a number of rules of thumb they thought could be used as the basis for a general guide to forecasting tornadoes, based on the observation of vertical instability and upper-air wind shear. But they hadn't cracked the mystery.

Except that Miller thought he had. At least he'd had a kind of intuition. He couldn't quantify it. He couldn't even describe it clearly—then or later. Fawbush, reviewing the same data, was never able to work out exactly what Miller thought he saw. But looking at all the charts, Miller had gradually evolved a sense that the forces at play in the atmosphere took on a characteristic shape just before a tornado descended. And when, on the morning of March 25, the two men prepared to show their results to General Borum, Miller suddenly became aware that the map for that day's weather was uncomfortably close to the pattern in his mind.

General Borum was something of a weather buff himself. He wasn't an expert meteorologist, but he did know the basics. He was also good with the station's old radar unit; he was often able to tweak it back to life after the weather officers had given up. Whenever bad storms came over the base, he liked to hang around the weather station and watch the melting glows of rain drift across the monitor screen. When he showed up at the weather station on the morning of the twenty-fifth, he took a look through the rules of thumb they had worked out over the last few days and had no trouble understanding them.

But what about Miller's intuition about the day's data? Borum then inspected the weather map. If he fully comprehended what Miller was talking about, he didn't say. Instead, he simply asked whether they were thinking of issuing a tornado forecast.

That was a bad moment for Fawbush. He took refuge in vagueness. He would only say that Miller was right about one thing: the day's map did look like the map from five days earlier.

Borum didn't press the point. He let Fawbush off the hook by asking when they would be sure.

There was a silence. An honest answer from Fawbush would probably have been "Never." As far as he knew, nobody had ever tried to predict a tornado for a specific place at a specific time, and he was positive that he did not want to be the first. Miller, meanwhile, was in fact quite sure of the forecast already, but he didn't have the nerve to speak up.

Borum tried again: When was the tornado likely to arrive?

That much Fawbush was willing to commit to. If it happened at all, it would come in with a storm front that was then beginning to take shape to the southwest. He said he could predict the movement of the front easily enough: the crucial hour for the airbase would be between 5:00 and 6:00 p.m.

Borum told them to make the late-afternoon forecast for severe thunderstorms. It would at least flag the possibility of violent weather and trigger the first phase of the base's new disaster preparedness plan.

Miller and Fawbush spent all that afternoon reading the reports coming off the Teletype. The line of severe storms had duly formed and was moving to the northeast. Conditions across the prairie were deteriorating in advance of the front. The winds were rising, cumulonimbus clouds were sprouting, a squall line was gathering strength. General Borum stopped by the station again around 2:00 p.m. He asked when the squall line would reach Tinker. They told him that it was right on schedule and would hit around 6:00 p.m. Then Borum asked the same question again: Were they going to issue a tornado forecast?

Fawbush tried the same answer: "It sure does look like the last one."

Borum told Fawbush he was sick of his sounding like a broken record. If they really believed they knew what they were doing, he said, then they had no choice but to issue the forecast.

Then Miller spoke up, but unexpectedly he urged caution. He pointed out that the chance of two tornadoes hitting the base inside of a week was beyond astronomical. Besides, he reminded the general, nobody had ever issued an operational tornado forecast before.

"You are about to set a precedent," Borum answered.

Fawbush reluctantly wrote out the forecast. Miller typed it and sent it on to base operations. It was formally issued to the base just before 3:00 p.m. After the general left the weather station, Miller remembered, he and Fawbush remained where they were, sunk in gloom, certain they were about to become laughingstocks. Miller was sure the blame was going to fall on them rather than on General Borum. "We couldn't win," he later wrote, "and the General couldn't lose." After all, what would happen when the forecast turned out to be a bust? "I figured General Borum wasn't about to say, 'I made them do it.' More likely it would be, 'Major Fawbush and Captain Miller thought it looked a great deal like the 20th—ask them.' I wondered how I would manage as a civilian, perhaps as an elevator operator. It seemed improbable that anyone would employ, as a weather forecaster, an idiot who issued a tornado forecast for a precise location."

Meanwhile, all over the base, in response to the forecast, work crews were guiding the aircraft into hangars, moving cars and trucks into garages, policing the grounds for stray objects. The air controllers were directing incoming planes to divert to other bases. As 6:00 p.m. approached, and the western sky was flickering with lightning, the controllers shut down the tower and moved to shelter.

Fawbush and Miller were still reading reports from weather stations. The line of storms was continuing its stately progress across the prairie toward Oklahoma City. But these still appeared to be ordinary spring thunderstorms. There were no reports of hail or high winds—much less any sightings of funnel clouds. The mood in the station grew funereal. The two men decided that they had only one chance to save their reputations: the national commander of the Air Weather Service might take mercy on them if only the thunderstorms were bad enough. "At this point," Miller wrote, "we would settle gratefully for a brilliant lightning display and a wind gust to 30 or 40 mph." At 5:00 p.m. the squall line passed over the Oklahoma City municipal airport: the report there was light rain, a scattering of pea-size hail, and wind gusts of a paltry 26 miles per hour.

It was the end of Miller's shift; he couldn't bear to stay on any longer, and he went home.

Miller lived in Midwest City, a suburb that had sprung up between Tinker and Oklahoma City. It was a low sprawl of shopping centers, ranch houses, and light-industrial factories. From his back patio Miller had an unbroken view of the southwestern skies. When he got home, he stood there for a long while watching the storm approaching. He told his wife, Beverly, what had happened. "She was reasonably sympathetic," he wrote, but he didn't feel even remotely consoled. Instead, "I sat down to aggravate my depression systematically." (By which he appears to mean that he started drinking.) Shortly after 6:00 p.m., the squall line passed over the base and neared Miller's house. Miller walked back out onto the patio. The sky was darker than he'd expected. Some areas of the cloud deck were agitated, and there were small white clouds darting beneath the base of the thunderhead. Then the rain started falling. He went back inside. His wife had turned on the radio. "I was in another part of the house," he recalled, "but I caught the words *destructive tornado* and *Tinker Field*."

His first thought was that the newscast was some kind of garbled replay from earlier in the week. "Good grief," he thought, "they're still talking about last week's tornado—but why break into the news?" He picked up the phone to call the base weather station. The line was dead. He felt "a strange unbelieving excitement." He told his wife he was going back to the base.

It turned out to be a tough expedition. The streetlights were out, and there was storm debris strewn all over the highway. He came to the base entrance to find a scene of chaos. Power lines were down everywhere; emergency floodlights had been brought in, and they were sweeping erratically across the endless pavements, revealing vistas heaped with wreckage.

Miller threaded his car slowly through the blocked streets of the base until he arrived at the weather station. The Operations Building was dark. Fawbush was standing outside the front door, smoking a cigarette. His mood, as Miller later described it, was "jubilant." He eagerly recounted what had taken place after Miller had left for home. When the main force of the squall line had come over the base around 6:00 p.m., he had gone outside to watch. Just above the southwest fences of the base, he saw what looked like two thunderclouds coming together and rotating. The sky around them turned greenish black. An enormous wing of a B-29 went sailing up languidly toward the clouds and disintegrated in midair. Then the funnel cloud descended.

The funnel was there and gone inside of a minute. Many planes that hadn't been securely braced were destroyed, but the total damage was barely half of what it had been a week earlier, and there were no injuries at all among the base personnel. That alone made Borum's tornado disaster plan a spectacular success in the eyes of the Pentagon. Fawbush and Miller were "instant heroes," Miller remembered. "In my case," he wrote, "the rest of my life would be intimately associated with tornadoes and severe thunderstorms."

On March 25, 1949, exactly one year after the operational forecast, Fawbush and Miller put out a second tornado warning. This one was for a large area of eastern Oklahoma south of Tulsa and east of McAlester.

They issued the warning at three in the afternoon. At nine in the evening, two tornadoes were spotted on the ground northeast of McAlester. A month later, on April 30, Fawbush and Miller issued a forecast for tornadoes in an area within thirty miles on either side of a line from the town of Altus to south of Tulsa. Thirteen tornadoes came down in eastern Oklahoma, and ten of them were within or close to the warning area. A week later, another forecast, for an area between Amarillo and Lubbock, Texas: two tornadoes touched down there. And another nine days later, for an area between Amarillo and Gage, Oklahoma: a very large and violent tornado touched down and destroyed a veterans' housing development with more than 170 units. Seven people died and eighty-two were injured.

These forecasts were all kept confidential. They were classified documents issued through the military's own communication network for the benefit of base personnel only. Fawbush and Miller didn't attempt to make them public. Public forecasting was the exclusive business of the civilian Weather Bureau. But they were quickly growing uncomfortable with their position. On the one hand, they didn't want to be court-martialed for leaking classified documents; on the other, they didn't want to be held responsible for civilian deaths because they'd failed to warn people of imminent danger.

Besides, the forecasts were beginning to leak out anyway. Military people in the know were calling their relatives and warning them if they were in a threat area. Discreetly, and only with the tacit sanction of their superiors, Fawbush and Miller began notifying certain civilian authorities like the Red Cross and the Oklahoma Highway Patrol whenever they issued a new forecast.

The results were only to be expected. A rumor began to spread through Oklahoma and its neighboring states that the air force had a secret method of predicting tornadoes. There was an immediate public outcry. As it happened, there was already a rumor circulating that tornadoes in the Great Plains were increasing in number and severity due to the nuclear tests in the southwestern desert. The idea that the government might be withholding knowledge of when and where these sinister new tornadoes would strike led to newspaper editorial campaigns demanding full disclosure and urgent congressional inquiries to the Weather Bureau about why this secret method wasn't being made public in order to protect the people of the heartland.

The Weather Bureau's response was halting and confused. It'd had little to say in public concerning the rumors about nuclear testing, other than to issue rote dismissals of the whole issue as nonsense. (The Pentagon hadn't commented at all; it maintained a solemn silence about everything involving America's nuclear arsenal.) Now, faced with this new flurry of criticism, it made some gestures at dealing with the question of tornado forecasting. In July 1950, the head of the bureau, Francis Reichelderfer, sent a memo to all its offices concerning the long-standing forecasting ban. The memo didn't so much lift the ban as wish away its whole existence. Reichelderfer urged the bureau's regional offices to remember that they had the authority to issue tornado forecasts whenever they deemed it appropriate. Also, he wrote, "Weather Bureau employees should avoid statements that can be interpreted as a negation of the Bureau's willingness or ability to make tornado forecasts."

Meanwhile, a meeting was arranged between senior Weather Bureau meteorologists and the team of weather officers from Tinker AFB. There Fawbush and Miller laid out their provisional tornado-forecasting guidelines in detail and explained their success with their operational forecast. The delegation from the Weather Bureau listened politely and then rejected the whole presentation out of hand.

The delegation didn't believe, first of all, that the success of the operational forecast had been anything more than a lucky guess. And as for the follow-up warnings issued by Fawbush and Miller—those struck the meteorologists as worse than useless. The meteorologists pointed out that unlike the operational forecast, the later warnings had been not for an exact geographic point like an air base but for very broad and vague areas of the Great Plains. And yet, even so, when the near hits outside the prediction zones were discounted, their accuracy rate had actually been less than 50 percent. So Fawbush and Miller's method would not lead to the issuance of clear advance warnings to specific communities. And that, as far as the bureau delegation was concerned, made the whole business a waste of time.

The effective position of the bureau remained exactly as it was. Despite its own chief's determination that the bureau do otherwise, no bureau forecaster was willing to take the risk of issuing a tornado forecast. The head of forecasting at the Washington, D.C., office even gave an interview in 1952 in which he declared that the policy would never change. "It is impossible," he said, "to pinpoint a tornado by forecast."

Fawbush and Miller remained at the Tinker Air Force Base weather station for the next few years after the operational forecast. The station was renamed the Severe Weather Warning Center and given specific authority to predict tornadoes and other violent weather for military bases across the Midwest from the Ohio valley to the Rockies. During its first year of operation, the center issued 156 forecasts, and there were confirmed tornado touchdowns in or near 102 of its warning areas. In 1956 the center was transferred to Kansas City. Fawbush retired; Miller stayed with the center for another twenty years, first as a senior officer and then (after mandatory retirement from the air force) as a civilian forecaster in the Pentagon's employ.

Miller's contempt for the Weather Bureau was not without its justice. In the years that followed the showdown between the bureau and Tinker's weather officers, the bureau began a reluctant progress toward tornado forecasting, but it seemed determined to go about it in the most self-defeating manner possible. When a TV weatherman in Tulsa, Oklahoma, took it upon himself in 1951 to issue an on-air tornado warning, thus demonstrably saving many lives, the immediate response of the bureau was to demand that he be arrested. "Warnings for the general public," the bureau said, "are, by law, a function of the United States Weather Bureau." (Eventually, it let the matter quietly drop.)

But its attitude began to loosen. A 1954 book, *Tornadoes of the United States,* by the bureau meteorologist Snowden Flora (this was the first book on tornadoes published in America during the twentieth century), gave a cautious but favorable summary of the tornado-forecasting guidelines worked out by Fawbush and Miller—exactly the same guidelines that the bureau had rejected a few years earlier. It also explained carefully why Fawbush and Miller's now-famous tornado warnings were intended for the military and couldn't be distributed to the general public. However, the author wrote, there was no need for the public to be concerned, because the bureau was now in constant communication with Fawbush and Miller; in fact, "one important forecaster center of the Weather Bureau in the Middle West has an unlisted telephone connection with Tinker Field for emergencies." In every way—or so the implicit message was—the bureau was now in the thick of tornado forecasting.

The bureau began encouraging the formation of amateur spotter networks in the Great Plains, along the lines of the military spotter networks set up during the war. The bureau sometimes disseminated warnings from spotters when they could be confirmed, and bureau spokesmen unbent enough to credit the spotters occasionally with saving lives. Then, too, the spread of radar technology to weather stations throughout the country made the amassing of reliable tornado data possible for the first time, and the bureau meteorologists became increasingly confident about identifying dangerous weather conditions that might lead to tornadoes. There were circumstances where even the most skeptical meteorologist would have to conclude that tornadoes were a strong possibility—in March 1952, for instance, when an exceptionally violent and unstable storm system crossed through the South. The bureau was sufficiently alarmed to issue a general tornado forecast for the entire region. The storm system spawned thirty-one tornadoes over the next two days.

By the end of the 1950s, the bureau had evolved what it thought was a workable method for dealing with tornadoes. It issued "forecasts" several hours ahead of time when it believed there was a possibility of tornadoes in a particular area; this was essentially what Fawbush and Miller had been doing (or for that matter John Finley, almost a century earlier), in that the forecast areas were very large and no specific communities were identified as being at risk. The bureau then issued "alerts" for individual locations when there was a confirmed report, either from radar or from a spotter, that a tornado was on the ground. When the public proved to find these terms confusing, "tornado forecast" was renamed "tornado watch," and "tornado alert" was renamed "tornado warning"—the terms still used today.

The value of this system was open to dispute. The accuracy rate of the tornado watches was about one in three; that was scarcely better than Fawbush and Miller's results, which the bureau had so vigorously scorned. The average lead time of the tornado warnings, meanwhile, was three to four minutes, which barely gave people ahead of the tornado time to take shelter. So what good was the bureau doing? When tornadoes failed to occur in the watch areas, they were attacked for crying wolf; when tornadoes were an imminent danger, they were attacked for staying silent until it was too late.

To be fair, the bureau was relying on volunteers to spread the alarm; their watches and warnings were distributed to local governmental authorities, newspapers, and radio and television stations, which were then supposed to alert the public. This was effectively a guarantee that warnings would arrive late or not at all. In most of the country, even in Tornado Alley, there were no emergency alert networks; few local TV stations in the country would interrupt their regular programming for any news bulletins involving severe weather. Even when the watches and warnings did get out, the most common response among the public was bafflement. No one understood the bulletins; even when warning sirens were sounded, no one knew what they meant.

The bureau believed the real problem was that the public didn't understand what tornadoes were. In the late 1950s and into the 1960s, bureau public affairs officers, school systems, law enforcement and other agencies of public safety, and newspapers and television stations began educating people about tornado safety. This was how a whole generation of American midwesterners first heard about opening the windows when a tornado approached and taking shelter in the southwest corner of the basement. They heard that tornadoes reached a top speed of five hundred miles an hour and that there was a vacuum at the heart of the funnel cloud that made houses explode. They heard, in fact, an accretion of old folklore, forgotten theories, and once-plausible but long-superseded guesswork dating back to John Finley's time and before, all of it passed off as the current scientific thinking only because there really wasn't any current scientific thinking on tornado safety. It was the sort of authoritative nonsense people had always associated with the Weather Bureau, the kind of thing that made those like Robert Miller wish the bureau would leave tornadoes to the real experts.

Certain great figures in the study of tornadoes, it has been observed in the *Bulletin of the American Meteorological Society,* "possess an ability to view the complex phenomena of the atmosphere with limited reliance on the theoretical underpinning of meteorology." The subject of the observation might have been James Espy, or John Finley, or even Benjamin Franklin, but in this case it was Miller. Miller, over his years at the Severe Weather Warning Center, acquired a reputation as the greatest practical meteorologist who ever lived. But he had never been particularly well-grounded in meteorological theory. From his success with the operational forecast onward, he relied on his intuition. He simply knew the shape of a tornado-spawning storm system when he saw it, even if he could not articulate the reasons why. Forecasters like Miller, the *Bulletin* concluded, were something like "human analog machines, with phenomenal memories of synoptic weather regimes."

Miller taught many cadets and junior weather officers in his years at the center, and they all remembered the extraordinary visual clarity he brought to the study of violent weather. They particularly recalled his weather maps, which he would draw freehand, with marvelous simplicity and force: they were, one forecaster remembered, "like architectural drawings." But his skill encompassed the specifics of daily forecasting as well. He had evolved through years of trial and error an almost infallible sense of how to transform a stream of raw data into a lucid and accurate forecast. In the 1960s, he was ultimately prevailed upon to put together a memorandum outlining his forecasting principles; he intended it only for in-house use, but it immediately began circulating throughout both the military and the civilian meteorological communities and is still considered a standard reference today. It is a brilliantly practical treatise on weather forecasting, but the most striking thing about it is that its underlying principles are essentially just ad hoc rules of thumb.

This is what made his guidelines for tornado forecasting so problematic. His own intuitions about tornadoes were still essentially based on the rules that he and Fawbush had arrived at in 1948: they depended on crude, direct observation of vertical instability and upper-air wind shear in a severe thunderstorm. Miller's contemporaries, on the other hand, were attempting to devise models of what they called tornadogenesis, involving complex patterns of downdrafts, vortices, and outflow. While both approaches had their value, neither seemed to get anywhere near a solution to the essential problem: determining which thunderstorms were actually going to produce tornadoes, and when, and where. That goal appeared to be out of reach—perhaps permanently. In all his years as a forecaster, Miller never again succeeded in making another tornado prediction as specific and accurate as his first operational forecast. But then, neither did anybody else.

The new theoretical approaches to meteorology left Miller at best indifferent and at worst enraged. His students observed that he didn't want to hear about any rival ideas and didn't want his students or assistants reading about them, either. His teaching method consisted of a relentless drilling in his own forecast guidelines. His goal was to train his students to visualize the large-scale three-dimensional shape of violent storms with exactly the same clarity as he did.

The sureness of his hand and the lucidity of his thought were accompanied by other personality traits that people found more difficult. Even those who came to feel affection and admiration for Miller thought him an intimidating, sometimes terrifying presence (particularly after Fawbush, always a tempering force, retired from the service). He was infamous for his brutal temper, his competitiveness, his toughness with his underlings, and his disdain for authority. He had a raging intolerance for error and a contempt for contrary views. He was infamous in his office for bellowing insults at those he had to work with; his kindest word for them was "dummies."

His attitude toward his old nemesis the Weather Bureau hardened into something like permanent fury. When the Weather Bureau set up its own office for storm prediction in Kansas City, called the Severe Local Storms Unit (known by the acronym SELS—the acronym remained even after the name changed to the National Severe Storms Forecast Center), Miller fiercely resisted cooperating with it. He routinely refused to share any data at all with SELS until he had issued his own predictions. He still blamed the Weather Bureau for rejecting his ideas, and the ones they hadn't rejected he believed they'd stolen. He wasn't necessarily wrong about this, either: in the early days, one prominent regional observer had been taking Miller's tornado forecasts, rewriting them, and surreptitiously passing them along to local newspapers and television stations as his own off-the-record insider information. On Miller's desk at the Severe Weather Warning Center, several people remembered, was a green telephone that was the direct unlisted line to his counterpart at the SELS office. They dreaded hearing it ring. Miller never picked that phone up willingly and often ended his calls by hurling it at the wall.

Miller retired from the Severe Weather Warning Center in 1975. He spent the next few years working as a weather consultant to private corporations. He didn't stay anywhere for long: he was in Maryland, then California, then Louisiana. For a good part of the time he was working under a NASA grant to study commercial applications of satellite weather data. He was never happy in this part of his career and was a poor fit with the white-collar corporate culture of his employers. He left professional meteorology at the end of the 1970s.

He reemerged in 1994, when he made a public appearance at the National Severe Storms Laboratory in Norman, Oklahoma. He was in extremely poor health, but he roused himself to give a speech about his famous forecast; the speech was described as "spirited" and one that "displayed his rough-hewn nature coupled with his undeniable charm." Shortly after his return home his health collapsed, and he was permanently confined to bed, where he died four years later. He had spent his last active years drafting his memoirs, which he titled "The Unfriendly Sky," and working part-time at a hobby shop specializing in military memorabilia.

19

Visible Effects of the Invisible

On September 26, 1948, a waterspout formed in Ariake Bay, off the island of Kyushu, the southwesternmost island in the Japanese archipelago, and rapidly came ashore. That area of Kyushu is today thoroughly urbanized, and the ancient farming villages only survive as the names of railroad stations, but in the 1940s it was still rural: the spout roared up and down hillsides that were terraced with rice paddies, and it shredded the scattered farmhouse roofs for six miles inland.

A few days later an expert arrived to survey the damage. His name was Tetsuya Fujita. He was twenty-seven years old; he'd been trained as a mechanical engineer and was now an assistant professor of physics at the Kyushu Institute of Technology. He had made a special study of damage patterns in catastrophic events. His most significant work had been a survey of the most catastrophic event in the island's history, the bombing of Nagasaki; he'd led a special team there in the weeks after the blast and analyzed the pattern of burn marks on the wreckage. (The dangers of radiation poisoning were still only dimly understood at that point; Fujita never showed any ill effects from his time spent at the disaster site, but several members of his team did get severely sick.) He had been able to deduce most of the physical properties of the bomb from his study; he had even managed to work out that it had detonated at roughly five hundred feet in the air.

But Fujita's real love was meteorology—in particular the physics of extremely violent weather. After the Nagasaki survey he'd gotten a grant from the government to train science teachers in the basics of the subject, which wasn't then much studied in Japan. He began his own researches with the thorny problem of the conflicting and variable surface winds often recorded during severe thunderstorms. He spent days at a mountain weather station, watching the storms cascade and surge and billow below him, to see if he could understand their internal logic. That was where he made his first major discovery: convective updrafts in thunderstorms were accompanied by equally powerful downdrafts. (He didn't know it until much later, but the same discovery was being made at around the same time by American meteorologists.)

Fujita's dream was to study the fundamental questions of meteorology full-time. He didn't see any opportunities for this in Japan; in the years after the war, America was the only place where basic meteorological research was being funded. But then America was also the country with the most violent and interesting weather. So Fujita wrote up his detailed observations of the damage trail of the waterspout, translated them into English (a typewriter with an English keyboard cost him more than a month's salary), and sent his report unsolicited to the meteorologist Horace Byers, a professor at the University of Chicago. He picked Byers only because he'd found the name on a meteorological paper that somebody in his college had thrown into a wastebasket.

In Chicago, Byers read Fujita's paper and was impressed with it. The two men struck up a correspondence. Fujita went on to get a doctorate in science from Tokyo University in 1950. A few years later, Byers was able to arrange for the University of Chicago to invite him to join the faculty.

Fujita departed for America in 1953. He landed in San Francisco and took a train across the Rockies and through the Great Plains to Chicago; it was his first glimpse of the vast theater of the atmosphere where he would spend the rest of his life. But what he remembered most about the trip was that he'd only been able to bring twenty-two dollars with him through customs at San Francisco. In order to survive during the three-day train ride, he'd spent all his money on a supply of Fig Newtons and Coca-Cola.

Fujita arrived in America at exactly the right time: in the boom years after the war, American universities were flush with government funding and were building up impressive new departments in the hard sciences.

There was also the unexpected technical bounty of radar equipment; the government was making available to university research labs at bargain rates the radar units from countless decommissioned military planes and ground weather stations. The flood of new data from these units meant that in the 1950s and 1960s, the basic conceptual model for violent storms was being rethought. It was increasingly understood that storms weren't static events but complex and rapidly evolving dynamic systems, with their own underlying logic and life cycle. The term that began to be used in the 1960s was "storm cell"; a storm front was seen as a kind of tidal wave, with individual thunderstorms flowering and dying all along its length like the curlicues of its crest. Certain cells were so strong and well organized that they became self-sustaining—repeatedly dwindling and regenerating again as they were carried across the landscape: these were called supercells, and it became clear over the years they were studied that these were the cells that most often spawned tornadoes.

Fujita's research projects were part of the vanguard of this new thinking. His first major project was an exhaustive analysis of a tornado that had passed through Fargo, North Dakota, in June 1957. He wanted to do what nobody had ever done before—document the full life cycle of a single tornado. He thought of a novel way of attempting it. It happened that this tornado had been unusually slow moving; it hadn't raced through Fargo but had almost dawdled, at an average speed of barely twenty miles an hour. This meant that almost everyone in town had stopped to watch it, and many of those people had time to bring out their cameras. With the help of a local television station, Fujita was able to gather more than 150 amateur photographs of the tornado. He used them to create a kind of filmstrip that showed the tornado at one-minute intervals over almost the entire duration of its existence. He then spent the next two years watching the filmstrip. At the end of that time, he had evolved the first model for a tornado's growth, maturity, and decay. Many of the most basic elements of a tornado's structure as it is understood today—such as its initial descent from a "wall cloud" within the supercell—were identified for the first time by Fujita in his filmstrip.

Fujita settled into being an American. He brought his wife and children over from Japan and bought a house in Chicago near the university. He became an American citizen. He grew to be a celebrity within the meteorological community, and he published often; his papers on tornadoes, hurricanes, and typhoons were regarded as consistently original and brilliant. He decided to publish under the name T. Theodore Fujita and was pleased when people called him Ted.

In the 1960s, Fujita made exhaustive studies of tornado damage tracks. Initially, he walked most of the tracks on foot, but he ultimately came to prefer being flown the length of the track in a high-wing Cessna. He was particularly insistent on that model because its unusual wing position didn't block his panoramic view of the damage. By his own count, he conducted detailed examinations of more than three hundred tracks. His published reports set an extraordinarily high standard. One man who accompanied Fujita on some of these flights, a professor of civil engineering named James McDonald, later wrote that Fujita "had an uncanny ability to sort out the damage indicators on the ground and come up with plausible flow patterns."

Through his exhaustive studies, and through his curious attentiveness to the exact nuances of destruction, he came up with an idea for a classification system for tornadoes based on how much damage they caused. He devised a scale of wind speed with twelve steps, like a musical scale, from calm winds to winds at the speed of sound, and he began assigning the tornadoes he studied to points along the scale. The steps began at category 0, with winds under a hundred miles an hour, causing damage that he classified as light. Category 1 was moderate damage, followed by considerable, severe, devastating, and incredible. Incredible damage was category 5, with estimated wind speeds topping three hundred miles an hour. That was where the scale stopped. Fujita believed that this was the upper limit of what was physically possible: damage that could be considered category 6 he called inconceivable. No tornado on record, not the Tri-state Tornado nor the strange moving mountain that destroyed Irving, Kansas, in 1879, could be rated a 6 or higher.

Fujita introduced his scale in 1971. It was immediately and universally accepted. It quickly became routine to speak of a given tornado as, say, a Fujita scale 2, or just an F2. But nobody imagined how soon the scale would turn out to be essential.

Around one o'clock on the afternoon of April 3, 1974, a tornado touched down deep within the Illinois farm country. It was an unseasonably hot and humid day; the forecast from the National Weather Service was for violent thunderstorms with possible tornadoes all through the heartland. But this tornado hardly counted as violent. It was a faint white sprite of the sultry air; it danced for a few hundred yards across the green depths of a gigantic cornfield and then dissolved against the backdrop of a purple thundercloud. It probably did no more damage than scatter a hayrick or knock over a road sign. For anybody who might have glimpsed it in the distance from an interstate highway, it was doubtless a memorable sight, but on the Fujita scale it rated on the lowest rung, F0. Among professional meteorologists it wouldn't have been remembered at all, if everything about that day hadn't turned out to be unforgettable.

The weather data for April 3 showed that there was a very large and powerful area of low pressure moving east across the country from the Rocky Mountains. At the surface, this system was drawing in a flow of warm humid air from the Gulf of Mexico. In the upper air it was drawing in hot dry air from the southwestern deserts. This was an unusual pattern. More typically what happens is that the upper-air winds come in from the north and are very cold. This causes a large falloff in temperature between the surface and the higher altitudes; convection columns form and bleed off their moisture in the form of clouds and rain—just as James Espy had envisaged more than a century before. But on April 3, both the surface air and the upper-level winds were warm, so something else happened. The convection columns didn't form; instead, the hot air remained near the surface. The atmosphere, as meteorologists have come to say, was "capped."

The cap remained in place as the day wore on. The cap was so strong, in fact, that it prevented the ordinary formation of clouds. This meant that the undiluted heat of the sun caused the trapped air at the surface to warm up even more. By early afternoon the potential energy within the system was spiking, and the atmosphere was becoming catastrophically unstable. Extremely hot and humid convection columns at last began punching up randomly through the cap, and cumulonimbus clouds bloomed in the skies all over the eastern Mississippi valley and the Deep South.

As the atmospheric cap disintegrated all across the eastern half of the country, exceptionally violent supercells swelled up, died off, and regenerated in the inexhaustible convective flow of released potential energy. By late afternoon tornadoes were spinning out of the clouds and touching down everywhere. There were dozens of them: long writhing snakes, gigantic black blasting chimneys, shapeless gray whirls of debris, vast churning cliff-face wall clouds, graceful tapering cones glowing with late-afternoon gold. By nightfall, tornadoes had touched down in thirteen states. At one point during the evening, so many tornadoes were simultaneously on the ground in Indiana (sixteen, by one count) that meteorologists in a move of desperation issued a single tornado warning for the entire state.

There had been outbreaks of tornadoes before. There were records of them as far back as the Enigma Outbreak of 1884. There had been two major outbreaks in 1953 alone—thirty-three tornadoes in the plains over three days in early May, forty-eight across the Great Lakes and New England a month later. But there had never been a case where so many violent tornadoes had touched down all at once. In Ohio, two tornadoes touched down simultaneously and swirled together into one large F5 funnel cloud about a half mile wide, which shortly afterward destroyed the town of Xenia. It picked up a school bus and dropped it through the roof of the school, where it fell directly onto an auditorium stage; the children had been rehearsing a play there a few minutes before. Roughly two hours later, the town of Tanner, Alabama, was destroyed by an F5 tornado, and as the survivors and rescuers searched frantically through the rubble, a second F5 tornado following the same path blasted through the town and leveled whatever was still standing. Another F5 tornado in Alabama was on the ground for almost two hours and traveled more than a hundred miles; it was one of the most powerful tornadoes recorded since the Tri-state Tornado of 1925.

By the end of the night, more than three hundred people were dead, thousands were injured, and there were tracks of damage and devastation from Illinois to the East Coast. Tornadoes were still touching down after midnight as the storm system was blown toward the Atlantic. One of the last trailing tornadoes touched down in Kingsport, Tennessee, around three in the morning. It was a mile wide, a vast bulging apparition of terror rumbling through the darkness, but it was little more than a hollow bag of gas. Its winds were well under a hundred miles an hour, and on the Fujita scale it rated an F0.

The Super Outbreak, as it quickly became known, was the worst single tornado event in American history. Almost 150 tornadoes touched down out of a single weather system. Fujita had thought that there might turn out to be an average in America of four or five major tornadoes annually—that is, tornadoes rating higher than an F3. In that one night, there had been twenty-four F4s and six F5s.

Fujita made the study of the Super Outbreak a major project. He assembled microscopically detailed surveys of the damage tracks of every tornado in the outbreak, and he mapped them all. The result was an extraordinarily rich image of the ever-shifting and fluid progress of a major storm system. The map also demonstrated that Fujita's own tornado scale had to be used judiciously. There was no steady and predictable path of destruction even with the strongest tornadoes. A tornado classed as an F5, for instance, usually had clusters and pockets of incredible calamity interspersed with large zones of much milder damage. The damage varied from mile to mile and sometimes from square foot to square foot: most of the houses on a block might be blown into splinters, leaving one in the middle completely untouched. Evidently, even the most violent tornadoes had weird areas of calm within them, while the weakest tornadoes might have pocket domains of uncontrolled fury.

Most meteorologists would have been inclined to write these variations off as random flukes, unpredictable and inexplicable. But Fujita had been struck by a novel—even hair-raisingly original—thought. Tornadoes were not solid, unitary objects. There wasn't necessarily one central vortex of low pressure at the heart of the funnel. A tornado might be made up of a dance of multiple vortices, spinning and weaving around a central core. The meandering motions of these vortices, as they approached and retreated from the ground back to the upper altitudes, were what created the intricately variable tangles of wreckage that the most powerful tornadoes left behind.

It was ideas like this that led people to start calling Fujita "Mr. Tornado."

Fujita studied wind damage patterns at hurricanes; he mastered satellite imagery analysis to describe cloud and debris evidence at major tornadoes. He was taken in a high-altitude research jet to circle thunderstorm tops as they rose and collapsed (he believed there was a correlation between a sinking thunderhead and tornado formation). But his most extended research project in his later years was the search for an explanation for a plane crash. On June 24, 1975, an Eastern Air Lines 727 was on final approach to Kennedy International Airport during a violent thunderstorm; without warning the plane swerved out of its flight path, struck the approach lights, burst into flames, and broke up on the ground. Of the 124 people on board, only 11 survived. Eastern Air Lines asked Fujita to find out what had gone wrong. Fujita's analysis of the data revealed a mystery: the plane had been buffeted by an extraordinarily violent gust of wind that hadn't been recorded anywhere else on the airfield. So where had the wind come from? He was struck by a radical new idea. Suppose an extremely concentrated downdraft had formed in the storm cell directly overhead. It might have been so localized that it wasn't even detectable a few hundred yards away, but the wind shear of its gust front, for the few seconds it lasted, would be strong enough to knock a commercial jetliner out of the sky. Fujita called it a microburst.

Fujita made use of a new piece of technology to test his theory—the Doppler radar. This was an advanced radar design that did more than passively reflect back the simple presence of objects; it discerned the way these objects were moving relative to the radar signal. When directed at storms, it allowed for the first time a fine-grain analysis of the complex movement of rain and winds within a thunderhead. Fujita spent the next several years using Doppler radar units to search for microbursts. Most of his colleagues were skeptical—if not openly contemptuous. It seemed absurd to them to suggest that there could be such a strong, complex, and violent phenomenon taking place within a thunderstorm that had somehow gone totally unnoticed throughout all of history. They were openly astonished when Fujita emerged from his multiyear study with Doppler images of microbursts erupting from storm cells, falling with extreme speed, and rapidly spreading and dissipating across the ground directly below, like milk poured out from a carton onto a tabletop. Fujita, with the backing of the entire meteorological community, used his evidence to lobby the aviation industry and the government for Doppler radar to be made standard equipment at airports.

Fujita always had his opponents. Few seem to have disliked him personally, but there were always complaints about how he got his results. He was not one for precision. He would guess. This made the exact calibrations of damage in the Fujita scale something of a sham, since his criteria for assessing the tornado were actually impressionistic, even poetic—what was, after all, the objective distinction between "devastating" and "incredible" damage? (After his death, the scale was revised, and it is now customary to refer to a tornado not as an F2 but as an EF-2, for "Enhanced Fujita.") Fujita was also notorious in his later years for refusing to use computers in order to model tornadoes. Computers, he liked to say, simply didn't understand these things.

At bottom he was another intuitionist, like Robert Miller, like John Finley, like James Espy. He was relying not on a ground of theoretical or mathematical knowledge but on a kind of imaginative sympathy for the storm itself. He made no secret of his fascination with the unquantifiable. Only the wildest and most free ranging of intellects could have conceived the dynamics of a thunderstorm in such a way as to suggest the existence of the multiple-vortex tornado and the microburst, but brilliantly illuminating as these ideas were, Fujita's models for them were hard for other scientists to use. They weren't so much convincing as stunning.

Fujita didn't entirely care. He said he would be more than satisfied if only half his ideas were found valuable. He called his memoirs *An Attempt to Unlock the Mystery of Severe Storms,* and he never claimed that his attempt had been successful. There were many aspects of tornadoes that he never fully engaged with. There was in particular the one issue that everybody else still believed was the sole and essential question: the exact mechanism of tornadogenesis. Fujita offered several models for it, but none of them were met with any lasting enthusiasm. He could also be reluctant to shed his own ideas when they were proven wrong. He had, for instance, begun with the general assumption shared by most meteorologists: that tornado damage was the result of a near vacuum within the funnel that caused buildings to explode. But there was never much empirical evidence to back up this theory; Fujita's own maps of damage tracks showed no sign of any exploded buildings. It gradually became obvious to the younger generation of meteorologists that Fujita and his colleagues had been mistaken, but Fujita himself, well into his sixties and seventies, remained convinced of the existence of a deadly vacuum at the tornado's heart.

But this was Fujita's great legacy: freeing up the minds of meteorologists to reconceive the nature of violent storms from scratch. It's understood now that tornadoes are so destructive not because of some catastrophic differential in air pressure but from the simple effects of wind. While there is an area of extremely low pressure within the tornado, this is incidental. There is in fact only one irreducible element in any tornado: the vortex that draws in winds from the surrounding atmosphere. It's the astonishing strength of these winds—technically known as surface inflow jets—together with the barrages of flying debris they carry with them, that causes all of the tornado's damage. Everything else we think of as characteristic of tornadoes—in particular the funnel cloud itself—is a secondary effect that is easily occluded or may not appear at all. The tornado isn't a peculiar kind of cloud but a certain configuration of the air, a moving vortex within the storm, which in its purest form is invisible.

In fact, as Fujita's followers and successors began to think of it, there was something fundamentally misleading about conceiving of tornadoes as distinct phenomena. They are only an aspect of the fantastically complex and violently evolving dynamics of a supercell thunderstorm. They are rarely singular. They form in clusters and waves; they breed and die off within the larger movement of a storm front like bubbles in the froth. The number of tornadoes that form or half form, that blur and merge and separate within any given storm cell, defies any exact count. The sheer chaos of a severe storm renders precision impossible.

This way of thinking about tornadoes has suggested a dire possibility to contemporary meteorologists: that true prediction of tornadoes might never be a practical reality. The problem of tornadogenesis will doubtless be solved, but the solution might not help. It could turn out that large, rapidly unfolding storm systems simply can't be modeled in sufficient detail to predict which cells will or won't spawn tornadoes and in what number. The ultimate goal of tornado forecasting, then, could turn out to be a will-o'-the-wisp.

But the study of tornadoes sooner or later breaks down any and all certainties. Even the most obvious truths about them eventually turn out to be backward. For decades after 1974, meteorologists took it as a self-evident fact that the Super Outbreak was a freak outlier, a "five-hundred-year event" (meaning something that might possibly happen once or twice a millennium). This certainty endured despite a growing mountain of evidence that major storm systems can routinely generate dozens of tornadoes in very brief periods of time. As a single storm system passed across Oklahoma and Kansas on May 3, 1999, for instance, there were 66 tornado touchdowns. Then, in April 2011, over the course of three days, a gigantic storm system sweeping across the eastern United States and Canada spawned more than 350 tornadoes. It became known as the Super Outbreak of 2011, and nobody talked any longer about five-hundred-year events. Instead, the suspicion grew that Super Outbreaks might not be rare at all but something closer to the norm.

Theodore Fujita died in Chicago in the fall of 1998, at the age of seventy-eight. In his later life, whenever he was asked what accomplishment he was most proud of, he'd say it was the campaign to install Doppler radar at airports for the detection of microbursts, which has in the last few decades saved hundreds and maybe even thousands of lives. But the microburst research project had also resulted in another, wholly private accomplishment, and this was the one that the people who knew him would often recall first when they talked about him.

It happened at the end of the spring in 1982. He was working then at Denver International Airport, a field notorious for its high winds and its unexpected and violent storms. Fujita considered it a highly promising ground for his microburst hunt. The research team was positioning three mobile Doppler units in the empty country north of the airport to see what distances and angles gave them the best coverage of the runways. Fujita himself never had much patience for that kind of grunt work; he tended to leave the calibration and data collection to his team and would instead spend his time driving around the back roads of Colorado by himself, watching for storms and trying to catch an unfolding microburst with his camera. But on June 12, Fujita did stop off briefly at one of the radar units. The team was tracking a line of thunderstorms advancing across the open country from the east. Fujita stood by himself, idly snapping photographs of the storm clouds. It was late afternoon; the western sky was still clear, and brilliant golden sunlight was falling across the landscape. The storm front was lit up in brilliant billows of white and purple. Then, just below the cloud deck, against a deep blue background, a frail white snake appeared that curved and bulged and undulated and melted back into nothingness.

Later that night the entire research team held a party to celebrate. It was the first time Fujita had seen an actual tornado.

Epilogue

The Wild Hunt

Irving, Kansas—the town where John Finley had done his first field report and where Dorothy Gale had lived and died—survived the mysterious double tornado of May 1879. Within a few years, the evidence of the disaster had largely been erased. The destroyed houses and stores had been rebuilt, and the scarred earth replanted. Life there resumed its old meandering and obscure course. At the end of the nineteenth century, Irving appeared to be indistinguishable from any of the other small market towns of northern Kansas. It prospered mainly because it was at the junction of two major railroad lines, the Union Pacific and the Missouri Pacific, and grew to be a natural gathering point for farmers and speculators from around the region. Irving had a strong and flourishing bank, which dealt almost entirely in agricultural loans, and a successful newspaper that published weather forecasts and crop prices. It had a dry-goods store, a feed store, a smithy, and a lawyer's office. It had a telegraph office, a postal express office, and a public library—not a bad showing for a town with a population of four hundred.

Irving went through its share of hard times with the new century. There were two catastrophic floods. There were economic convulsions: panics and bank failures, collapses of the regional economy. And there was the Dust Bowl—the inevitable consequence of the destruction of the old prairie. When the long droughts came in the 1930s, the drying and crumbling topsoil was no longer held in place by the yards-deep mats of the grass roots. Instead, the winds blew the topsoil away, acre after acre, windstorm after windstorm. More than a hundred million acres of arable land were scoured clean, and the topsoil was sifting down as gritty dust all across eastern America and falling on ships in the Atlantic Ocean. Irving and its surrounding farms somehow hung on, just on the edge of the zone of greatest devastation; western Kansas and the Texas and Oklahoma Panhandles were as broken and lifeless as the deserts of Mars.

The decades that followed were green, a time of abundant rainfall and flourishing crops. The region's water table, which had gone down almost to sea level during the drought, came back up to its old level in the 1940s. Irving should have thrived. But the great harvests of the 1950s drove down agricultural prices almost to nothing, and farmers to survive had to get their crops to the buyers as cheaply as possible. That meant transport by truck on the new interstate highways, rather than by the old railroads. It was Irving's bad luck that it was nowhere near any interstate on-ramp. The small farms around it began to fail and were sold out to gigantic agricultural corporations. In the late 1950s, many of the last surviving farms were bought out for the construction of a dam and an artificial lake. The town dwindled down to a few crossroads stores and a post office. By the end of the decade the stores had gone out of business and the post office had closed. Irving became a ghost town.

In the early 1990s, people began showing up in Irving again. They didn't stay; there was nowhere to stay. They would come down the old highway to the crossroads, and they would park for a long look around. They traveled in odd caravans—lines of battered minivans and SUVs, some of them bristling with antennas and small satellite disks. Their passengers all wore jeans and work shirts; they carried laptops and video cameras. They would pace around the meadowland and lay out picnics in the scattered stands of trees, and they would gesture at the horizon and argue about where the tornadoes of 1879 had come from.

The chasers are on the road every spring, driving hundreds of miles a day, toward any place where the skies are growing turbulent and the thunderheads are sprouting. The weather tourists who pay to ride with the chasers are never guaranteed the sight of a tornado, and many of them do the tours for years without a glimpse. The closest some ever get is the spectacle of a gigantic supercell wall cloud rotating languidly across half the sky and then trailing off into inconsequential downpours.

What people mainly see on those trips is the blank prairie land-scape fanning out on either side of the interstates, spreading around main highways, and enfolding the wandering tracks of county roads. There are unimaginably large expanses of cultivated fields, dotted here and there with curved tin sheds like miniature army barracks; there are the endlessly unwinding franchise strips: fast-food restaurants, an auto parts store, a furniture outlet, and a scattering of hulking, nameless warehouses, all islanded in wastes of freshly laid asphalt.

Sometimes the highway grows shabbier, and the roadside clutter thickens into a town. A down-at-the-heels place: the businesses along the main street are dime stores, liquor stores, discount clothing stores, bargain appliance stores, dry cleaners, and Laundromats. A shoe store has huge cardboard bins of unsorted shoes sitting out on the sidewalk. The grocery store has a mechanical coin-operated rocking horse in front. The traffic lights are antiques—knobby yellow cubes that dangle from wires, drooping over the intersections like Japanese lanterns. Lunch is at a counter in a dime store. Hot dogs wrapped in white-bread toast, a tangle of crinkle-cut fries limp as caterpillars, two pale circlets of pickle, and the local cola served in a paper cone in a metal holder. On the store shelves are dolls staring from behind yellowed cellophane wrappers.

After sunset the landscapes deepen into vagueness: shapeless wood-lands, vast blurs of farmlands, mysterious glows of subdivisions hidden behind the horizon. In the middle depths there are always the silhou-ettes of power pylons and radio masts—complicated black cutouts tipped with slow red pulsing lights. Dinner means burgers at a back table at a truck stop bar, where the chasers pour out pitchers of beer and argue about the next day's hunt. Later, long after midnight, two of them might meet by the ice machine in a motel parking lot, next to the deserted swimming pool; maybe they'd see a flicker of lightning along the horizon and wonder if tomorrow their luck would change.

And maybe tomorrow it would. The morning would be unusually humid, skin already sticking to the seats in the van as soon as the sun is up. A day unwinding through small towns crisscrossed by power lines and marked by water towers and steeples. Roads dwindling into two-lane, ragged-shouldered blacktops that rose and fell for hours through the sultry green hill country. Fences fantastically twisting, fences spiked and thorny lines of unpainted wood. At the intersections are totem poles displaying a clutter of rusted road designation signs—county roads, U.S. highways, the red-white-and-blue interstate shield—with arrows pointing off in wild directions. All the while, stipples of cloud bulge low over the landscape, now and then emitting spatters of warm rain.

Then in late afternoon the air gets dark. The rain thickens, and mingling among its steady hiss are flicks and taps as though tiny glass beads are striking the windows. The tapping turns into banging and cracking and thunking. Hailstones skitter down the windshield and hop around on the hood like popcorn. The rain seethes over the windows. A blare of light and a blast of thunder in front of the caravan; another to the side; another right behind. Everybody sits frozen, except for the guides, who mutter numbers they're reading off the glowing panels of their laptops. Now and then they call over their shoulders, "Hold on, folks!" One passenger talks to himself in an irritated monotone, as though trying to remember some lesson in class where he hadn't been paying attention: "Now, do we get out of the car or not? Is it safer in here if we don't touch anything metal? Should we try to wait this out or not?" The windows drown in froth as though inside a car wash.

Then the light changes. The fields and woodlands outside the window begin to regain their solidity. The runnels of rain down the windows fray away to nothing. The sign totem reappears in its expected spot; the cornstalks nod and bob together. Down the road, something is gliding sidewise through the middle distance, a vast ghost of filthy brown and black. The sun comes out in the western sky and illuminates a gigantic gliding cloud moving away with lumbering grace, crowned by brilliant white cauliflower domes and strewing dragon tails of lightning in all directions. At its base, amid a turmoil of black earth like the wake of a furious motorboat, is a curving, tapered funnel cloud, glowing reddish gold in the late-afternoon light. Above in the dazzlingly clear air is a half-formed rainbow. Reaching up overhead are a scattering of contrails crisscrossing through the highest promontories of the thunderhead. Lightning flickers there, like the glare and smoke of an eternal battle, Godzilla versus the military, drifting on endlessly toward the horizon.

The beginnings of the modern tornado chase go back to an incident that took place in April 1953 at a civilian radar project jointly run by the Illinois state government and the University of Illinois. The project used a military-surplus radar unit to measure rainfall and water levels in local streams and lakes. The unit was being tested at an airport weather station in Champaign, Illinois. The tester, an electrical engineer named Donald Staggs, happened to be at work one afternoon when a large wave of thunderstorms passed nearby. Staggs was so fascinated by the complicated patterns of blurs and specters on the radar monitor that he stayed into the evening to watch for more. Some time after sunset another line passed, and Staggs saw a mysteriously sharp and well-defined shape appear amid a cluster of rain echoes. It was like a large hook gliding through the dark in the depths of the storm. The radar unit happened to be fitted with a camera that filmed the images on the monitor; later analysis of the film showed that the mysterious hook could be matched up exactly with the track of a passing tornado. Other radar units would later record the same hook in other storms, and it eventually acquired a name: the tornado vortex signature. It typically appears at the heart of a thundercloud about twenty minutes before a tornado descends.

The news that tornadoes could be detected before they touched the ground caused a revolution in the study of severe weather. When the new generation of Doppler radars first came into use at the end of the 1960s, research scientists began actively hunting for tornadoes in zones of violent atmospheric disturbance. In May 1973, storm intercept teams from the National Severe Storms Laboratory tracked a tornado as it approached and destroyed the small town of Union City, Oklahoma. The chasers were able to spot the tornado as it was forming and follow it through its complete life cycle, from the first stirrings of its debris cloud on the ground and the will-o'-the-wisp of its embryonic funnel to its black grandly swollen maturity to the final sinuous twists of its dissipation, while a Doppler radar simultaneously recorded the movement of the tornado vortex signature within the parent storm.

Chasers in those days were scientists from the Weather Service or professors and grad students from local universities. They drove battered station wagons and communicated by walkie-talkie and shortwave radio. Their navigation was done by means of crumpled, coffee-stained road maps kept in glove compartments. Their first results were unimpressive by today's standards: grainy home movies taken through car windows, distant photographs snapped from the highway shoulder. Only gradually on their chases were they joined by amateur tornado buffs who brought their own lavish equipment. By the 1990s and early years of the twenty-first century, there were entrepreneurs of the tornado safari who brought in weather tourists from all over the world. Today the caravans are customized trucks and vans and SUVs with armoring and shatterproof glass, carrying a carapace of antennas and dishes and Plexiglas observation bubbles and built-in video cameras. Sometimes tornadoes in the open country are encircled by multiple chase teams, made up of government meteorologists and tornado video companies, all recording real-time data from portable Doppler units. It's often said the major danger of tornado hunting now is of a head-on collision with another pursuit car.

The chasers speak their own lingo unintelligible to the locals. Part of it is the technical vocabulary of the professional meteorologists— all about dry lines and CAPEs and rear-flanking downdraft columns, mesocyclonic rotation, and vertical instability. But they also have their own ad hoc terms that come from their direct observations of the weird and multiform manifestations of the tornado cloud. (Orthodox meteorologists resisted using this slang for years, because they thought it was unscientific; now chaser lingo creeps into the most stolid research papers.) They talk about the wall cloud and the beaver tail, the debris ball and the barber pole. The gigantic rotating mass of a supercell cloud is the mother ship. The tornado funnel is a tube or a wedge or a cigar or a stovepipe or an elephant trunk, and when it dwindles during its last minutes into a thin undulating snake, they say it is roping out.

The chasers have also amassed a huge inchoate library of tornado images—first film and then digital video, much of it posted to You-Tube: a genre sometimes called "torn porn." The videos show tornadoes in countless forms, squat buzzing whirlwinds and vast soul-catching curves, blurry churns of black smoke and white fluted vases smooth as pewter. What they do not show are the bizarre and inexplicable sights that have been reported by generations of eyewitnesses. Torn porn has brought an end to hundreds of years of tornado folklore.

Where, for instance, are the strange lights so often reported around the funnel? The sparkling fire, the multicolored glows, the ruby-red eye at the funnel's heart? Not once have they been caught on video, and most chasers doubt they ever existed. The sickly green cloud color just before the funnel descends, on the other hand, has been documented. But the thinking now is that it's caused by dense cloud cover and has nothing to do with tornadoes in particular. The most surprising finding has been that tornadoes do not repeatedly rise and fall or skip over the landscape like a stone in a pond; as the hundreds of videos unmistakably show, a tornado on the ground stays there until it ropes out. (It's possible that what the eyewitnesses interpret as a rise and fall is actually a tornado breaking up and a new tornado forming in its place.)

What else has been debunked? Hiding in the southwest corner of the basement. As is amply demonstrated by torn porn, and repeatedly confirmed by new analyses of damage tracks, the greatest danger in a tornado is flying debris. (At three hundred miles an hour, even a piece of cardboard can be fatal.) No corner of the average basement is particularly safe; what you need is a windowless room, preferably a bathroom (the pipes in the walls provide extra protection). In open country, it's suicidal to take shelter beneath a freeway overpass, which acts something like a wind tunnel: the least bad choice is to lie facedown in a ditch in a field and hope for the best. And with the new understanding that houses do not explode when a tornado passes over them has come an end to the advice about equalizing the air pressure. "Don't bother opening the windows," the experts like to say now. "The tornado will do that for you."

The new assurance about tornadoes, the authoritative expertise with which both chasers and meteorologists currently speak, can give the impression that the danger of tornadoes—well, if it's not ended altogether, at least now has been routinized and is being managed by professionals. For a tornado to touch down outside a National Weather Service watch area is essentially unheard of today; the effective time for a tornado warning has been stretched to twenty minutes or more.

Tornadoes approaching major metropolitan areas are followed on the ground by chase teams and swarmed in the air by helicopters; their progress is now-cast on TV stations and tracked by real-time Doppler radar on the Web. Some tornadoes have been so closely monitored that the warnings for them have practically been issued street by street.

And yet that feeling of complacency can be cured by almost any successful tornado chase. There is a moment when the chase caravan approaches the fresh damage track of an active tornado and the awe and the exhilaration of the pursuit suddenly collapse into sickened horror. The lead car slows and begins threading through scatterings of debris— shredded sheets of plasterboard, splinters of furniture, the twisted shell of a water heater like a crashed missile; a pastoral roadside diner or gas station has been cratered; the tornado receding beyond the tree lines is suddenly lit up by silent flares of white light as power lines are torn, while around the cone of the funnel are the whirling black scraps of wrecked rooftops and shattered cars. The experienced chasers know what's coming: everything ahead on the road is going to be worse.

On May 22, 2011, an unusually powerful EF-5 tornado approached Joplin, Missouri. Everything about the professional response happened exactly as it was supposed to. The watch had been issued hours earlier; the warnings were going out with a lead time of more than twenty minutes; the helicopters of the local TV stations were in flight; the chase teams were hurtling down the highways, not only transmitting real-time data and video about the tornado, but stopping to warn the police on the ground that it was coming. Then the storm engulfed the city. The sky was a chaos of rapid black low-hanging clouds; wild contrary winds swept through the subdivisions and along the franchise strips; blasts of rain reduced visibility to a few feet. From everywhere came the moan of the civil-defense sirens, which seemed to have panicked and baffled the townspeople; many remained paralyzed by indecision in their front yards or by their cars in mall parking lots, unwilling to take shelter until it was too late. But then, there was for the most part nowhere to take shelter: Joplin, like most midwestern towns and cities, had been rapidly built up over the preceding decades without anything resembling storm cellars. Most new houses and businesses didn't even have basements.

People in the last few seconds before the tornado passed over them were huddling within the walk-in freezers of franchise restaurants or the storage rooms of convenience stores.

By the time the tornado crossed into the city core, it was more than a mile wide, a gigantic gaunt apparition shrouded within torrential downpours of rain. Some people didn't realize what it was until it was directly on top of them. The inflowing winds were so fierce they scoured the bark off trees and carried trucks through the air for more than a city block. A hundred and sixty people died—which made it the single deadliest American tornado in more than sixty years. Accurate counting and identification of the remains proved difficult because some of those killed in the cannonades of flying debris had been torn apart in midair and their body parts scattered among the ruins. In the aftermath, the chaser teams glided through endless blocks of death and destruction; one estimate was that more than half the buildings in town had been damaged. The franchises of the strip malls had collapsed in on themselves; the rows of subdivisions were reduced to their foundations; the parking lots were piled high with wrecked cars, and the open fields were mountain ranges of construction debris. It was hard to think that there had been any progress at all since the time of the Tri-state Tornado.

One popular book on science in the late nineteenth century offered a novel explanation for the featureless sameness of the prairies: there were no trees or other prominences because the tornadoes continually scoured the land clean. This was a colorful theory that was hopeless nonsense; after all, on average no specific location in Tornado Alley is touched by a tornado more than once every thousand years. But then, the theory wouldn't work even if tornadoes descended to earth with every single thunderstorm. Tornadoes simply don't do enough damage to the land. They rarely leave lasting scars. The old rule of thumb in the wilderness days was that a windroad through the forest lasted a generation; now the traces of a tornado are obliterated in a few years or even a few months. The debris is cleared, the insurance is paid off, the houses and schools and strip malls and franchise restaurants are rebuilt; it's a rare thing even for a monument to be left behind to record what had once happened there during a few horrible minutes one faraway spring afternoon.

The scars they leave on the collective memory are even more ephemeral. The inexorable settlement of the prairie has been built on a kind of cultural denial of its history; even at the heart of Tornado Alley the development of the land is continuing with heedless abandon. Few of the new buildings have storm cellars or any kind of shelter from violent weather. The new residents of Tornado Alley are reported to be baffled by the meaning of the tornado sirens.

The tornado chasers don't usually show all that much interest in history, either. Names like James Espy and John Finley invariably draw a blank. But there are a few monuments here and there, and some chasers do know where to look for them. They will sometimes pay visits on idle days of high pressure and low dew point, when the wind socks hang idle in the rural airports and the skies are dotted by fair-weather cumulus. They might, for instance, drive all day off their main hunting trails on the interstates up through the forests of Wisconsin, to reach the little town of Peshtigo north of Green Bay. There is a small white church on a crooked side street near the river, amid a scattering of clapboard houses, greasy-spoon restaurants, and gas stations. The church was built on the spot where Father Pernin's old church had once stood. Next to it is a cemetery with ancient, weather-stained stone markers. On a large green mound is a sign identifying this as the mass grave for the unidentifiable victims of the fire tornado.

In the suburbs of Oklahoma City there is another marker. It's on the grounds of Tinker Air Force Base: a tall rectangle of polished granite on a pebbled square of ground near the airfields. This was where the old Operations Building stood—which housed the weather station where Miller and Fawbush had worked. The marker is inscribed "First Tornado Forecast." A few of the chasers like to joke that it should read "First (and Only)."

In Irving, Kansas, there is nothing now but a few concrete foundations, a scattering of fence posts—and a solitary marker. It stands at the location of the old post office. It's a low piece of carved stone like a crypt from a Victorian mausoleum, bearing the single word "Irving."

Behind it stands an old-fashioned rural mailbox, like a birdhouse on a tall pole. Sometimes the chasers open up the mailbox idly to see if there's anything inside. And sometimes there is: a scrap of paper bearing a message from another chaser. It might be the name and URL of the chaser's video company, or the boastful news of some great tornado he'd pursued, or just some flippant insult directed at any and all rivals. Of course the chaser who found the message has to write out a reply. The message is left for the next chaser to find, or for some anonymous collector to preserve. Or maybe now and then someone finds the box stuffed full and empties all the messages onto the ground, for the wind to scatter as it wills.

A Note on Sources

Introduction: Ghost Riders

For the physics of tornadoes I've used Edwin Kessler, ed., *Thunderstorm Morphology and Dynamics,* 2nd ed. (Norman: University of Oklahoma Press, 1992). Readers who'd prefer to skip vector calculus should consult T. P. Grazulis's relatively nontechnical book *The Tornado: Nature's Ultimate Windstorm* (Norman: University of Oklahoma Press, 2001). For the general history of tornado forecasting, I have relied heavily on two works by Marlene Bradford: "Historical Roots of Modern Tornado Forecasts and Warnings," *Weather and Forecasting* 14, no. 4 (1999); and *Scanning the Skies: A History of Tornado Forecasting* (Norman: University of Oklahoma Press, 2001).

Prologue: The Pillar in the Storm

The story of the Cambridge whirlwind is told in Increase Mather's book *An Essay for the Recording of Illustrious Providences: Wherein an Account Is Given of Many Remarkable and Very Memorable Events, Which Have Hapned This Last Age, Especially in New England*; I've used the text reprinted in the nineteenth century (London: Reeves and Turner, 1890). The version of the events in Mather's letter to the Royal Society (published in its *Philosophical Transactions*) varies in several details but is not essentially different.

Part I: The Thunder House

By far the clearest accounts of Franklin's investigations are his own letters; quotations are from the texts in the volume of scientific letters and publications included in his 1838 collected works. For the electricians and the general history of electrical research in the eighteenth century, I've also consulted William E. Burns, *Science and Technology in Colonial America* (Westport, Conn.: Greenwood, 2005); Michael Brian Schiffer, *Draw the Lightning Down: Benjamin Franklin and Electrical Technology in the Age of Enlightenment* (Berkeley: University of California Press, 2003); and James Delbourgo, *A Most Amazing Scene of Wonders: Electricity and Enlightenment in Early America* (Cambridge, Mass.: Harvard University Press, 2006). The first debates about tornadoes in North America, together with some early accounts of the windroads, are reprinted in David M. Ludlum, *Early American Tornadoes, 1586–1870* (Boston:

American Meteorological Society, 1970). The fullest account of the 1805 tornado in southern Illinois is in John Reynolds, *The Pioneer History of Illinois, Containing the Discovery in 1673, and the History of the Country to the Year 1818* (Chicago: Fergus, 1887).

Part II: The Storm War

The best analysis of the "storm war" is in James Rodger Fleming, *Meteorology in America, 1800–1870* (Baltimore: Johns Hopkins University Press, 1990). Fleming's main concern is with the questions the war raised about the theory and practice of science, particularly the debate about "Baconianism"; readers interested in this issue, which I have largely scanted, should immediately seek out his book. There is also a shorter and less technical account of the war in Ludlum's *Early American Tornadoes,* along with good biographical sketches of the major participants. The published writings of the storm war have never been collected and are scattered among several repositories—chief among them the early volumes of the *Journal of the Franklin Institute,* the *Proceedings of the American Philosophical Society,* and the *Proceedings of the American Association for the Advancement of Science.* Doubtless there are others I didn't find. Robert Hare and William Redfield often published their assorted replies and counter-replies to each other as pamphlets, which now survive in many variant forms (typically a stack of them would be bound into a one-off volume for a library or a private collector). There is a thorough survey of both the pamphlets and the journal publications by the principals in James Fleming's book.

There has been no full biography of James Espy. The closest thing to one is the brief memoir by Mrs. L. M. Morehead, *A Few Incidents in the Life of Professor James P. Espy* (privately printed, 1888). Espy's own major literary work, which has some autobiographical passages along with a vivid account of the development of his early ideas, is *The Philosophy of Storms* (Boston: Little and Brown, 1841). The account of the Franklin Institute derives from Bruce Sinclair, *Philadelphia's Philosopher Mechanics: A History of the Franklin Institute, 1824–1865* (Baltimore: Johns Hopkins University Press, 1974). For a good general history of the lyceum movement, see Carl Bode, *The American Lyceum: Town Meeting of the Mind* (New York: Oxford University Press, 1956). Espy's most detailed descriptions of his rainmaking proposals (as well as his directives for navigating in hurricanes) are in his contributions to the annual *Reports of the Smithsonian Institution to Congress,* which were reprinted in *The Smithsonian Institution: Documents Relative to Its Origin and History, 1835–1899* (Washington, D.C.: Government Printing Office, 1901). Espy's ideas about artificial rain are set in a wider historical context in Clark C. Spence, *The Rainmakers: American "Pluviculture" to World War II* (Lincoln: University of Nebraska Press, 1980). The account of Espy in his old age is from *Autobiography of Samuel D. Gross, with Sketches of His Contemporaries* (Philadelphia: George Barrie, 1887). His unfinished work on moral philosophy was published after his death as *The Human Will: A Series of Posthumous Essays on Moral Accountability, the Legitimate Object of Punishment, and the Powers of the Will* (Cincinnati: Dial, 1860). William Redfield's life is partially told in his son's unfinished autobiography, *Recollections of John Howard Redfield* (privately printed,

1900), and there is also a vivid memorial of him in Denison Olmsted, *Address on the Scientific Life and Labors of William C. Redfield* (New Haven, Conn.: E. Hayes, 1857). There is a biography of Robert Hare by Edgar Fahs Smith, *The Life of Robert Hare: An American Chemist, 1781–1858* (Philadelphia: Lippincott, 1917); it is assembled almost entirely out of Hare's professional and technical correspondence, but it does, perhaps inadvertently, offer a vivid glimpse of his personality. Hare's fullest account of his spiritualist research is in his book *Experimental Investigation of the Spirit Manifestations, Demonstrating the Existence of Spirits and Their Communion with Mortals* (New York: Partridge & Brittan, 1855).

What exactly happened during the Peshtigo firestorm remains unclear. My account derives as much as possible from eyewitness testimony, primarily Peter Pernin's memoir, *The Finger of God Is There,* reprinted as *The Great Peshtigo Fire: An Eyewitness Account* (Madison: State Historical Society of Wisconsin, 1999); as well as Edgar Johnson Goodspeed, *History of the Great Fires in Chicago and the West* (n.p., 1871); Alfred L. Sewell, *Great Calamity! Scenes, Incidents, and Lessons of the Great Chicago Fire and the Burning of Peshtigo, Wisconsin* (Chicago: Sewell, 1871); and Frank Luzerne, *Through the Flames and Beyond,* which was also published as *The Lost City! Drama of the Fire Fiend* (New York: Wells, 1872). I have also used the modern history *Embers of October,* by Robert W. Wells (Peshtigo, Wis.: Peshtigo Historical Society, 1995). The 1925 fire tornado is described in Noel F. Busch, *Two Minutes to Noon* (New York: Simon and Schuster, 1962). Readers interested in a modern analysis of an EF-2 tornado occurring within a major firestorm should consult Michael Fromm et al., "Violent Pyro-convective Storm Devastates Australia's Capital," *Geophysical Research Letters* 33 (2006).

Part III: Red Wind and Tornado Green

The description of the prairie is based on travelers' accounts in the mid-nineteenth century, in particular the narratives collected in Henry Howe, ed., *Historical Collections of the Great West* (Cincinnati: E. Morgan, 1855), and James Hewitt, ed., *Eye-Witnesses to Wagon Trains West* (New York: Scribner, 1973); as well as John Hanson Beadle, *The Undeveloped West; or, Five Years in the Territories* (Philadelphia: National Publishing, 1873); Fitz Hugh Ludlow, *The Heart of the Continent: A Record of Travel Across the Plains and in Oregon* (New York: Hurd and Houghton, 1870); William Shepherd, *Prairie Experiences in Handling Cattle and Sheep* (London: Chapman and Hall, 1884); and Albert Deane Richardson, *Beyond the Mississippi: From the Great River to the Great Ocean* (Hartford, Conn.: American Publishing, 1869). The best general history of the settlement of the prairie is Everett Dick, *The Sod-House Frontier, 1854–1890* (New York: Appleton-Century, 1937). The account of the spread of horses through the West is from Colin G. Calloway, *One Vast Winter Count: The Native American West Before Lewis and Clark* (Lincoln: University of Nebraska Press, 2003). Ely Moore's story of the tornado is retold in Daniel Fitzgerald, *Sound and Fury: A History of Kansas Tornadoes, 1854–2008* (Dan Fitzgerald Company, 2009).

For John Finley's life, I have depended heavily on a biographical sketch by Joseph G. Galway, "J. P. Finley: The First Severe Storms Forecaster," *Bulletin of the American*

Meteorological Society, November 1985, and Finley's own autobiographical account, dating from 1922, "Personal View of John P. Finley," which is unpublished but can be found in the online historical archive of the National Oceanic and Atmospheric Administration (NOAA). Finley's field reports and historical studies of tornadoes were published in the series *Professional Papers of the Signal Service,* from the U.S. Government Printing Office. He told the story of his experiences in the Philippines in "Race Development by Industrial Means Among the Moros and Pagans of the Southern Philippines," *Journal of Race Development* 3, no. 3 (1913). Pershing's opinion of Finley is quoted from Frank Everson Vandiver, *Black Jack: The Life and Times of John J. Pershing* (College Station: Texas A&M University Press, 1977).

The general description of the Signal Corps is based on "The Beginning of the National Weather Service: The Signal Years (1870–1891), as Viewed by Early Weather Pioneers," an unpublished written collection edited by Gary K. Grice, in the NOAA historical archive, as well as Rebecca Robbins Raines, *Getting the Message Through: A Branch History of the U.S. Army Signal Corps* (Washington, D.C.: U.S. Army Center of Military History, 1996). The specific projects pursued by the Signal Corps in those years, including Finley's experiments in tornado prediction, are summarized in detail in the annual *Reports of the Chief Signal Officer to the Secretary of War,* published by the U.S. Government Printing Office. The early history of the Pike's Peak weather station is described in Phyllis Smith, *Weather Pioneers: The Signal Corps Station at Pikes Peak* (Athens: Ohio University Press, 1993). The sketch of the Washington City headquarters derives from Mary Clemmer Ames, *Ten Years in Washington: Life and Scenes in the National Capital, as a Woman Sees Them* (Hartford, Conn.: A. D. Worthington, 1873).

There are many contemporary accounts of the Greely expedition, of varying degrees of believability. A good modern retelling is Leonard F. Guttridge, *Ghosts of Cape Sabine: The Harrowing True Story of the Greely Expedition* (New York: Putnam, 2000). The story of Hazen, Lincoln, and the court-martial is based on *The Hazen Court-Martial: The Responsibility for the Disaster to the Lady Franklin Bay Polar Expedition Definitely Established, with Proposed Reforms in the Law and Practice of Courts-Martial* (New York: Van Nostrand, 1885), which has a complete trial transcript together with a very long (and indignant) introduction by Hazen's attorney, Thomas Jefferson Mackey. Quotations from the Allison Commission hearings are from *Testimony Before the Joint Commission to Consider the Present Organizations of the Signal Service, Geological Survey, Coast and Geodetic Survey, and the Hydrographic Office of the Navy Department, with a View to Secure Greater Efficiency and Economy of Administration of the Public Service in Said Bureaus* (Washington, D.C.: Government Printing Office, 1886).

The Louisville tornado is described in Keven McQueen, *The Great Louisville Tornado of 1890* (Charleston, S.C.: History Press, 2010); the St. Louis tornado in Julian Curzon, ed., *The Great Cyclone at St. Louis and East St. Louis, May 27, 1896* (St. Louis: Cyclone Publishing, 1896). Professor Henry Hazen's views on tornadoes and tornado safety are outlined in his book *The Tornado* (New York: N. D. C. Hodges, 1890). For the Trans-Mississippi Exposition, I have used James B. Haynes, *History of the Trans-Mississippi and International Exposition of 1898* (printed by the Exposition

Committee, 1910), and Jess R. Peterson, *Omaha's Trans-Mississippi Exposition* (Chicago: Arcadia, 2003). The story of L. Frank Baum's inspiration for *The Wizard of Oz* is based on Katharine M. Rogers, *L. Frank Baum, Creator of Oz: A Biography* (New York: St. Martin's Press, 2002).

The general description of Egypt is based on C. William Horrell, Henry Dan Piper, and John W. Voigt, *Land Between the Rivers: The Southern Illinois Country* (Carbondale: Southern Illinois University Press, 1973). The description of the Tri-state Tornado is based on Alfred J. Henry, "The Tornadoes of March 18, 1925," *Monthly Weather Review,* April 1925; on two modern histories, Peter S. Felknor, *The Tri-state Tornado: The Story of America's Greatest Tornado Disaster* (iUniverse, 2004), and Wallace Akin, *The Forgotten Storm: The Great Tri-state Tornado of 1925* (Guilford, Conn.: Lyons Press, 2002); and on the oral histories collected in Vickie Frost, ed., *When the Whole World Changed: Voices from Murphysboro, Illinois* (Murphysboro Pride Group, 1993).

Part IV: The Mystery of Severe Storms

The loss of the *Shenandoah* is told in Aaron J. Keirns, *America's Forgotten Airship Disaster: The Crash of the USS* Shenandoah (Howard, Ohio: Little River, 2010). The account of the civilian Weather Service and its critics is based on two institutional histories: Donald R. Whitnah, *A History of the United States Weather Bureau* (Urbana: University of Illinois Press, 1961); and Patrick Hughes, *A Century of Weather Service: A History of the Birth and Growth of the National Weather Service, 1870–1970* (New York: Gordon and Breach, 1970). The development of military meteorology is described in *Weather Training in the AAF, 1937–1945,* U.S. Air Force Historical Study No. 56 (Air University, 1952), a declassified report prepared by the USAF Historical Division.

Robert Miller's life is recounted in John M. Lewis, Robert A. Maddox, and Charlie A. Crisp, "Architect of Severe Storm Forecasting: Colonel Robert C. Miller," *Bulletin of the American Meteorological Society,* April 2006. Miller's own autobiography, "The Unfriendly Sky," was left unfinished at his death; there are extended excerpts from the unpublished manuscript in the NOAA archive, including a detailed account of his famous operational forecast. A modern reanalysis of the forecast is Robert A. Maddox and Charlie A. Crisp, "The Tinker AFB Tornadoes of March 1848," *Weather and Forecasting* 14, no. 4 (1999).

For T. Theodore Fujita, I have used the special memorial issue of the *Bulletin of the American Meteorological Society* 82, no. 1 (2001), particularly James R. McDonald, "T. Theodore Fujita: His Contribution to Tornado Knowledge Through Damage Documentation and the Fujita Scale"; Gregory S. Forbes and Howard B. Bluestein, "Tornadoes, Tornadic Thunderstorms, and Photogrammetry: A Review of the Contributions by T. T. Fujita"; and James W. Wilson and Robert M. Wakimoto, "The Discovery of the Downburst: T. T. Fujita's Contribution"; as well as the memorial page to Fujita by Tim Marshall at stormtrack.org. Fujita's analysis of the Super Outbreak is collected in Edwin Kessler, ed., *The Thunderstorm in Human Affairs* (Norman: University of Oklahoma Press, 1983).

Epilogue: The Wild Hunt

There are countless books and videos now about tornado chasing; the best remains Howard Bluestein, *Tornado Alley: Monster Storms of the Great Plains* (New York: Oxford University Press, 2006). The summary of current thinking about tornadoes is as accurate as I could make it as of the present writing (June 2012), but readers should be aware that tornadoes have a way of turning the established into the ephemeral very quickly.

Acknowledgments

Copious thanks are due to my editor, Tim O'Connell, and everyone at Pantheon who went an extra mile or two on this project—particularly the publicity manager, Michiko Clark, as well as Kate Welsh, Kelly Blair, Altie Karper, Catherine Courtade, and Sheila Klee. Closer to home, I owe thanks to my indefatigable agent, Danielle Egan-Miller, and to Joanna MacKenzie and Shelbey Campbell at Browne & Miller Literary Associates, and also to my invaluable assistant, Molly Walsh.

Printed in the United States
by Baker & Taylor Publisher Services